Routledge
New York and London

RATIONAL CHOICE THEORY AND RELIGION

Summary and Assessment

Edited by

Lawrence A. Young

Published in 1997
by Routledge
29 West 35th Street
New York, NY 10001

Published in
Great Britain by
Routledge
11 New Fetter Lane
London EC4P 4EE

Copyright © 1997 by
Routledge
Printed in the
United States of America
on acid-free paper.

Library of Congress Cataloging-in-Publication-Data
Rational choice theory and religion / edited by
    Lawrence A. Young,
        p.   cm.
    includes bibliographical references and index.
    ISBN: 0-415-91191-5 (cl.) — ISBN: 0-415-91192-3 (pbk.)
    1. Religion.   2. Rational choice theory.
I. Young, Lawrence A. (Lawrence Alfred), 1955–   .
BL 48. R296   1996
306.6—dc20   96–25169
                                    CIP

CONTENTS

CONTENTS

CONTRIBUTORS

Nancy T. American is Professor of Sociology of Religion at the Center for Social and Religious Research, Hartford Seminary. She is the author of the forthcoming *Congregation and Community: Stability and Change in American Religion* (New Brunswick, NJ: Rutgers University.)

Randall Collins is Professor of Sociology at the University of California–Riverside. His books include *Weberian Sociological Theory* (1986) and *Theoretical Sociology* (1988). He is currently completing a project on the comparative sociology of philosophies.

Roger Finke is Associate Professor of Sociology at Purdue University. He co-authored (with Rodney Stark), *The Churching of America, 1776–1990: Winners and Losers in Our Religious Economy* and his work has appeared in journals such as the *American Sociological Review* and the *Journal for the Scientific Study of Religion*.

Michael Hechter is Fellow of New College, Oxford and Professor of Sociology at the University of Arizona. He is currently at work on a book about nationalism.

Laurence R. Iannaccone received his Ph.D. in economics from the University of Chicago and is currently Associate Professor of Economics at Santa Clara. His research on economic/rational choice models of religious behavior has appeared in numerous journals, including the *American Journal of Sociology, Economic Inquiry,* the *Journal of Political Economy, Social Forces,* and the *Journal for the Scientific Study of Religion.*

Peter Mueser is Associate Professor of Economics at the University of Missouri–Columbia. His research includes the workings of the labor market and labor migration. He is currently investigating apparent violations of rational choice theory in experimental environments.

Mary Jo Neitz is Professor of Sociology and Women's Studies at the University of Missouri–Columbia. She is interested in religion and gender, qualitative methods, and feminist theories. She is currently working on an ethnography of modern witchcraft.

Darren E. Sherkat is Assistant Professor in the Department of Sociology and the Graduate Department of Religion at Vanderbilt University. He received his Ph.D. from Duke University in 1991. His work has focused on the sociology of religion and social movements, and his recent articles appear in *American Sociological Review, Social Forces, Social Science Research, Journal for the Scientific Study of Religion,* and *Youth and Society* among other places. He is currently working on a general theory of cultural markets.

Rodney Stark is Professor of Sociology and Comparative Religion at the University of Washington. His most recent book is *The Rise of Christianity: A Sociologist Reconsiders History* (Princeton, 1996).

R. Stephen Warner is Professor of Sociology at the University of Illinois at Chicago, where he teaches sociological theory and ethnographic methods in addition to sociology of religion. From 1993 to 1996, he was Director of the New Ethnic and Immigrant Congregations Project, a research training and support program funded by the Lilly Endowment and the Pew Charitable Trusts.

Lawrence A. Young received his Ph.D. from the University of Wisconsin and is currently Associate Professor of Sociology at Brigham Young University. He is co-author of *Full Pews and Empty Alters* (1993) and co-editor of *Contemporary Mormonism: Social Science Perspectives* (1994).

INTRODUCTION

Lawrence A. Young

RATIONAL CHOICE theory has emerged as a major item on the agenda of most social scientists in the 1990s. Its proponents have formed a section within the American Sociological Association and the leading journal in the area argues that "The *paradigm of rational action* is the one paradigm that offers the promise of bringing a greater theoretical unity among social science disciplines such as economics, sociology, cognitive psychology, political science, moral philosophy and law."[1]

The impact of rational choice theory on the social scientific study of religion during the past decade has been dramatic. Its strongest advocates argue that it represents a new paradigm within the sociology of religion. The approach has important implications for a broad range of macro, organizational, and individual level phenomenon on both the supply-side and demand-side of the equation. For example, rational choice theorists have considered issues such as:

—Who will make contributions to religious organizations?

—Why do many individuals opt to participate in strict denominations?

—What type of religious switching behaviors are likely to take place in interfaith marriages?

—Why do some religious organizations grow in membership and vitality while others become marginal over time?

—What is the difference between competitive religious markets and religious monopolies?

The capacity of the model to deal with a broad range of issues makes it one of the most important developments in the social scientific study of religion during the past several decades. In fact, the rational choice model has the potential to replace secularization theory as the dominant theoretical frame of reference within the social scientific study of religion. Furthermore, the development of rational choice theories of religion has implications for sociology in general, since rational choice theory has possibly enjoyed its strongest substantive application within the subdiscipline of the sociology of religion.

In April 1994, a group of social scientists gathered in the mountains at Sundance, Utah to consider the emergence of the rational choice approach within the sociology of religion. This book grows out of that earlier meeting and brings together many of the major proponents of the approach as well as additional scholars identified with the sociology of religion and social theory. Together, they summarize and assess the development of rational choice theory within the sociology of religion.

The essays in Part I of this volume provide a summary of the rational choice approach. No one has been more closely associated with this approach than *Rodney Stark* (University of Washington). It is appropriate that a book devoted to summarizing and assessing rational choice theories of religion begins with an essay by the leading figure within the tradition. Stark's essay (Chapter 1) is autobiographical, unfolding the emergence and development of the rational choice approach within the sociology of religion. At the heart of Chapter 1 is the assessment that too much of the sociological enterprise is non-scientific because it has proceeded without rigorous attention to formal theory. Stark suggests that his work, as well as the emergence of the rational choice approach more generally, can best be understood as an effort to bring deductive theory back into the service of a scientifically grounded sociology. He illustrates this effort by summarizing the development and content of his formal theory of religion.

Economists frequently complain that sociological applications of rational models function more as motifs than rigorous theory. Although such critiques are open to challenge, the emergence of the rational choice approach within religion has benefited from the work of the economist *Laurence Iannaccone* (Santa Clara University), who has applied rigorous economic techniques to the assessment of religion. In Chapter 2, he demonstrates how rational choice models build from the foundation of rational action to predict and explain individual, household, organizational and societal religious processes.

Roger Finke (Purdue University) explores the supply-side of religious change in Chapter 3, assessing the consequences of religious competition. While most approaches to explaining religious change focus on the consequences of changes in religious demands, Finke turns the equation on its head and helps articulate the consequences of unregulated competitive markets. In the process, he has participated in the re-writing of the history of religion in the United States.

In Chapter 4, *Darren Sherkat* (Vanderbilt University) focuses on individual preferences in outlining a theory of religious choice. His work illustrates the direction in which young scholars are taking the rational choice approach to religion. For example, while Sherkat is informed by the work of Stark, Iannaccone, and Finke, his work is also clearly rooted in the broader sociological tradition of rational choice theory. Consequently, he draws as much from the works of social scientists like Jon Elster and Amartya Sen as from the sociology of religion tradition.

Chapter 5 presents *R. Stephen Warner's* (University of Illinois–Chicago) autobiographical account of how someone involved with a major research agenda in the sociology of religion—that was conceptualized as grounded in a theoretical approach different from rational choice theory—inductively came to see his work, as well as the work of many others, as coalescing around an emerging new paradigm that is heavily informed by rational choice models of religion. This journey of self-discovery resulted in a major *American Journal of Sociology* review essay and broadened the domain of those who are viewed as pursuing a rational choice approach within the sociology of religion.

Part II of this volume seeks to assess the development of rational choice theory within the social scientific study of religion. The first three chapters of Part II are written by individuals who perceive rational choice models of religion to be useful but somewhat limited. Each of these chapters seeks to explore what is not addressed by rational models of religion. In Chapter 6, *Mary Jo Neitz* and *Peter Mueser* (both at the University of Missouri) suggest that while the major insights of the rational choice approach to religion are congruent with their own findings derived from ethnographic studies of charismatic Catholics and contemporary NeoPagens, other theoretical perspectives suggest additional questions not addressed by rational choice theory that are essential for a complete understanding of religion in society. Chapter 7 draws upon data from a recent study of congregations conducted by *Nancy Ammerman* (Hartford Seminary) in order to explore the relationship between available choices, varying levels of demand and religious commitment. In the process, she raises questions about the various effects of different configurations of choices and argues that rational choice theory does not account for all of the effects. In Chapter 8, *Lawrence A. Young* (Brigham Young University) summarizes the phenomenological approach to religion, a tradition within the sociology of religion which he argues is dependent upon neither secularization theory nor rational choice models of religion. He argues that this phenomenological approach remains vital and insightful and then explores the possibility of integration between phenomenological images of religion and rational choice models.

Although much of the current research on rational choice models of religion has enjoyed high visibility within the social scientific study of religion, its influence beyond those doing the sociology of religion has been somewhat limited. This is unfortunate given the prominence of rational choice theory within the sociology of religion. The last two chapters in the book seek to broaden the audience.

Michael Hechter (University of Oxford and University of Arizona), who is a founder and past chair of the Rational Choice Section of the American Sociological Association, assesses the potential positive contribution of rational choice theory for the study of religion as well as the very real contribution that the sociology of religion can make to the development of rational choice theory. In Chapter 9, he argues that rational models of religion must include both instrumental values and immanent values if they are to accurately reflect reality. While traditional rational choice approaches have studied instrumental values extensively, Hechter points out that the study of immanent values represents the cutting edge of rational choice theory and that social scientists who study religion can and should be involved in this exploration of immanent values in a rational choice context.

Randall Collins (University of California–Riverside), author of numerous books on social theory and founding editor of *Sociological Theory*, compares the Stark and Bainbridge theory of religion with the work of Emile Durkheim and Max Weber in Chapter 10. Although he argues that all three approaches are too simple, he suggests that the work of Stark and Bainbridge is a landmark approach that makes valuable contributions and is an important achievement along the path to an adequate theory of religion that should give scholars the confidence to continue their efforts.

In the end we are left with a picture of exciting theoretical developments that are reshaping our understanding of religion. Because rational choice theories of religion have much to contribute, they will persist and continue to inform our thinking. Nevertheless, this volume points out limits of rational choice approaches to religion. What remains to be seen is whether rational choice theory simply needs additional time to solve these limitations or if rational choice theory needs to be augmented by additional theoretical approaches in presenting a complete picture of the sociology of religion. The essays that follow should equip readers to enter into the conversation.

NOTES

[1] The quote is taken from a recent advertisement for *Rationality and Society*.

SUMMARY

BRINGING THEORY BACK IN

Rodney Stark

I GREATLY appreciate this opportunity to survey the recent renaissance of theorizing in the sociology of religion—a development of such significance that Stephen Warner (1993: 1044) has correctly described it as a "paradigm shift in progress." I do not think it too immodest to agree with Warner that I played a major role in these developments. Therefore, I found it useful to organize my survey on an autobiographical framework.

Several years before I began graduate school—while completing my military service and then working as a reporter for the *Oakland Tribune*—I became very interested in the philosophy of science. I read everyone important, but no one influenced me more than Karl Popper. Although I first read it more than 30 years ago, my reaction to Popper's essay, "Philosophy of Science: A Personal Report" (1957), which subsequently became the first chapter in his *Conjectures and Refutations* (1968), is entirely vivid.

The start of the essay recounts Popper's student days in Vienna in 1919 when four theories dominated student discussion: Marx's theory of history, Freud's psychoanalysis, Alfred Adler's individual psychology, and Einstein's theory of relativity. Popper became increasingly uneasy with the scientific standing of the first three, but not because they were less mathematical and exact. Rather, he came to the conclusion that, because of their logical structure, each was merely posing as a scientific theory. In fact, as he put it, each of the three "resembled astrology rather than astronomy" (1968: 34). In particular, he faulted these theories because they appeared to have *too much* explanatory capacity. Thus, while that year Eddington had journeyed to an island just west of Africa to observe an eclipse of the sun—hoping thereby to *falsify* Einstein's theory—Popper's friends who advocated Marx, Freud, or Adler claimed the power of each theory lay in its capacity to incorporate all possible events and outcomes. That is, these theories always fit the data. Popper wrote, "they were always confirmed—which in the eyes of their admirers constituted the strongest argument in favour of these theories. It began to dawn on me that this apparent strength was in fact their weakness" (p. 35). Thus did Popper discover, or at least make explicit, the proposition that a real theory must be "incompatible with certain possible results of observation." Aside from Einstein and his handful of followers, no one at this time really believed that light was influenced by gravity. Therefore, scientists around the world assumed that Eddington would not observe light to bend when an eclipse made the appropriate observation possible. But Einstein's theory did not predict that light might or might not bend, but that it *must* bend. Had it not done so, the theory of relativity would have been falsified.

Thus I learned from Popper and from many other philosophers of science that a real theory must predict and prohibit certain observations, and that some outcomes must be incompatible with the theory. Systems of thought that could accommodate all possible observations explained nothing because ahead of time they were of no predictive use—they were merely *post hoc* classification schemes capable only of description or codification.

Popper and his colleagues also taught me that theories should begin with abstract, general statements, or axioms, from which a set of propositions could be derived, and that one tested such theories by testing empirical predictions derived from the propositions. Moreover, one does not attempt to establish the truth of the axioms inductively or to induct axioms from observations, since universal statements cannot be induced—a point that Hume had irrefutably established by the middle of the eighteenth century. So, when I began graduate studies at Berkeley I regarded these views of theory not only to be self-evident, but to have long since become the prevailing wisdom. This assumption was correct insofar as the philosophy department was concerned, but the sociology department was quite another matter.

At that time, two semesters of theory and two semesters of methods were required of all first-year sociology students at Berkeley. It took me only a few days to discover that we would read no theories during the first semester theory course which was instead a history of social thought. It took me not much longer to realize that the faculty in the first semester methods course had no notion of what a theory was either. One of them told our class that "theory is the baloney you put at the front of a paper so the intellectuals have to publish it." He reported that in his experience one could usually get by just fine by using Robert Merton's "means/ends typology" as one's theory.[1]

Things got much worse in the second semester when I discovered we would read no theories, as I understood that term, in modern social theory. For, in the early 1960s, theory sometimes meant Marxism, but usually theory meant structural functionalism and the premier theorist was Talcott Parsons. So I paid my dues by reading *The Structure of Social Action* and *The Social System*. My fellow inmates complained about how badly written these books were, and how dense and muddled the prose. I would have forgiven all of that had they included any effort at theorizing. But they did not. The thing about the structural functionalists was that they did not constitute a theoretical school at all because they never theorized. This massive body of concepts and definitional statements contains not one contingent, or falsifiable statement that I ever was able to discover. Structural functionalism was, as with Freudianism, Marxism, and Adlerism, far more like astrology than astronomy.

Not being entirely unperceptive, even I soon learned not to express such views—as I might as well express faith that the earth is flat. Indeed, as I passed around excerpts from Popper to some of my peers, they treated it as a species of pornography—exciting to read, but one must not be detected doing so. Nevertheless, I remained determined that one day I would write some social theories.

In 1964, I went to Montreal for the ASA meetings and heard George Homans give his famous (some said infamous) presidential address, "Bringing Men Back In"—a title I intentionally echoed for this essay. Having been introduced by Neil Smelser, Homans devoted the first part of his address to trashing structural functionalism, in part by showing that the first 65 or so pages of Smelser's book on the industrial revolution of the cotton industry in Great Britain were entirely superfluous to the explanations that followed. These initial "theoretical" pages introduced a structural–functionalist account of change and modernization. But, Homans crowed, since there wasn't a single contingent statement in the theory, nothing was predicted about what would be found in the analysis; hence nothing of explanatory value would be lost simply by excising that portion and getting on with the analysis that made up the remainder of the book. Moreover, Homans noted, when Smelser actually turned to the explanatory task, all the conceptual boxes and all "four functional exigencies" disappeared, to be replaced by references to rational actors—albeit these statements seem intentionally cloudy. Homans then proceeded to clarify what a real scientific theory is and to argue, convincingly, why the rational choice axiom is fundamental to any social scientific theory—hence the need to bring humans back into social theory.

I was delighted by the entire performance, and not least by the theatricality of Homan's delivery. At the time, I knew who Homans was but had not read him—he had barely been mentioned in any class or seminar I took at Berkeley, George Herbert Mead still being regarded as *the* social psychologist. Once back in Berkeley, I quickly read the first edition of *Social Behavior: Its Elementary Forms* (1961). I found it exciting and disappointing. The good part was that Homans had constructed an authentic social theory, albeit borrowing a lot from the Skinnerian version of behaviorism. But the book ended many chapters too soon. I shall never understand why Homans was content to settle for so very little. That is, as soon as he got people interacting and thereby beginning to like one another, he quit. He failed to take what seemed to me to be obvious next steps by which he could have deduced how interactions must generate norms, how interaction among larger numbers of actors must produce social structures, how increasingly complex culture is accumulated and thereby forces a division of labor, and on and on. That is, if Homans seemed determined to explain to us what we ought to do and where to start, he also seemed to have had no real stomach for the job at hand.

But at least he got me tinkering in spare moments with theoretical exercises. Soon I thought I might have found a real theorist more ambitious than Homans when I ordered a copy of Gerhard Lenski's *Power and Privilege* (1966), which was billed as a propositional theory of stratification. Lenski was in fact far more ambitious than Homans and, in the beginning of the book, he did pursue a deductive theory. But, seemingly out of a concern to cover his flanks against inductionist critics, he made the theory increasingly specific and inductive as he went along and eventually the system became circular and descriptive. Even if I ultimately found the book wanting, I had many exciting moments while reading it, and I found it to be a very instructive example of how to organize a large, abstract, deductive system for a social scientific audience.

In 1967, I began a three-volume work on religious behavior with Charles Glock. The first volume appeared in 1968. It was a largely conceptual and descriptive book called *American Piety: The Nature of Religious Commitment*. The scheduled second volume was to focus on sources of religious commitment, and the third was to be concerned with the consequences of religious commitment. Neither the second nor the third volume ever appeared. And theory was a major reason.[2]

When I wrote the second volume, I began it with a deductive theory of religious commitment that was not much different from one included in the essay, "Towards a Theory of Religion: Religious Commitment," that William Sims Bainbridge and I (1980) published more than a decade later. I began with a rational choice axiom: *Humans seek what they perceive to be rewards and avoid what they per-*

ceive to be costs. Another axiom explicitly introduced human cognition: *Human action is directed by a complex information-processing system that functions to identify problems and attempt solutions to them.* I pause here to point out that, from the very beginning, my theoretical work has always included an explicit and significant cognitive component, something frequently overlooked by those who worry that I rely too much on exchange theory (cf. Garrett, 1990).

Another axiom imposed scarcity upon the concept of rewards: *Some desired rewards are limited in supply, including some that simply do not exist (in the physical world).* I also introduced the notion of *compensators.* I have never liked that word. It carries unmeant negative connotations, but I have not yet found a more suitable alternative. Compensators are a sort of substitute for desired rewards. That is, they provide an explanation about how the desired reward (or an equivalent alternative) actually can be obtained, but propose a method for attaining the reward that is rather elaborate and lengthy. Often the actual attainment will be in the distant future or even in another reality, and the truth of the explanation will be very difficult, if not impossible, to ascertain in advance. When a child asks for a bike and a parent proposes that the child keep his or her room clean for a year and get no grade below B during the same period, whereupon the bike will appear, a compensator has been issued in lieu of the desired reward. We can distinguish compensators from rewards because one is the thing wanted, and the other is a proposal about gaining the reward.

As reward-seeking beings, humans will always prefer the reward to the compensator, but they often will have no choice because some things we want can't be had in sufficient supply by some people and some rewards cannot be had, here and now, by anyone. Compensators abound in all areas of life, but my primary interest has been in religious compensators. Let me note only the most obvious example. Most people desire immortality. No one knows how to achieve that here and now—the Fountain of Youth remains elusive. But many religions offer instructions about how that reward can be achieved over the longer term. When one's behavior is guided by such a set of instructions one has accepted a compensator. One also is exhibiting religious commitment, since the instructions always entail certain requirements vis-à-vis the divine. Indeed, it usually is necessary to enter into a long-term exchange relationship with the divine and with divinely inspired institutions, in order to follow the instructions: churches rest upon these underlying exchange relationships.

I want it to be clear that the theory does not, and should not, imply anything about the truth or falsity of religious compensators. It merely postulates the process of rational choices by which humans value and exchange these compensators.

By logically manipulating the axioms and definitions of the theory, I was able to reach what I thought were some striking deductions concerning the relationship between power and piety. Noting that religious compensators typically include both scarce and unavailable rewards, we can see that:

1. *The power of an individual or group will be negatively associated with accepting religious compensators for rewards that are only scarce.* That is, powerful people will simply pursue the rewards—material luxuries, for example. Less powerful people will tend to accept compensators that, for example, assure them that by forgoing luxury now they are piling up riches in the life to come. We might call this the sectlike form of religious commitment.

2. *The power of an individual or group will be positively associated with control of religious organizations and with gaining the rewards available from religious organizations.* Here I deduced what could be called the churchlike form of religious commitment.

But it is the third deduction that has always interested me most:

3. *Regardless of power, persons and groups will tend to accept religious compensators for rewards that do not exist in this life.* Here I noted that in some regards everyone is deprived and everyone has a motive for being religious—that since everyone faces death, doctrines of an afterlife appeal to all. We could call this the universal form of religious commitment.

Finally, I introduced the concept of socialization to condition human perceptions and actions, including their religious commitment.

These three simple deductions, or propositions, seemed of great utility. First of all, they are very parsimonious. All human attributes related to variations in individual or group power, including all status attributes such as sex and race, are covered by these three propositions, with specific predictions and prohibitions being evident. Thus an immense literature of known correlations neatly fits beneath them. Second, by reference to the axioms, the propositions are *explained*. We know *why* things are this way.

With this deductive system as my guide, in the remainder of the book I tested these propositions with considerable success, using not only the large data bases Glock and I had collected, but also the pertinent empirical literature.

In 1969, when the book was done, I gave a copy to Glock, anticipating that I would get it back in a month or two with minor proof editing—that was the way we collaborated. But this time the months stretched on and on. Since I was busy writing a book on the police, I did not press him. Finally, he put a note in my box to the effect that as usual the book looked great, but it would not be wise to include the first chapter. He counselled me that theory, and especially deductive theory, seemed to put people off. Why didn't we just stick to testing well-known hypotheses about correlates of religious commitment such as "poor people tend to pray more than rich people" or "rich people are more likely to belong to and attend church than are poor people"? The problem with this approach is, of course, that the hypotheses were intellectual orphans in that there was no higher order explanation of why these hypothesis should hold, or even why they should be formulated or tested. In fact, these "hypotheses" were derived from earlier empirical results (cf. Demerath, 1965) and therefore were in some sense *post hoc*. It seemed to me far more important to say why and how these differential patterns existed, for they turn up not just for income, but for other status-related variables such as IQ, education, and race. It seemed silly to continue to resort to dozens of *ad hoc* interpretations, one for each of these correlations, when a parsimonious explanatory model was at hand.

This second volume never appeared because I was not prepared to pull in my horns and Glock was not willing to stick out his neck. As it turned out, he was undoubtedly right about the wiser course over the short run. But, at that point in my career, I had published five books, not one of which was important. Enough of that. And, while I was at it, I decided I'd had enough of Berkeley, too. So I accepted an appointment at the University of Washington.

As soon as I had adjusted to my new role as professor, I spent a wonderfully rainy weekend in Seattle adding a summary of the pertinent empirical evidence to the end of the chapter containing the theory of commitment and submitted it as a paper to a major journal. It came back almost immediately by return mail with a lengthy explanation that deductive theories are inappropriate for the social sciences. When I pointed to Homan's presidential address, I was given to understand that presidential addresses are not subject to the review process. Just to make sure, I sent the essay off to the other major journal. This time, I was told that what was needed was empirical proof of the truth of the axioms before it would be appropriate to assess empirical data merely concerning the derived propositions. I despaired of bringing real theories into sociology. I put the essay on a shelf, along with the manuscript of the second volume, and on and off for the next several years I gave serious thought to leaving academia.

Fortunately, there were signs that some sociologists did know what theories were and were prepared to try to create them. In particular, Peter Blau and James S. Coleman were doing very impressive theoretical work, although neither seemed willing to try for the "big theory"—to take up where Homans had stopped and try to make social systems emerge from micro-axioms. Moreover, even these established stars seemed to be having hard going bringing theory back in. For example, in a major theoretical essay in the *American Sociological Review*, after a lengthy explanation of the logical structure of deductive theories and how one does not test the axioms, but rather tests the lower-order empirical predictions derived from the axioms, Blau (1970) then devoted the remainder of the paper to ignoring everything he had just written, as he tried to demonstrate that his axioms *could be induced* from empirical data. This led me to think that he had been ambushed by the same reviewers who had demanded that I induce my axioms, and that for some reason he had been willing to go along. It was as if David Hume had never lived. I also noted that Blau and Coleman both did their best theoretical work in books, where reviewers could not meddle. From this I concluded that if I wanted to do theory, I should probably do books. I also concluded that I should avoid the hue and cry over Marxism, causal models, grounded theories, symbolic interaction, and all the rest by concentrating my theoretical efforts in a subfield where I might be able to exploit my skills at conceptualization and empirical research—and my early reputation—to force a forum for my theoretical work. And then, in 1975, William Sims Bainbridge came to Seattle.

When Bill arrived from Harvard as a brand new assistant professor, we hit it off immediately. Each of us has many interests that bore the other silly, but that has merely added to the fun (and breadth) of our collaboration. In the beginning, our discussions of religious behavior centered on the book he was completing about a new religious movement, in which he made considerable use of my work on religious conversion. With that book in press (*Satan's Power*, 1978), we began our first efforts at collaboration, and I soon gave him the essay containing my deductive theory of commitment. After careful study, he noted that much greater power and clarity could be gained by adding an additional axiom, which became axiom A1 in all of our subsequent work: *Human perception and action take place through time, from the past into the future.* He then defined the *past* as the universe of conditions which can be known but not influenced, and the *future* as the universe of conditions which can be influenced but not known. What could be more obvious? Yet, by explicitly placing human behavior in time, many of our subsequent efforts to explain religious phenomena were clarified and simplified. Thus did I discover Bill's gifts for abstract thought, and I knew I had found someone crazy enough to agree to collaborate on a full-length deductive theory of religion.

It has struck many as odd that we would collaborate on an activity so seemingly singular as deductive theorizing. But there are immense virtues in doing such work as a collaboration. Let me explain. When one is not able to formalize a theory, that is, express it in symbolic or mathematical form, the deductive process is fraught with risks, and it grows more difficult as the deductive chains lengthen. It is very easy to think one has deduced a set of propositions when, in fact, one has simply jumped to them without having reached them in an unbroken logical chain. Such gaps usually are relatively easy to spot when the chains are symbolic, but it is very difficult to spot them when the chains are in plain English. To combat this problem, we divided the labor. I did the first drafts. Then Bill worked through each step independently, seeing if he could retrace my path without hitting a gap in the chain. When he found what he thought was a gap, we would get together and go over the logical steps until they were closed—although he would often have provided the closure before we consulted. In addition, Bill often found implications I had entirely overlooked and he extended many branches from the main line to produce important propositions on a number of vital issues. In the end, neither of us knows for sure who did what.

But we do know that our colleagues were little interested in so-called "grand theories" about anything. Early on, we submitted the axiomatic theory of religious commitment to the *Journal of Scientific Study of Religion*. In Phillip Hammond we found a receptive editor, and no significant revisions were required.[3] That, however, does not alter the fact that this is the only paper Bill and I ever published for which we did not receive a single request for a reprint. In any event, by the time this first fragment of the theory was published in June 1980, Bill and I had a relatively complete draft of the whole theory. We submitted a copy to Grant Barnes at the University of California Press, a friend who had previously published books by each of us. The reviews he received were rather surprising. John Lofland, as true-blue a symbolic interactionist as has ever lived, wrote an astonishingly favorable review. His enthusiasm was not shared by two anonymous "theorists," one of whom condemned the whole approach on the grounds that it was well-known that theories aping the physical sciences could not deal with the ambiguities and nuances of social science. I believe Grant Barnes would have published the book anyway, but at that point Bill and I decided to adopt a Fabian strategy. We would delay sending our theory into a hostile world, meanwhile teasing our opponents and tempting possible supporters by revealing fragments of the theory in essays constituting empirical tests of some of its more significant propositions. Through these means we hoped to create a climate of opinion willing to give theory a chance.

From 1980 through 1983, Bainbridge and I published 19 co-authored journal articles, in addition to other articles that each of us wrote alone. And in time, our advertisements of coming theoretical attractions did begin to create interest among sociologists of religion. Indeed, some people began to write attacks on our theory despite never having read it (cf. Wallis and Bruce, 1984). So, in 1984 we turned 22 of these essays into a book which Grant Barnes arranged to publish the next year. *The Future of Religion* was well received—it even won the Society for the Scientific Study of Religion distinguished book award. So at last it seemed time to publish our theory of religion. We returned to the manuscript, which had been in a drawer for about five years, and gave it a final going through. We both were rusty and it was very hard going. Worse yet, since 1982 Bill had been back at Harvard which made our collaboration rather more cumbersome. But eventually the book was done.

A Theory of Religion appeared in 1987. It consists of seven axioms, each of which is a very simple statement about humans or the human condition. In addition to those reported earlier in this essay, others are such uncontroversial claims as:

Rewards vary in kind, value, and generality.
Most rewards sought by humans are destroyed when they are used.

It would be difficult to think of more obvious statements. But, when combined with the 104 concepts defined in our theoretical system, we managed to derive 344 contingent propositions, including the three derived for the theory of commitment. As a necessary preliminary to explaining religion, some of these propositions account for the emergence of norms and values; others explain the division of labor (or specialization); and others deduce stratification, cultural evolution and a whole host of primary social phenomena.

A major source of satisfaction was our ability to deduce within our axiomatic system propositions embodying the social scientific study of religion's most respected theories of the middle range.

Consider Malinowski's celebrated proposition that "primitives" never resort to magic when they possess means for achieving their goals directly. For example, they never resort to magic to remove weeds from their fields or to fix their fences. But there are forces, such as bad weather or plant blight, that thwart their best efforts and exceed their knowledge. "To control these influences and only these," the primitive agriculturist "employs magic" (Malinowski, [1925] 1964: 29). In our deductive system, Malinowski's proposition is generalized beyond magic and beyond primitive cultures and takes the form of Proposition 58: *People will not exchange with the gods when a cheaper or more efficient alternative is known and available.*

Another example is Durkheim's (1915: 44) famous claim that "*There is no church of magic.*" Since I regard this as by far the most original and important insight in Durkheim's otherwise quite overvalued work on religion, let me trace his argument. He began by distinguishing between religion and magic. While both are made up of beliefs and rites, myths and dogmas, magic differs by stressing technical and utilitarian ends and fails to address basic theological concerns: "[magic] does not waste its time in pure speculation" (p.42). Moreover, Durkheim noted the "marked repugnance of religion for magic, and in return, the hostility of the second for the first. Magic takes a sort of professional pleasure in profaning holy things…On its side, religion, when it has not condemned and prohibited magic rites, has always looked upon them with disfavor" (p. 43). Finally, Durkheim noted that "Between the magician and the individuals who consult him, as between these individuals themselves, there are no lasting bonds…The magician has a clientele and not a church, and it is very possible that his clients have no other relations between each other, or even do not know each other; even the relations which they have with him are generally accidental and transient; they are just like those of a sick man with his physician" (p. 44).

Here is how these insights appeared in our theory. First were some key definitions:

Definition 18: *Compensators* are postulations of reward according to explanations that are not readily susceptible to unambiguous evaluation.

Definition 19: Compensators which substitute for single, specific rewards are called *specific compensators*.

Definition 20: Compensators which substitute for a cluster of many rewards and for rewards of great scope and value are called *general compensators*.

Definition 22: *Religion* refers to systems of general compensators based on supernatural assumptions.

Let me note here that among the rewards of greatest scope are explanations of the human condition: Does life have purpose? Why are we here? What can we hope? Is death the end? Why do we suffer? Does justice exist? How did the universe come into being? Moreover, answers to such questions constitute what are often called theologies.

Definition 52: *Magic* refers to specific compensators that promise to provide desired rewards without regard for evidence concerning the designated means.

Definition 53: Cultural specialists whose main activity is providing specific compensators are *magicians*.

These definitions are consistent with Durkheim. Now see how the rest of Durkheim's assertions about religion and magic fall out as deductions within our system:

Proposition 91: *Magic is more vulnerable than religion to disconfirmation.*

Proposition 92: *It is not in the interest of religious specialists to risk disconfirmation of the compensators they supply.*

Proposition 93: *Religious specialists will, over time, tend to reduce the amount of magic they supply.*

Proposition 94: *To the extent that the demand for magic continues after religious specialists have ceased providing it, others will specialize in providing it.*

Proposition 95: *The roles of religious specialist and magician will tend to be differentiated, as will religious and magical culture generally.*

Proposition 96: *Magicians cannot require others to engage in long-term, stable patterns of exchange* (an earlier proposition asserted that religious specialists *can* require such patterns of exchange).

Proposition 97: *In the absence of long-term, stable patterns of exchange, an organization composed of magicians and a committed laity cannot be sustained.*

Proposition 98: *Magicians will serve individual clients, not lead an organization.*

Proposition 99: *Magicians are much less powerful than religious specialists.*

We then proceeded to explain Durkheim's perception of antagonism between religion and magic and also to show why this antagonism is often very minor. If, for whatever reason, the prevailing religious institutions in a society continue to offer their own brand of magic (as was the case with the medieval church) we deduced in Proposition 104: *...religion...will tend to oppose magic outside its system.* This explains witchcraft trials. But, in Proposition 105, we deduced that when religious institutions do not deal in magic, they will tolerate magic outside their system. This is the pattern found throughout most of the East where priests and magicians live in symbiotic balance.

In similar fashion we deduced the evolution of the gods. Many scholars have noted the tendency for religions to evolve in the direction of monotheism (Swanson, 1960; Bellah, 1964; Lenski, 1970). We thus deduced:

Proposition 61: *As societies become older, larger, and more cosmopolitan they will worship fewer gods of greater scope.*

Here, however, is an instance when the logical processes of deduction produced novelty. For we discovered that, given our axioms and definitions, the end product of this evolution is not *monotheism*, defined as belief in only one god (supernatural being) of infinite scope. Viewed within our system, such a god would necessarily be conceived of either as almost wholly remote from human concerns and affairs (as exemplified by Unitarianism and the versions of Buddhism sustained by Chinese court philosophers) or as dangerously capricious in the manner of the Greek pantheon. Here the issue is rationality, not only on the part of believers, but on the part of the gods. And we deduced that evil supernatural forces (such as Satan) are essential to the most rational conception of divinity.

Proposition 107: *Explanations that assume the gods are rational offer greater certainty of reward than explanations that assume the gods are irrational.*

Definition 54: *Rationality* is marked by consistent, goal–oriented activity.

Proposition 108: *Distinguishing the supernatural into two classes—good and evil—offers a rational portrait of the gods.*

Definition 55: *Good* and *evil* refer to the intentions of the gods in their exchanges with humans. *Good* consists of the intention to allow humans to profit from exchanges. *Evil* consists of the intention to inflict coercive exchanges or deceptions upon humans, leading to losses for the humans.

Thus we deduced the necessity either to conceive of a single god who is above the question of good or evil by virtue of being remote from any exchanges with humans (the Tao is not a fit exchange partner), or to admit the existence of more than one supernatural being. Thus we see that good and evil reflect the possible goal-orientations of the gods—to give more than they take, or to take more than they give. A god holding either of these intentions is more rational than a god who holds both intentions.

We therefore deduced:

Proposition 109: *The more complex the culture, the clearer the distinction drawn between good and evil gods.*

Proposition 110: *The older, larger, and more cosmopolitan societies become, the clearer the distinction drawn between good and evil gods.*

Proposition 111: *Humans seek to exchange with good gods, and to avoid exchanging with evil gods.*

Proposition 112: *Good gods will be preferred who are thought to protect humans from exchanges with evil gods.*

Proposition 113: *The more complex the culture, the more likely is belief in good gods that are more powerful than evil gods.*

Proposition 114: *The older, larger, and more cosmopolitan societies become, the more likely they are to believe in good gods that are more powerful than evil gods.*

In other propositions, we were able to deduce a fully-articulated control theory of deviance as our mechanism for explaining why and how people create, convert to, and defect from religious movements. We also produced propositions to account for the birth of sects and the conditions under which sects evolve into churches, for the occurrence of religious revivals and for dozens of other things about which much was already known to our fellow scholars. What we tried to do was not so much discover new knowledge, but to carefully codify the wealth of what already was known and unite it under one theoretical system in order to discover the connections among all of these insights.

It may be appropriate here to mention briefly the implications of theorizing about religion for the plausibility of religious doctrines. It would be entirely wrong to claim that by offering rational explanations of why religions will, for example, tend to conceive of the gods in rational terms, the truth of religious doctrines is called into question—that religious phenomena are reduced thereby to naturalistic explanations. On the contrary, if the supernatural is as described by traditional Jewish–Christian–Moslem theology, then we live in a reality in which our theory about the nature of the gods *ought* to hold. That is, the God of Abraham is presented as the merciful and forgiving creator of an orderly, lawful universe. The idea that social science can comprehend religion *because* God is rational is entirely parallel with the notion that the laws of physics are susceptible to reason and discovery, because, as Einstein reminded the world, "God does not play at dice." Moreover, our deductions about the need for a separation of good and evil are entirely consistent with millennia of theological thought.

I recognize that many omissions and shortcomings mark our first effort at a theory of religion, but I am proud that we finally got serious theoretical activity going again in the sociology of religion. Suddenly, there are a number of other people, especially young scholars, doing creative and original work on theories of religion and many more who are testing and refining pieces of these theories. For me, the most satisfying part of these developments has been the privilege to encourage, learn from, and often collaborate with these younger scholars.

One of these scholars is, of course, Laurence Iannaccone. Just before Christmas in 1985 I received a letter from an assistant professor of economics at Santa Clara University. He explained that the enclosed essay, which consisted of a formal model of church and sect, had been on his shelf since the summer of 1980 because neither his dissertation advisor nor "anyone else in Chicago's economics department deemed the subject worthy of an economist's attention." He asked what I thought of his model and where I thought he might send it. I wrote him immediate encouragement because his paper was wonderful—not the least of its virtues being that it was entirely compatible with the work Bainbridge and I were about to publish. My judgment of the paper was soon ratified by others, and it appeared in a special issue of the *American Journal of Sociology* devoted to economic sociology.

Since then, Larry Iannacconne has become a well-known figure in the social scientific study of religion, and his applications of rational choice theory as developed in micro-economics have been major contributions to very basic issues, such as why strict churches are strong. Moreover, Larry's work has already closed very serious theoretical gaps at the micro level that were left by Bainbridge and myself. The truth is that, although from the very first I have constructed deductive theories from what primarily are micro-axioms and have derived macro sociology from micro origins, I always have been more interested in the macro level of analysis.

Hence, beginning in 1985, with the theory book drafted and launched on its nearly interminable journey into print, I began to extend and refine the theory at the most macro level of analysis. Things rapidly began to come together when I struck upon the notion of religious economies. A *religious economy* consists of all the religious activity going on in any society. Religious economies are like commercial economies in that they consist of a market of current and potential customers, a set of firms seeking to serve that market, and the religious "product lines" offered by the various firms (Stark, 1985). The use of market language to discuss things often thought to be sacred was not, and is not, meant to offend, but to enable me to import some basic insights from economics to help explain religious phenomena.

Among the many innovations made possible by this approach is the capacity to focus on the behavior of religious *firms* rather than only upon religious *consumers*. Let me give an example of what this shift in focus offers. Past discussions of secularization usually postulate a decline in the *demand* for religion, claiming that potential consumers in a modern, enlightened age no longer find a need for faith in the supernatural. In contrast, in new essays written with Larry Iannaccone (1993; 1994), we focus not so much on religious consumers as on religious *suppliers*. We ask, under what conditions are religious firms able to *create a demand* Or, what happens when only a few, lazy religious firms confront the potential religious consumer? More concretely, does the low level of religious mobilization in Scandinavia, for instance, primarily reflect weak demand, or an unattractive product, badly marketed, within a highly regulated and distorted religious economy?

As I pondered the workings of religious economies I soon recognized that the most decisive factor involved is whether they are free markets or whether the government regulates the economy in the direction of monopoly. Bainbridge and I already had deduced that a religious organization would be motivated to seek monopoly standing and that often the state finds that its interests are best served by supporting a religious monopoly. Starting anew, I extended the theory thus:

> Proposition 1: *The capacity of a single religious firm to monopolize a religious economy depends upon the degree to which the state uses coercive force to regulate the religious economy.*

> Proposition 2: *To the degree that a religious economy is unregulated, it will tend to be very pluralistic.*

Pluralism refers to the number of firms active in the economy: the more firms having a significant market-share, the greater the degree of pluralism.

I shall not deal here with why pluralism must arise in free markets. Rather I shall focus on my realization that competitive pluralism is not the evil force that saps the vigor from religion. To the contrary, where there is greater pluralism and competition, religious organizations are stronger, and the overall level of religious participation is higher (Stark, 1985). This led me to formulate the next two propositions:

Proposition 3: *To the degree that a religious economy is pluralistic, firms will specialize.*

To *specialize*, a firm caters to the special needs and tastes of specific market segments.

Proposition 4: *To the degree that a religious economy is competitive and pluralistic, overall levels of religious participation will tend to be high. Conversely, to the degree that a religious economy is monopolized by one or two state-supported firms, overall levels of participation will tend to be low.*

Economists take it for granted that a set of specialized firms will, together, be able to appeal to a far greater proportion of consumers than can a solitary unspecialized firm. The same principle applies to religion. Moreover, because so much of the religious product necessarily is intangible and concerns the far distant future, vigorous marketing activity is needed to achieve high levels of consumption. But that is not how state-supported monopoly firms function. It is a major proposition of economics that such firms tend to be inefficient. Writing in 1776 about established religions in general and the Church of England in particular, Adam Smith noted their lack of "exertion" and "zeal":

> [T]he clergy, reposing themselves upon their benefices, had neglected to keep up the fervour of faith and devotion of the great body of the people; and having given themselves up to indolence, were incapable of making vigorous exertion in defence even of their own establishment. ([1776] 1937: 741)

Having begun to use economic language and to apply basic economic principles, my acquaintance with Larry allowed me to discuss these things with a trained economist. Interestingly enough, this economist was more interested in micro issues that might have been of greater interest to sociologists and psychologists. During the past several years Larry and I have collaborated, and often our papers move from micro to macro theorizing. I have contributed an occasional point and examples to the micro portions of these essays and Larry has done the same to the macro portions.

In any event, the extension of the macro level of theorizing about religious economies has yielded many quite controversial results. For example, the theory forces the conclusion that the so-called secularization thesis is simply wrong—that levels of religious mobilization vary in response to pluralism, not to the spread of modernity and scientific sophistication. The deduction that religious mobilization must be low when a religious economy is essentially monopolized required us to examine history and to discover that the received wisdom about the universal piety of medieval Europe is mythical and that the medieval masses were scarcely religious at all. The theory even predicts the churching of Europe, should the religious economies of those nations be effectively deregulated.

These new theoretical developments at the macro level have also been important in my collaboration with another of the gifted young scholars who have recently taken up the social scientific study of religion—Roger Finke.

I have been blessed with some good graduate students, but for many years I never had one of appreciable talent who had much interest in religion. Mostly, I have trained criminologists, and in the beginning Roger worked with me on criminological topics. In 1983, for instance, he was one of my co-authors on an essay called "Crime and Delinquency in the Roaring Twenties." But Roger soon decided he wanted to specialize in the sociology of religion. Instantly, whatever have been my failings in terms of the quantity of sociologists of religion I have trained, I became beyond reproach in terms of their quality.

My collaboration with Roger was not initially focused on theory. Together we had begun to explore the wonderful and neglected religious census studies. When it turned out to be possible to construct equations to predict church membership in 1850, 1860, and 1870 from data on the seating capacity and finances of each congregation, Roger realized he could do his dissertation on the churching of America. *Churching* is the appropriate verb because in 1850 only a third of Americans actually belonged to a church, while by 1980 almost two-thirds belonged. In addition to describing these changes and comparing the relative fate of various religious denominations during the process, Roger made the first major effort to test the deduction that pluralism invigorates religious "firms" and thus results in higher overall levels of religious participation. His findings were very strongly positive: as pluralism grew, levels of American church membership grew accordingly. With his dissertation completed, Roger left Washington and our future collaboration depended upon long distance communication. But, continue we did and over the next several years, as we worked together, what had once seemed a carefully delimited dissertation project sprawled into a major undertaking in which we used quantification and theory to challenge many chapters in the standard narrative of American religious history. In the end, we both had to read a lot of musty books and dig in a lot of diaries and documents to extend our grasp of American religious history in order to be careful to get things right. So, *The Churching of America, 1976–1990: Winners and Losers in Our Religious Economy* did not appear until 1992. In the meantime, Roger, Larry and I have been involved in a number of three-way and two-way collaborations.

In their essays, Larry Iannaccone and Roger Finke summarize their own work in far greater detail. Moreover, they mention others who have, and are, contributing to the task of bringing theory back in. As for me, I am continuing to analyze religious economies. I hope soon to offer a theory of religious conflict and civility in which I try to explain why and when religious economies will be torn by religious strife and to discover the basis for peaceful civility among distinctly different religions. I am also building a theory of the dynamics and stability in religious economies by close examination of the demand side. My aim is to identify the natural and relatively stable set of religious market niches that exist in societies—that is, segments of potential adherents sharing particular religious needs, tastes and expectations.

Meanwhile, I have used portions of the theory to sustain me in another foray into history. This time, I have tried to reconstruct the rise of Christianity. The project has served as a cherished hobby for about eight years and I have published parts of it as I have gone along. As a result, I have come to know a number of historians of the early church and of Greco-Roman times. What wonderful, dedicated scholars they are, and generous with both praise and help. I finished the book last month. I probably could have been done several years earlier, but I was reluctant to finish because now I will lack an excuse to continue reading the marvelous work being produced by scholars in this area. Lest you think I am referring primarily to works of textual analysis, I offer a recent essay by Roger Bagnall of Columbia who used a Gini index to calculate inequality in landholding in Roman Egypt, based on surviving tax records from the year 350. Bagnall is a classicist who specializes in ancient papyri. But his statistical sophistication is equal to anyone in sociology, and his respect for hypothesis testing (as opposed to raw empiricism) exceeds most. Indeed, Bagnall's results shed light on a major historical question: why did so few people from Egypt rise to the Roman aristocracy, as compared with people from other parts of the empire? In Bagnall's words: "Perhaps the most striking feature of all, in fact, is the absence of really great landed fortunes in the hands of the curial class, fortunes that might support a rise from municipal status to the aristocracy of the empire" (1992: 143).

These historians of the early church do not need me to teach them how to analyze quantitative data. So then, what was my role? To introduce them to real social scientific theories. And my favorable reception among them is the result of their ability to see that when concrete events can be cast as instances of a general class of phenomena, governed by general axioms, that is far more satisfactory than *ad hoc* explanations. Now, if we can just convince sociologists that science is a theory-driven enterprise.

Finally, given the focus of this conference, it should be asked, if sociology is to be theory-driven, must these be rational choice theories? That depends upon what it means to call something a rational choice theory. If it merely means that all efficient social theories will include an axiom postulating that humans seek to maximize, which is to say, humans will attempt to act rationally, then undoubtedly the future of sociological theory rests on a rational choice approach (Coleman, 1990). But if we place greater limits than that on what we will call Rational Choice Theories (as is implied when the words are capitalized), then the future of social theory may be far broader. To conclude this essay, I would like to explore this matter in greater depth.

For far too many sociologists, theoretical "work" is a form of ancestor worship. That is, theory is believed to consist of the opinions, prejudices, insights, analyses, and metaphors about social life contained in the works of dead founders, especially Marx, Durkheim, and Weber. These collections of thought are often referred to as "perspectives" and most books and articles identified as "theory" or "theoretical" involve efforts to explicate or to compare these perspectives. Most sociologists experience some pressure to identify with a particular perspective. Unfortunately, once sociologists are identified with any given perspective they have, in a very important sense, been deactivated. That is, if a scholar is known to be a Weberian or a Marxist, he or she easily is placed within an array of distinctive perspectives and the bases for disputes among these perspectives are well-known and regarded as *beyond resolution*. Since, as Popper noted, perspectives do not give rise to contingent (falsifiable) predictions, they can never be disconfirmed and hence they endure in splendid, if hermetic, majesty. That is, each perspective is assumed to have a sufficient claim to validity so that all can and must exist in endless, sterile disputation. That being the case, no serious progress is possible beyond mere fiddling with details of a given perspective. Moreover, the fate of perspectives is governed not by the results of research, but by fashion, taste, esthetics, or effective moral exhortation.

We must be very careful not to let our efforts to bring real theories into sociology be compromised by being labelled as the Rational Choice "approach" or "perspective." For then our work becomes just another one of the field's "theoretical" sects. But, as Voltaire pointed out, "There are no sects in geometry." And there are no sects in real theory, either.

To test this assertion, examine any university catalogue. You will find no course on the thought of Newton or Einstein in any physics department. Nor will you find a course on the thought of Copernicus in an astronomy department. And no courses on the thought of Darwin appear in biology department listings. Truly theoretical fields remember their ancestors only in ceremonial ways—no matter how illustrious their achievements—because real theories continue to evolve and, therefore, ancestors are always out-of-date.

My goal is to bring real theories into sociology, not to found a new theoretical sect. So, rather than suggest that rational choice theories are the future of sociology, I would suggest instead that for the future of sociology, theory is the only rational choice!

NOTES

[1] He also claimed that when he was in a hurry he didn't read a paper, but just looked at the tables, since that's really all of interest that the author could report.

[2] For other reasons see my ASR presidential address (1984).

[3] Phil did ask that we cut the essay from the 32 pages we submitted to his new, non-negotiable limit of 25 pages. But in the days before people were familiar with the power of word-processing (the machines available in those pre-micro computer days cost $12,000 or more and required extensive operator training), we solved this problem by having the font slightly reduced in size and slightly decreasing the margins.

REFERENCES

Bainbridge, William Sims. 1978. Satan's Power: *Ethnography of a Deviant Psychotherapy Cult.* Berkeley: University of California Press.

Bagnall, Roger S. 1992. "Landholding in Late Roman Egypt: The Distribution of Wealth." *The Journal of Roman Studies.* LXXXII: 128–149.

Bellah, Robert N. 1964. "Religious Evolution." *American Sociological Review* 29: 358–374.

Blau, Peter M. 1970. "A Formal Theory of Differentiation in Organizations." *American Sociological Review* 35: 201–218.

Coleman, James S. 1990. *Foundations of Social Theory.* Cambridge: The Belknap Press of Harvard University Press.

Demerath, N.J. III. 1965. *Social Class in American Protestantism.* Chicago: Rand McNally.

Finke, Roger, and Rodney Stark. 1992. *The Churching of America: 1776–1990.* New Brunswick, NJ: Rutgers University Press.

Garrett, William R. 1990. "Sociology and New Testament Studies: A Critical Evaluation of Rodney Stark's Contributions." *Journal for the Scientific Study of Religion* 29: 377–384.

Homans, George. 1961. *Social Behavior: Its Elementary Forms.* New York: Harcourt, Brace & World.

———1964. "Bringing Men Back In." *American Sociological Review* 29: 809–818.

Lenski, Gerhard. 1966. *Power and Privilege: A Theory of Social Stratification.* New York: McGraw-Hill.

———1970. *Human Societies.* New York: McGraw-Hill.

Popper, Karl R. 1957. "Philosophy of Science: A Personal Report." In C.A. Mace, ed., *British Philosophy in Mid-Century.* Oxford: Oxford University Press.

———1968. *Conjectures and Refutations.* New York: Harper Torchbooks.

Smith, Adam. [1776] 1937. *The Wealth of Nations.* New York: The Modern Library.

Stark, Rodney. 1984. "Religion and Conformity: Reaffirming a *Sociology* of Religion." *Sociological Analysis* 46: 18–27.

———1985. "From Church-Sect to Religious Economies." In Phillip E. Hammond, ed., *The Sacred in a Post-Secular Age.* Berkeley: University of California Press: 139–149.

Stark, Rodney, and William Sims Bainbridge. 1987. *A Theory of Religion.* New York and Bern: Peter Lang.

———1985. *The Future of Religion: Secularization, Revival, and Cult Formation.* Berkeley: University of California Press.

———1980. "Towards a Theory of Religion: Religious Commitment." *Journal for the Scientific Study of Religion* 19: 114–128.

Stark, Rodney, William Sims Bainbridge, Robert Crutchfield, Daniel P. Doyle, and Roger Finke, "Crime and Delinquency in the Roaring Twenties." *Journal of Research in Crime and Delinquency* 20: 4–23.

Stark, Rodney, and Charles Y. Glock. 1968. *American Piety: The Nature of Religious Commitment.* Berkeley: University of California Press.

Stark, Rodney, and Laurence R. Iannaccone. 1992. "Sociology of Religion." In Edgar F. Borgatta, editor-in-chief, and Marie L. Borgatta, managing editor, *Encyclopedia of Sociology.* New York: Macmillan: 2029–2037.

RATIONAL CHOICE

Framework for the
Scientific Study of Religion[1]

Laurence R. Iannaccone

Stark, Rodney, and Laurence R. Iannaccone. 1993. "Rational Choice Propositions About Religious Movements," in David G. Bromley and Jeffrey K. Hadden, eds., *Handbook on Cults and Sects in America.* Greenwich, CT: JAI Press: 109–125.

———1994. "A Supply-Side Reinterpretation of the 'Secularization' of Europe." *Journal for the Scientific Study of Religion* 33: 230–252.

Swanson, Guy E. 1960. *The Birth of the Gods.* Ann Arbor: University of Michigan Press.

Wallis, Roy, and Steve Bruce. 1984. "The Stark-Bainbridge Theory of Religion: A Critical Analysis of Counter Proposals." *Sociological Analysis* 45: 11–28.

Warner, R. Stephen. 1993. "Work in Progress Towards a New Paradigm for the Sociological Study of Religion in the United States." *American Journal of Sociology* 98: 1044–1093.

SINCE FINISHING my thesis in 1984, I have had the good fortune to find an employer willing to subsidize my research on the economics of religion, colleagues willing to read my papers and take them seriously, and collaborators with interests and agendas that complement my own. Rightly or wrongly, this run of luck has left me ever more convinced that rational choice theory offers a new framework for the social scientific study of religion. I find rational choice approaches to be both theoretically rigorous and empirically fruitful. They explain and integrate much of what is already known about religious participation, generate new predictions that suggest new avenues for empirical research, yield policy implications about the welfare effects of government intervention in the religious marketplace, and forge links between religious research and a growing body of rational choice research on other "nonmarket" institutions and activities.

This essay reviews the rational choice approach to religion, drawing from my own research to illustrate both general principles and specific applications. I will not defend the approach against its standard criticisms, having done so in another paper (Iannaccone, 1995a), nor will I venture a comprehensive survey. Instead, this essay provides something approximating an illustrated "how-to" manual for those interested in the approach. Starting with a brief overview, the essay traces rational choice through progressively higher levels of aggregation)—from households, to groups, to entire religious "markets"—always emphasizing the general assumptions underpinning the approach.

THE RATIONAL CHOICE APPROACH

Gary Becker (1976: 5) has aptly characterized the "heart" of the rational choice approach as "the combined assumptions of maximizing behavior, market equilibrium, and stable preferences, used relentlessly and unflinchingly." It was this broad and ambitious view of economics that drew me to the field,[2] and in many ways my subsequent research has remained unabashedly "Beckerian." Frankly, I cannot imagine a meaningful rational choice model of religion that does not ultimately rest upon these three assumptions:

> Assumption 1: *Individuals act rationally, weighing the costs and benefits of potential actions, and choosing those actions that maximize their net benefits.*

> Assumption 2: *The ultimate preferences (or "needs") that individuals use to assess costs and benefits tend not to vary much from person to person or time to time.*

> Assumption 3: *Social outcomes constitute the equilibria that emerge from the aggregation and interaction of individual actions.*

Of these three assumptions, maximizing behavior is fundamental. One must, however, emphasize its status as a simplifying *assumption* to be employed and assessed within the context of predictive models that are themselves simplified representations of reality. One may assert its usefulness without for a moment believing that people always act logically, efficiently, or in accordance with their own self-interest. I do not claim to *know* that people truly are rational. I simply know that rational choice assumptions have borne considerable fruit in the social sciences, particularly economics; that rational choice theory is well suited to the task of building and testing formal models of human behavior; and that the rational choice approach to religion has until recently gone largely untried.[3]

Rational choice theorists assume that people approach all actions in the same way, evaluating costs and benefits and acting so as to maximize their net benefits. Hence people choose what religion, if any, they will accept and how extensively they will participate in it. Over time, most people modify their religious choices in significant ways, varying their rates of religious participation and modifying its character, or even switching religions altogether. Given the assumption of stable preferences, the rational choice theorist is almost never content to explain such changes with reference to changed tastes, norms, or beliefs. The theorist seeks instead to model behavioral changes (and interpersonal differences) as optimal responses to varying circumstances—different prices, incomes, skills, experiences, technologies, resource constraints, and the like.

Similar assumptions apply to religion's supply side. Religious "producers" are also viewed as optimizers—maximizing members, net resources, government support, or some other basic determinant of institutional success. Evolutionary forces will favor maximizing behaviors even if religious firms do not consciously strive for "success," since the individuals, organizations, and policies that yield greater resources are more likely to survive and grow. The actions of church and clergy are thus modeled as rational responses to the constraints and opportunities found in the religious marketplace.

The combined actions of religious consumers and religious producers form a *religious market* which, like other markets, tends toward a steady-state equilibrium. As in other markets, the consumers' freedom to choose constrains the producers of religion. A "seller" (whether of automobiles or absolution) cannot long survive without the steady support of "buyers" (whether money-paying customers, dues-paying members, contributors and coworkers, or governmental subsidizers). Consumer preferences thus shape the content of religious commodities and the structure of the institutions that provide them. These effects are felt more strongly where religion is less regulated and competition among religious firms is more pronounced. In a highly competitive environment, religions have little choice but to abandon inefficient modes of production and unpopular products in favor of more attractive and profitable alternatives.

Finally, the rational choice approach presupposes a commitment to the goals and methods of science in general. This does not imply that narrative and metaphor have no place in a rational choice argument (McCloskey, 1985) or that qualitative field work must play second fiddle to quantitative survey data. But it does involve a search for behavioral laws that satisfy the criteria of objectivity, reproducibility, and refutability. (For more on this subject, see Rodney Stark's essay in this volume.)

THE HOUSEHOLD BEHAVIOR MODEL

Rational choice models have a distinctive logical structure. They explain religious behavior as the consequence of actions designed to solve one or more problems of the following form:

> **choose:**　　　　{*actions*}
> **that maximize:**　{*objective*}
> **subject to:**　　 {*constraints*}

To make any headway, a theorist must therefore state the actors' objective in a manner that is both analytically tractable and relevant to the question at hand. For example, in a model designed to predict church attendance, religious participation may appear as a separate source of utility while numerous other activities (recreation, transportation, dining, sleep, and social interactions) are lumped under a broad heading such as "other sources of satisfaction." Another model, designed to explore the interactions between religious "firms" and their "customers" may isolate different facets of religious participation, classifying some acts (such as preaching) as production and others (such as listening to a sermon) as consumption. Finding a level of abstraction that balances generality and clarity against practical relevance and predictive detail is always important and rarely easy.[4] (I am reminded of Albert Einstein's maxim that "theories should be as simple as possible, but not more so.") In practice, standard economic models of households, firms, or markets provide a natural starting point; the trick is finding an appropriate modification of an already fruitful approach.

Although the theorist will often experiment with different levels of abstraction, the actors' *ultimate* objectives, variously labeled "tastes" or "preferences," are assumed to remain stable. This assumption has both a philosophical basis (the conviction that fundamental human needs really do not differ much over time and place) and a pragmatic basis (the fact that we lack, as yet, any objective way to model and measure taste formation). In practice, it means that a rational choice model must explain changing behavior in terms of changing constraints. The assumptions of rational choice and stable preferences thus have the following corollary:

> *Behavioral changes (over time) are the consequence of changed constraints; behavioral differences (across individuals) are the consequence of differing constraints.*

Prices and incomes constitute the typical model's most *salient* constraints, but the overall state of technology and the actors' state of knowledge, ability, experience, and social position function as additional constraints. The theorist seeks to explain and predict behavior as optimal responses to changes in these constraints—price increase here, an income shift there, a technological innovation, or a difference in native ability or investment capital. This strategy can work only if one embraces a broad view of concepts like "price," "production," and "capital." Prices and costs refer to anything that must be sacrificed, regardless of its form—money, time, status, and so forth. Production occurs in the household just as it does in the factory, yielding both tangible commodities like home repairs and intangibles like relaxation. Educational and on-the-job investments in "human capital" (knowledge and skills) enhance productivity just like physical capital (machinery and structures). It is this perspective more than anything else that distinguishes the "new home economics" pioneered by Becker and his associates from traditional, commerce-oriented economics on the one hand and traditional sociology on the other.

> Assumption 4: *Constraints take a wide variety of forms—explicit and implicit prices, income and ability, physical and capital, technology governing both commercial and household production, and so forth.*

Starting Simple: Household Production

The simplest models of religious behavior ignore interactions and equilibrium, focusing instead on the behavior of individuals and households (e.g., Azzi and Ehrenberg, 1975). Viewing religion as just one of many household commodities, one may then analyze religious participation as a standard consumer choice problem:

> **choose:** {*the amounts of time and money to devote to religious versus secular activities*}
>
> **to maximize:** {*the overall utility derived from secular and religious commodities*}
>
> **subject to:** {*constraints on the total stock of household resources*}

One must, however, emphasize that most religious commodities are not tangible goods like cars or computers that can be manufactured, packaged, and sold in stores. Nor are they commercial services like haircuts or banking that we have others do for us. Rather, they fall into a third category that economists have labeled "household commodities"—valued goods and services that families and individuals produce for their own consumption (Becker, 1976: 89–114).

Household commodities may be as concrete as meals and laundry or as abstract as relaxation and love. Like the products of a commercial firm, household commodities are produced with scarce resources—purchased goods, household labor, and human skill. Hence even though we cannot quantify the relaxation and enjoyment derived from a commodity like "recreation," we may usefully speak of households "producing" this commodity by combining purchased inputs (such as ski equipment, automobile services, or VCRs, televisions, and stereos) with their own skills and time.

To model religious practice as a productive process, note that households routinely combine purchased goods and household time to "produce" religious satisfaction in much the same way that they produce meals, health, offspring, and recreation. To be sure, religious products are complex and largely unobservable (though possibly no more so than recreational enjoyment). Nevertheless, the principal *inputs* to religious production—time and money—are measurable and indeed are already routinely measured by researchers. Time inputs include the time spent attending and traveling to and from church services, devotional time spent praying, meditating, and reading scriptures, and time and effort required for religious charity or other religious activities. Money inputs include religious expenditures for Sunday attire, transportation to religious services, Bibles and other religious items, sacrificial offerings, and, above all, contributions that pay for religion's staff, services, and charitable works. (The knowledge, skills, and experiences specific to one's religion constitute a third class of inputs, which I will discuss in the next section.)

> Assumption 5: *Individuals and households produce religious "commodities" by combining money inputs (that pay for physical goods and services) with inputs of their own time.*

Despite its apparent simplicity, the household production model generates noteworthy predictions. Consider, for example, the concept of *input substitution* as it applies to religious production. Virtually all productive activities, whether household or commercial, concrete or abstract, require both time and money inputs. But the ratio of these inputs can often be varied. Home-cooked meals and restaurant meals can be equally good (or bad), but the former require greater inputs of household time relative to purchased goods. In like manner, lawns can be watered by hand or by automated sprinklers, trips can be taken by car or by plane, and children can be cared for by parents or preschools. In each of these cases, the efficient method of production will depend on the monetary value of the household's time. The higher the value of time, the more likely it is that the household will substitute time-saving, *money-intensive* forms of production for money-saving, *time-intensive* forms. Hence, it comes as no surprise that high income households are more likely to dine out, install sprinklers, travel by air, and send their children to preschools.

Applied to religion, the concept of input substitution implies that people with high monetary values of time will tend to engage in money-intensive religious practices. In particular, their money contributions will be high relative to their rates of attendance and vice versa. People with low monetary values of time will adopt more time-intensive practices and contribute relatively less money. To the best of my knowledge, these predictions have no precedent within traditional models of religious participation. They are, however, confirmed by survey results on church attendance and contributions (Iannaccone, 1990: 309). Although the surveys do not specify the ways in which people substitute money for time, casual observation suggests that richer congregations opt for a variety of time-saving, money-intensive practices: shorter services, more reliance on professional staff (such as clergy, custodians, choir directors, and paid soloists), larger and more costly facilities (permitting less use of members' homes for special meetings), less reliance on volunteered labor, and more reliance on purchased goods and services (such as catered meals in place of potlucks).

A second set of predictions concern religious contributions, and more specifically the *distribution* of contributions within congregations and across the entire population. A spate of recent research identifies "skewness" as the most striking unexplained feature of church contributions. According to Hoge (1993: 2), the highly skewed distribution of contributions "is an empirical finding in every study, and it is considered a bedrock rule of thumb by professional fund-raisers." In practice, this means that a mere twenty percent of church members provide up to eighty percent of the financial support in most congregations. Unfortunately, "past tradition in thinking about religious giving...has proven unsuited to explain...the highly skewed distribution of individual contributions in a typical church" (Hoge, 1993: 35).

To explain skewness in terms of household production, it suffices to recall that church attendance and contributions constitute the principle "expenditures" made in order to obtain religious commodities. Standard expenditure surveys and standard utility maximization models both suggest that: (1) the amount of money that a particular household devotes to any broad category of commodities tends to correlate very strongly with its income, (2) corresponding expenditures of time are relatively insensitive to changes in income (because the total amount of available time remains constant), and (3) a household's underlying propensity to consume broad categories of commodities depends on a wide range of factors that are largely unobservable, uncorrelated, and independent of income. Applied to a secular activity, such as vacationing, these facts lead us to (correctly) predict that richer people spend a great deal more *money* on their vacations (traveling to exotic locations, renting expensive equipment, and purchasing expensive meals and accommodations) but that they are not likely to consume much more vacation *time* (per year) than members of the middle class.

Similar predictions apply to religious activities. (1) Household contributions—the amount of money devoted to religion—will correlate very strongly with household income, but the contributed *share* of household income will be much less strongly linked to income.[5] (2) Income will have much less impact on church attendance—the amount of time devoted to religion. And (3) numerous other random factors will determine a person's overall propensity to participate in religious activities, raising or lowering both contributions and attendance while having little impact on their ratio.

It follows that dollar contributions will depend upon two distinct causal factors—household income and underlying religiosity—and that these two factors tend to interact *multiplicatively*. In contrast, church attendance will depend mostly upon a single factor—underlying religiosity. Drawing upon two additional facts (the empirical fact that the actual distributions of incomes tends to be skewed and the statistical fact that the product of independent, non-negative distributions tends to be more skewed than the underlying distributions), we can conclude that church contributions are virtually guaranteed to follow a distribution that is far more skewed than the distribution of church attendance, income, or underlying religiosity. The apparent mystery of skewness is thus solved by modeling church contributions as a particular class of commodity expenditures. For more on this subject, see Iannaccone (1993).

Complicating Things: Experience Effects

The most fruitful rational choice models of religious behavior spring from a marriage of abstract theory and empirical insight. Economics often can supply the theory, but the results are generally uninteresting (and sometimes absurd) if they ignore sociological observations.[6] As an economist and student of Becker, I was immediately drawn to the concept of religious commodity production, but it was my own familiarity with religion and the sociological research on religious participation that highlighted the importance of religious upbringing, social networks, and denominational ties. I developed the concept of *religious human capital* to bring these other determinants within the household production framework.

Religious capital denotes a person's accumulated stock of religious knowledge, skills, and sensitivities. It is an abstraction designed to encompass church ritual, doctrinal knowledge, friendships with fellow worshipers, and even faith (insofar as it is the product of experience). The term *human capital* is borrowed from labor economics, which introduced it to explain patterns in wages, career choice, and occupational mobility. In the case of religion, however, the distinction between a productivity-enhancing stock of "capital" and a taste-altering stock of "habits" is largely semantic (Iannaccone, 1984: 7).[7] The critical feature, regardless of terminology, is this: experience enhances the (real or perceived) value of religious activities, thereby raising rates of religious participation. Moreover, since most religious experience is "context specific" (relevant only to the particular congregation, denomination, or religious tradition in which it arose), human capital also shapes patterns of religious affiliation.

> Assumption 6: *As individuals and households produce religious commodities, they also accumulate a stock of "religious human capital" that enhances the satisfaction they derive from subsequent religious activity.*

Assumption 7: *Most religious human capital is "context specific," enhancing the real or perceived value of the particular activities, group, and religion that occasioned its accumulation.*

The human capital model yields predictions concerning denominational mobility, religious intermarriage, the timing of conversions, the influence of religious upbringing, the impact of mixed-faith marriage, and the age-profile of religiosity. For example, the similarities between religious capital and professional capital lead us to predict that most conversions and religious mobility will, like career choices and job mobility, occur at relatively young ages. Conversions and switching reflect people's efforts to find a better match between their religious capital and the context in which they will produce religious commodities. Over time, the gains from continued searching diminish, just as the benefits of job switching diminishes with age. Rates of intergenerational mobility tend to be low, particularly within distinctive religious traditions, since most children accumulate their religious capital in a (home and church) context determined by their parents. Switching will be most prevalent between relatively similar denominations (which allow the switchers to conserve on the value of their previous religious investments). Religious intermarriage will follow similar patterns, as people seek out partners whose religious human capital complements their own. The complementarity inherent in shared-faith marriages will lead to higher levels of church attendance and contributions. Churchgoers tend to accumulate religious capital as they age, and this leads to age-increasing patterns of religious participation. Survey data support all these predictions (Iannaccone, 1990; cf. Sherkat and Wilson, 1993).

More Complications: Religious Risk

Having begun with a simple model of religious commodity production, and having complicated it to take account of experience effects, we may complicate things further still by incorporating what Stark and Bainbridge (1985: 8) view as a defining feature of religion—its reliance on supernatural forces.

The supernatural imbues religious commodities with unique advantages and disadvantages, for although it can offer the prospect of otherwise unobtainable rewards (eternal life, peace on earth, unending bliss), the rewards are inherently risky, the existence and efficacy of these rewards must be taken on faith. Religion thus confronts its would-be producers and consumers with an obvious dilemma.

Assumption 7: *Most religious commodities are risky, promising large but uncertain benefits.*

Insights from the economics of uncertainty help us understand the activities and institutions that arise in response to this dilemma. After all, risk itself is hardly unique to religion, as any stock market investor or heart bypass candidate will readily attest. Secular markets and secular consumers deal with risk in various ways. In the case of stock market investments, the standard strategy is to diversify one's portfolio. In the case of heart surgery, the standard strategy is quite the opposite. Patients are well advised to identify a single, highly qualified specialist with whom they can develop a long-term relationship and to whom they will take all their business. As I will argue below, these two strategies have religious analogues that lead to different types of religious organizations and different patterns of religious practice. Risk thus paves the way from models of individual behavior to models of religious groups.

RELIGIOUS GROUPS[8]

Problems of risk arise whenever the attributes of a commodity cannot be fully determined prior to its purchase. problems prove especially serious when the commodity is expensive, hard to evaluate even after purchase, and impossible to return. Used cars embody all these features, as many a disappointed buyer will attest. Since potential buyers have difficulty assessing the quality of a used car in advance of purchase, used car sellers are tempted to overstate the value of their merchandise and to disguise its true nature. Knowing this, buyers will endeavor to reduce the odds of deception. They may demand guarantees, seek information from third parties, investigate the seller's reputation, and so forth. This motivates sellers to provide, or at least appear to provide, proof that their claims are true.

The uncertainty surrounding most religious goods is far greater than that which surrounds used cars. No amount of personal experience suffices fully to evaluate a religion's claims. Hence we can predict the emergence of institutions and arrangements designed to increase information (or at least the appearance of information) and reduce fraud.

Examples are not hard to find. Testimonials are commonplace in religion and, predictably, are more common in those variants that place greater emphasis on material blessings. Testimonies are more likely to be believed when they come from a trusted source, such as a personal acquaintance or a respected figure. They are especially credible when testifiers have relatively little to gain (or, better yet, much to lose) from having their claims heard and believed. This helps to explain why the character of religious activity is so often *collective* and the structure of religious organizations is so often *congregational*.[9] Fellow members are more trustworthy than strangers. They also have less incentive to overstate the benefits of the religion than do members of the clergy, whose livelihood depends on a steady stream of "sales." The clergy, in turn, are more persuasive when they do not benefit materially from their followers' faith or when they receive low salaries relative to their level of training.

Rational choice theory thus explains several distinctive features of religious institutions in terms of their ability to reduce the risk of consumer fraud. These include: a minimal professional staff whose financial compensation is low or independent of customer contributions/payments; heavy reliance on part-time and volunteer workers (and thus reliance on payments of time and service rather than money); a congregational structure, which limits the need for full-time professionals and provides a source of credible product endorsements; and collective activities, which provide continuous assurance through the enthusiasm, devotion, conviction, and testimony of fellow members.

> Assumption 8: *Collective production tends to reduce the risk and raise the value associated with religious activities.*

Congregations and Free-riders

Congregational structure has costs as well as benefits. It does indeed reduce the risk of fraud, thereby making religion more compelling and attractive, but it also makes it more vulnerable to "free-rider" problems. Such problems arise wherever individuals find it possible to reap the benefits of other people's efforts without expending a corresponding effort of their own.

One need not look far to find examples of anemic congregations plagued by free-riding—a visit to the nearest old-line Protestant church usually will suffice. However, far more striking examples are found in cults and communes. In such groups, which can only survive with high levels of commitment, the costs of free-riding are laid bare. Consider, for example, the Shakers' problems with transient members, or the Moonies' struggles with "exploiters" who joined the movement for "inexpensive room and board, money,...or sex" (Lofland, 1977: 152). Kanter (1973: 157–158) documents the "commitment problems" that plagued most nineteenth-century communes and quotes Charles Guide's observation that "these colonies are threatened as much by success as by failure...[for] if they attain prosperity they attract a crowd of members who lack the enthusiasm and faith of the earlier ones." The same perverse dynamic threatens *all* groups engaged in the production of collective goods.

> Assumption 9: *Collective religious activities are susceptible to free-rider problems.*

It would seem that religions are caught on the horns of a dilemma. On the one hand, a congregational structure which relies on the collective action of numerous volunteers is needed to make the religion credible. On the other hand, that same congregational structure threatens to undermine the level of commitment and contributions needed to make a religion viable.

Costly demands offer a solution to the dilemma (Iannaccone, 1992, 1994). The costs are not the standard costs associated with the production or purchase of secular commodities. Rather, they are apparently *gratuitous* costs—sacrifice and stigma—such as: burnt offerings, which destroy valued resources; distinctive dress and grooming that invite ridicule or scorn; dietary and sexual prohibitions that limit opportunities for pleasure; restrictions on the use of modern medicine or technology. The list goes on. Such costs are present to some degree in all religions, but they are especially pronounced in cults and sects.

Costly demands mitigate the free-rider problems that otherwise undermine a religious group. They do so for two reasons. First, they create a social barrier that tends to screen out half-hearted members. No longer is it possible simply to drop by and reap the benefits of attendance or membership. To take part, one must pay a price, bearing the stigma and sacrifice demanded of all members. Second, they increase the relative value of group activities, thereby stimulating participation among those who do join the group. Social stigmas make it costly (or even impossible) to engage in activities outside the group, and as the price of external activities rises, the demand for internal substitutes increases. To put the matter crudely: a comprehensive ban on dances, movies, gambling, drinking, and "worldly" friendships will turn Friday church socials into the highlight of one's week.

Cost-benefit analysis thus reveals why strict churches survive and flourish. Strictures mitigate free-rider problems. Potential members are forced to choose: participate fully or not at all. The seductive middle-ground is eliminated; average levels of commitment and participation increase; and, strange as it may seem, many members come out ahead. Efficient religions may thus embrace stigma, self-sacrifice, and bizarre behavioral standards; and perfectly rational people can be drawn to decidedly unconventional groups. This conclusion is in extreme contrast with the view, prevalent among psychiatrists, clinical psychologists, and the media, that conversion to religious cults or sects is inherently pathological, the consequence of psychological abnormality or coercive "brainwashing."

The proposed model of cost-induced commitment leads to a formal theory of church and sect (Iannaccone, 1988, 1992). By characterizing numerous religious demands as functionally equivalent solutions to free-rider problems, the model implicitly categorizes religions according to the extent to which they limit the consumption opportunities of their members. Groups that demand similar levels of sacrifice should display similar behavior despite differences in organization, history, and theology. Mainstream "churches" and extremist "sects" thus emerge as analytically distinct modes of religious organization rather than *ad hoc* descriptive categories, and the empirical correlates of sectarianism—strict behavioral standards, dramatic conversions, high levels of religious participation, resistance to social change, lower-class and minority appeal—emerge as formal consequences of a sectarian strategy. This single framework explains numerous empirical regularities that have fascinated religious scholars for most of a century.

Religious Portfolios

We have traced the consequences of religious risk down a lengthy path: from collective activities and congregational structures, to free-rider problems, to sacrifice and stigma, to a religious market equilibrium encompassing both low-cost "churches" and high-cost "sects."

There is, however, an alternative response to risk familiar to any market investor—*diversification*. One may reduce risk by spreading investments over a *portfolio* of assets.

To apply the portfolio concept to religious behavior, recall that many religious activities have the character of risky investments, sacrificing concrete resources for uncertain rewards. Note also that most people have access to a variety of different religions or different classes of religious acts within a single religious tradition. This situation gives religious "investors" a strong incentive to assemble *diversified portfolios of competing religious assets*. Such investors might hedge their religious bets by going to confession on Sunday, consulting a medium on Monday, and engaging in transcendental meditation on Wednesday.

Assumption 10: *Diversification can reduce the perceived risk associated with religious commodities.*

One is tempted to dismiss this line of thought as a case of economic logic pushed to the brink of absurdity. The typical American churchgoer is, after all, firmly wedded to a single religious tradition, a single denomination, and a single congregation. If the demand for diversification is as great as the preceding argument suggests, then why does competition not force churches to accommodate it? How do churches demand, and maintain, the sort of brand loyalty that secular producers only dream of?

The answer is that some religions *do* permit diversification, but these religions employ a very different "production technology" than that which characterizes standard American religion. The technology of religious production may be either "collective" or "private," and only the latter lends itself to diversification.

Assumption 11: *Religious commodities may* be either *"collective" (benefiting group)* or *"private" (benefiting individual consumers).*[10]

Most Western religions rely on collective, congregational production. In describing the risk-reducing advantages of the collective approach, I have emphasized that such religions must limit free-riding. Many do so through costly demands that effectively isolate members from competing groups. The demands can be sustained, despite competition from other religions, because the costs of exclusivity are for many people more than balanced by the gains from collective action. But exclusivity and diversification do not mix. A church cannot isolate its members and at the same time permit them to participate in competing groups— the two strategies are incompatible. Hence, congregationally-oriented religions can (and generally do) limit their members' involvement in competing religions. These limitations are most extensive in highly sectarian groups such as the Mormons, Jehovah's Witnesses, Adventists, Krishnas, Moonies, and fundamentalist Christian denominations.

But not all religions are congregationally oriented. Some deal in "private commodities" analogous to standard consumer products. These private commodities can be transferred directly from an individual producer to an individual consumer without recourse to a mediating group. Most New Age products fall into this category—books, tapes, and seminars; herbs, crystals, and pyramids; and techniques for meditation. Production and distribution of these products are not hampered by free-rider problems. Hence the costly strategies described in the previous section—exclusivity, sacrifice, and stigma—are not needed. Indeed, a producer of private commodities who employs these strategies will suffer a competitive disadvantage relative to other private-commodity producers, since the former imposes a cost upon his or her customers but can offer no special benefit in return. Religious firms that deal in private commodities are thus forced to sell their products "with no strings attached." It follows that their customers will patronize other firms so as to diversify their portfolio of religious assets. We may summarize the argument with a pair of propositions about the types of religious firms that can exist in equilibrium:

> Proposition 1: *Wherever religious firms exist to provide* private *commodities, competitive forces and risk aversion will lead consumers to patronize multiple firms, thereby diversifying their religious portfolios.*

> Proposition 2: *Wherever religious firms exist to facilitate the production of* collective *commodities, the firm and its patrons will demand exclusivity to mitigate the free-rider problems.*

Proposition 2 does not assert that a collective setting alters people's tastes. It is not their *desire* for a diversified portfolio that is diminished, only their *opportunity* to indulge that desire. In the absence of institutional constraints, people will yield to the temptation to free-ride and to diversify, and this in turn will undermine the collective. Hence, only those firms that maintain sufficient exclusivity (by means of strictness, monitoring, and the like) can remain viable producers of collective commodities. The members' impulse to diversify will be accommodated only in a limited sense and *only within the individual firm*. It follows that these firms will be under pressure to take a department store approach to religion—comprehensive belief systems, cradle to grave services, extensive and varied social networks, and so forth. In contrast, religious firms that produce private goods and services will be under no pressure to provide a full range of products. The forces of competition will, in fact, drive them to specialize, much as secular firms tend to specialize. Hence, private commodity firms over time will come to resemble highly specialized boutiques.

If propositions 1 and 2 are correct, then the degree to which a religious firm provides its customers/members with collective versus private goods should correlate with its tendency to make exclusive versus non-exclusive demands. The comprehensiveness of the firm's product line should also correlate. Even the content and financial strategies of the religion will be affected. Private religion will usually deal in specific goods and services, items that can be produced by one set of individuals and sold to another. Collective religion will deal in collective action and collective services—commodities that blur the line between producer and consumer and that do not lend themselves to buying and selling. The distinction between private and collective goods thus helps explain why some religions organize around client/practitioner or buyer/seller relationships whereas others organize as collectives in which all members are, to varying degrees, coworkers and co-consumers.

Empirical support for these predictions appears at many levels—within the United States, across the globe, and throughout history (Iannaccone, 1995b). Traditional Western religions, particularly their more sectarian variants, exemplify collective religion. In contrast, New Age religions exemplify what I am calling *private* religion. They are less susceptible to free-rider problems, but also less capable of generating commitment. They attract many "customers" but few real "members." Their practices center on client/practitioner relationships or fee-for-service transactions, and consumers tend not to form exclusive attachments to a single religion or religious firm. Monetary payments for services rendered tend to overshadow costly demands for an austere, deviant, or sacrificial lifestyle. Asian religions, in general, and Japanese Shintoism and Buddhism, in particular, exhibit similar features. Within the Greco-Roman Empire, Paganism manifested many, if not all, of the attributes of private, portfolio religions. In contrast, Early Christianity and Hellenistic Judaism were "classic" examples of exclusive, collective religions.

RELIGIOUS MARKETS: MONOPOLY VERSUS COMPETITION

The preceding propositions about collective and private commodities concern the types of religious firms that can survive in a state of long-run equilibrium. But economic theory has much more to say about equilibrium, particularly as it relates to different market structures.

To account for the appearance of religious markets, it suffices to note that gains from trade and specialization exist in religion as in virtually all other areas of life. People differ in their underlying capacities to produce religious commodities, and even those with similar abilities and endowments can dramatically increase their productivity by forgoing self-sufficiency in exchange for specialized training and market exchange. Firms specializing in the production of religious goods and services thus arise naturally and inevitably.

The simplest models of religious markets abstract from the special characteristics of religious commodities such as risk, human capital, and household production. Demand-side decisions then become a relatively simple matter of choosing the optimal level of religious consumption at the going price. Supply-side assumptions may be kept correspondingly simple. Thus:

> Assumption 12: *Churches are profit-maximizing firms specializing in the production of religious goods and services. Church workers are motivated by the same sort of self-interest that motivates secular workers.*

These are by *no means* the most realistic assumptions that one might adopt. I have chosen them over more "nuanced" formulations merely to keep the analysis tractable, thereby allowing the model to be judged against its formal predictions.

The concepts of religious supply and demand tap directly into a huge body of economic theory and data pertaining to markets, competition, and regulation. If church members act as utility-maximizing demanders and churches as profit-maximizing suppliers, then market forces constrain churches just as they do secular firms, and the benefits of religious competition, the burdens of monopoly, and the hazards of government regulation are as real as in any other sector of the economy. The market model thus predicts that pluralistic competition will stimulate religious markets just as it does secular markets, forcing suppliers to efficiently produce a wide range of alternative faiths well adapted to the specific needs of consumers. On the other hand, a state-sponsored religious monopoly will provide only the appearance of piety—an ineffective clergy and an apathetic population lie just below the surface.

Beginning with Finke and Stark's (1988) analysis of church membership in turn-of-the-century American cities, evidence for "the market model" has piled up with surprising speed. Finke and Stark found higher rates of religious affiliation and activity in cities with higher rates of religious diversity. Hamberg and Pettersson (1994) document a similar pattern across the provinces of Sweden. My own study of religious participation in seventeen Western nations finds significantly higher rates of church attendance and religious belief in countries with more religious pluralism (Iannaccone, 1991, cf., Chaves and Cann, 1992). Stark and McCann's (1989) analysis of data from one hundred American Catholic dioceses finds a strong negative correlation between Catholic market share and the fraction of Catholic males entering the priesthood. Iannaccone and Finke (1993) document the importance of religious regulation in America, Europe, and Japan. Martin (1990: 13) traces back the recent "explosion" of Protestantism to the elimination of state-established Catholic monopoly and "the general deregulation of religion" (cf., Gill, 1992). The demise of the Communist Party's repressive secular monopoly has ushered in a similar explosion of old and new religious faiths in Eastern Europe and Russia.

Historical research provides further evidence of the weakness of monopoly faiths and the vigor that comes with competition. It is becoming clear that Europe's so-called "age of faith" was in fact an era of widespread religious apathy, and that American rates of church membership and religious practice rose steadily as the established churches of the original colonies gave way to a free and increasingly diverse market of competing denominations (Finke and Stark, 1992). Econometric estimates by Kelly Olds (1994) document the increased demand for clergy that followed the disestablishment of religion in colonial New England.

CONCLUSIONS

Rational models of religion have begun to make good on their promises—integrating predictions, providing new explanations for observed regularities, and generating new hypotheses to guide future empirical research. This essay has traced the rational choice approach from simple models of individual behavior, to arguments about religious groups, to generalizations about religious markets. At each step, I have emphasized the assumptions that give the approach its distinctive character and provide the conceptual basis for further research. At the same time, I have tried to highlight the interplay between theoretical analysis and empirical insights.

Continued progress depends on this interplay. Economists have much to offer in the way of theory, but other social scientists have generated virtually all the survey data, ethnographic research, and studies of textual material. Economic theorists cannot simply assemble models from the bits of information that others have unearthed; one needs a "feel" for religion to know what to retain and what to abstract. Sociologists of religion have an overwhelming comparative advantage when it comes to empirical insights of this sort.

The models described in this essay cry out for additional empirical work. Some has begun to appear (in recent tests of the relationship between pluralism and religious participation). But I fear that long-standing debates over secularization and pluralism threaten to crowd out more basic research. Despite the obvious importance of these and other "macro" debates, I would urge more attention to micro-level questions. Do people really perceive some religions as more costly or risky than others, and are these perceptions consistent enough to justify cost-benefit analyses? Do individuals and organizations actually trade off between time and money when they "produce" religious commodities? How much time and money do people actually devote to religion, and how do these amounts vary across different groups? Do the consumers of "private" religion really hold religious portfolios? Do the producers of different types of religions finance their activities in systematically different ways? Until now, most rational choice research has made do with old data that happened to address the questions at hand. The rate of return to this research has proved high enough to justify investing in new empirical studies aimed squarely at the theory and its predictions. Traditional, psychologically-oriented scales of religious attitudes and behavior should be augmented by new measures of time and money, human capital, costs and benefits, collective versus private commodities, religious firms and their products, market competition, and religious regulation. The field is wide open, and any number can play.

NOTES

[1] Preparing this chapter has heightened my sense of indebtedness to colleagues who have provided continuing encouragement, assistance, and constructive criticism: Gary Becker, Roger Finke, Benton Johnson, Carrie Miles, Daniel Olson, Rodney Stark, Stephen Warner, and many others.

[2] The standard undergraduate approach to economics left me cold—so much so that after repeatedly enrolling in introductory economics (and always quitting after the first few lectures), I abandoned the subject in favor of the far more interesting social science offerings in sociology, anthropology, psychology, and political science. It was only after receiving a Masters in mathematics at the University of Chicago and sampling graduate lectures by Gary Becker, Milton Friedman, and George Stigler that I decided to give economics a second try.

[3] The rational choice approach may eventually give way to models that employ more complex assumptions about human behavior, but we are not likely to develop such models without first working out the strengths and weaknesses of rational choice. The rapidly growing body of research in "behavioral economics" and "behavioral finance" exemplifies this sequence (Thaler, 1992).

[4] For an impressive example of this balancing act, see Montgomery's (1994) rational choice model of denominational transformation.

[5] Recent empirical research conclusively verifies both of these predictions. In survey after survey, income is by far the strongest single predictor of church contributions—richer people do give more. But the *share* of income given is only weakly (and somewhat negatively) related to income. Hence, the rich contribute a slightly smaller percentage of their income to religion.

[6] The problem arises because theory fails to identify the objects of satisfaction in any given model. Azzi and Ehrenberg's (1975) model of religious participation, which posited "afterlife consumption" as the principle motivation for church attendance, illustrates this problem. Their failure to take account of sociological research on the empirical determinants of church attendance seriously weakens an otherwise ingenious application of household production theory.

[7] The mathematical model is identical in either case. Elsewhere, I used the same model to analyze habit formation (Iannaccone, 1986), and Becker and Murphy (1990) extended the model in their theory of "rational addiction."

[8] The following discussion draws heavily from Iannaccone (1992 and forthcoming).

[9] These observations parallel long-standing insights into the sociology of religion, such as Durkheim's (1965: 62) definition of religion as a collective phenomenon based on group rituals and shared meanings, and Berger's (1969: 46) claim that a religion cannot remain plausible unless it is embedded within a community that shares and reinforces its worldview.

[10] Here and throughout the paper, I adopt the standard economic definitions of the terms "private" and "collective." A commodity is said to be "private" if its benefits can be limited to a single individual or select group of individuals and if its use by that one person (or select group) precludes use by others. Most standard goods and services fall into this category— meals, haircuts, the use of a car, and so forth. A commodity is said to be "collective," "public," or "quasi-public" if it naturally benefits an entire group or population and if its use or consumption by one member of that group does not preclude its use by other members. Common examples include fire protection, national defense, public parks, and TV transmissions.

REFERENCES

Azzi, Corry, and Ronald Ehrenberg. 1975. "Household Allocation of Time and Church Attendance." *Journal of Political Economy* 84 (3): 27–56.

Becker, Gary S. 1976. *The Economic Approach to Human Behavior*. Chicago: University of Chicago Press.

Becker, Gary S., and Kevin Murphy. 1990. "A Theory of Rational Addiction." *Journal of Political Economy*.

Chaves, Mark, and David E. Cann. 1992. "Regulation, Pluralism, and Religious Market Structure: Explaining Religion's Vitality." *Rationality and Society* 4 (3).

Finke, Roger, and Rodney Stark. 1988. "Religious Economies and Sacred Canopies: Religious Mobilization in American Cities, 1906." *American Sociological Review* 53 (1): 41–49.

———1992. *The Churching of America 1776–1990: Winners and Losers in our Religious Economy*. New Brunswick, NJ: Rutgers University Press.

Gill, Anthony J. 1992. "Responses to Authoritarianism: Religious Competition and Church-State Relations in Latin America." Paper presented at the meetings of the Western Political Science Association, San Francisco, CA.

Hamberg, Eva M., and Thorleif Pettersson. 1994. "The Religious Market: Denominational Competition and Religious Participation in Contemporary Sweden." *Journal for the Scientific Study of Religion* 33 (3): 205–216.

Hoge, Dean. 1993. "Theoretical Approaches for Explaining Levels of Financial Giving by Church Members." Unpublished Paper. Washington, DC: Catholic University.

Iannaccone, Laurence R. 1984. "Consumption Capital and Habit Formation with an Application to Religious Participation." PhD dissertation, University of Chicago.

———1988. "A Formal Model of Church and Sect." *American Journal of Sociology* 94 (supplement): s241–s268.

———1990. "Religious Participation: A Human Capital Approach." *Journal of the Scientific Study of Religion* 29 (3): 297–314.

———1991. "The Consequences of Religious Market Structure: Adam Smith and the Economics of Religion." *Rationality and Society* 3 (2): 156–177.

———1992. "Sacrifice and Stigma: Reducing Free-Riding in Cults, Communes, and Other Collectives." *Journal of Political Economy* 100 (2): 271–291.

———1993. "Modeling the Determinants of Church Contributions." Working paper.

———1994. "Why Strict Churches are Strong." *American Journal of Sociology 99* (5): 1180–1211.

———1995a. "Voodoo Economics? Defending the Rational Choice Approach to Religion." *Journal for the Scientific Study of Religion* 34 (1): 76–88.

———1995b. "Risk, Rationality, and Religious Portfolios." *Economic Inquiry* 33 (2): 285–295.

Iannaccone, Laurence R., and Roger Finke. 1993. "The Illusion of Shifting Demand: Supply-Side Explanations for Trends and Change in the American Religious Marketplace." *The Annals of the American Association of Political and Social Science* 527 (May): 27–39.

Kanter, Rosabeth Moss. 1973. *Commitment and Community: Communes and Utopias in Sociological Perspective*. Cambridge: Harvard University Press.

Lofland, John. *Doomsday Cult*. 1977. New York: Wil

Martin, David. 1990. *Tongues of Fire: The Explosion of Protestantism in Latin America*. Oxford, England: Basil Blackwell.

McCloskey, Donald N. 1985. *The Rhetoric of Economics*. Madison, WI: University of Wisconsin Press.

Olds, Kelly. 1994. "Privatizing the Church: Disestablishment in Connecticut and Massachusetts." *Journal of Political Economy* 102 (2): 277–297.

Sherkat, Darren E., and John Wilson. 1993. "Preferences and Choice in Religious Markets: An Examination of Religious Switching and Apostasy." Mimeo: Vanderbilt University, 1993.

Stark, Rodney, and William Sims Bainbridge. 1985. *The Future of Religion*. Berkeley: University of California Press.

Thaler, Richard H. 1992. *The Winner's Curse: Paradoxes and Anomalies of Economic Life*. New York: The Free Press.

THE CONSEQUENCES OF RELIGIOUS COMPETITION

Supply-side Explanations for Religious Change

Roger Finke

WHEN EUROPEAN scholars and church leaders visited nineteenth-century America, they were quick to comment on what they called the "voluntary principle." Using explicit market terms, they described the unique "religious economy" and the open competition that resulted from separating church and state. Andrew Reed (1835: 127), who was sent by the Congregational Union of England and Wales to assess the church of America, offered this bold pronouncement on America's "Religious Economy which may be denominated *temporal*":

> Deliberately, but without hesitation, I say, *the result is in everything and every where most favourable to the voluntary, and against the compulsory principle*...Fact is universally in its favour (Reed, 1835: 137, 141).

Reed confidently added: "I need not, I presume, enter into detail on this particular; for none will arise to contradict the assertion" (Reed, 1835: 141). Philip Schaff ([1855] 1961: 96, 99), born in Switzerland and educated in Germany, offered similar praise for the new principle, but cautioned that it "changes the peaceful kingdom of God into a battlefield," describing America as the "classic land of sects." For Reed and Schaff the "facts" seemed obvious: separating church and state invigorated local churches and increased religious competition by introducing a host of new sects. Current scholars, however, have overlooked many of their keen insights on the implications of separating church and state.

This essay will review and extend recent theoretical work on the consequences of deregulating religious markets. Like the European visitors, I will discuss religious changes in market terms and give careful attention to the religious competition resulting from deregulation. I'll begin by clarifying why recent theoretical work on religious markets emphasizes supply-side changes, rather than the demand-side changes highlighted by other approaches. Then I'll discuss how regulation restricts competition by changing the incentives and opportunities of religious producers and the options for religious consumers. Finally, I'll devote the latter half of the essay to propositions on competition and pluralism in local religious markets. Here I'll explain why competition and pluralism result in more efficient religious organizations, lead to market niches, and mobilize a high percentage of the population into churches.

SUPPLY-SIDE EXPLANATION[1]

Explanations of religious change have focused almost exclusively on the changing *demand* for religion. The secularization model, long the dominant theory in the sociology of religion, is based on the premise that religion will decline as modernity erodes the demand for traditional religious beliefs (cf., Wilson, 1966, 1982). This confines the model in two ways. First, since the model forecasts only a decline in religious demand, it fails to explain increases in religious activity (Hadden, 1987; Finke, 1992). Second, and more relevant to this essay, it fails to address the impact of changing supply. What happens when the number and type of available religions change?

But the secularization model is not the only theory that ignores the supply side of religious change. Most explanations offered by historians and social scientists assume that fluctuations in religious activity are due to a shifting demand for religion. The source of this new demand is often vaguely attributed to cultural realignments, a change in the national psyche, economic cycles, or an escapist flight from modernity, with little attention given to changing supplies.[2]

A supply-side approach turns this assumption on its head and asserts that the most significant changes in religion derive from shifting *supply*, not shifting demand. Let me offer a couple of examples from my own research with Rodney

Stark and Larry Iannaccone (Finke and Stark, 1992; Finke and Iannaccone, 1993; Iannaccone, Finke, and Stark, forthcoming).

General histories of American religion devote much attention to the so-called "Great Awakenings" that ran from approximately 1730 to 1760 and 1800 to 1830. The First Great Awakening is best known for the enormously successful revivals of George Whitefield during 1739 and 1740. Whitefield attracted unprecedented numbers to his revivals throughout the colonies. Indeed, when he bid farewell in Boston, the crowd was estimated at 30,000—at a time when the total population of Boston was approximately 20,000. As for the Second Great Awakening, the revivals of Finney and others are well chronicled, but the most remarkable feature was the rapid growth of upstart sects and their ability to expand the market. Between 1776 and 1850 the national rate of adherence doubled, from 17 to 34 percent.

So what explains the success of Whitefield's revivals or the phenomenal growth of the upstart sects? As the term "awakening" suggests, scholars view these years as periods of surging demand. For example, William McLoughlin (1978: 2) describes awakenings as "cultural transformations affecting all Americans" and claims that they "begin in periods of cultural distortion and grave personal stress, when we lose faith in the legitimacy of our norms, the viability of our institutions, and the authority of our leaders in church and state." The argument is clear: the flurry of revivalistic activity was a response to a shift in religious demand.

But I would argue that this surge in revivals and the growth of organized religion was due to a shift in supply, not demand. As the colonial establishments lost support, upstart sects gained freedoms. With the restrictions on new sects and itinerants reduced, a new wave of religious suppliers emerged—suppliers that aggressively marketed their product to the masses. Whitefield's crowds didn't materialize out of nowhere, they responded to the publicity, press releases, and sermons circulated in their communities up to two years in advance (Lambert, 1990, 1994; Stout, 1991). The so-called Second Great Awakening was nothing more (nor less) than the successful marketing campaigns of "upstart" evangelical Protestants. Thus early American religion flourished in response to religious *deregulation*.

The effects of regulation, moreover, are not confined to one nation or time period. Post World War II Japan serves as one of many other examples. Before the end of World War II, the government strictly controlled religious activity in Japan. The state subsidized Shinto shrines and participation in Shinto ceremonies was a matter of civic duty. Alternative religions required government recognition to legally exist, and once recognized, they faced interference, suppression, and persecution from the state (McFarland, 1967; Hardacre, 1989). But the Japanese defeat and Allied Occupation in 1945 led to the immediate repeal of all laws controlling religion, disestablished the Shinto religion, and granted unprecedented religious freedom (Nakano, 1987).

The response was overwhelming. The period immediately following 1945 is called *kamigami no rasshu awa*, the "rush hour of the gods." It was said that "New Religions rose like mushrooms after a rainfall" (quoted in McFarland, 1967: 4).[3] By 1949, 403 new religious groups were founded, and 1,546 other groups established independence through secession from the shrines, temples, or churches to which they had previously belonged. In contrast, only 31 religious groups had received official recognition in the decades before 1945—13 Shinto sects, 28 Buddhist denominations, and two Christian groups (Nakano, 1987: 131). Some have argued that it was the *demand* for religion, not supply, that shifted most dramatically in the wake of World War II. This explanation, sometimes called the "cargo cult theory", suggests that when people are faced with frustrated expectations, social instability, and a loss of faith in traditional institutions, they will seek out new religions offering new answers (see Shupe, 1973). Like the Great Awakening thesis proposed by American historians, this theory suggests that the surge of new religions was driven by a sudden change in religious demand.

I reject this argument for several reasons. First, Japanese defeat did not trigger widespread spiritual escapism; the traditional religions did not experience an increase in membership or devotion. Second, the growth of new religions continued long after the Japanese economy recovered and continues even today. Third, Germany shared Japan's defeat, but its religious economy remained highly regulated and did not experience a post-war boom in new religions. On the other hand, when South Korea was liberated from Japanese rule and Japanese religious restrictions, it displayed a similar flowering of new religions, with a sharp increase in the level of active membership.[4]

These are but two of many examples where a prominent shift in regulation brought about rapid religious change. But the effects of regulation are not confined to prominent shifts. In other work, as I have shown, subtle revisions in existing rules have led to a change in the supply and activity of religious producers. American evangelical preachers rushed to the airwaves when a new Federal Communication Commission ruling facilitated their entry, and Eastern religions gained a committed following in late 1960s America when a new law allowed their teachers to immigrate. In each case, a supply-side shift explains what many claimed was a change in market demand.

This emphasis on supply-side changes, however, does *not* deny the importance of religious demand. I recognize that religious markets owe their outcomes to the forces of both supply *and* demand, with religious pluralism resulting from the inherent segmenting of religious demand in any religious market. Still, I emphasize the supply side because it is so often ignored and because I believe that the underlying determinants of religious demand are far more stable than past research would suggest. Whether they be the historical examples offered above, or contemporary religious changes in Russia, Latin America, and the Philippines, the neglected supply-side approach holds the key to understanding specific religious developments.

REGULATING INCENTIVES AND OPPORTUNITIES

As illustrated by the examples just given, regulations play a key role in defining how religious economies operate and in predicting the level of religious activity. Yet knowing that a decrease in regulation increases supply and participation doesn't explain why it occurs. To understand how regulation shapes the outcome of religious economies, we need to step closer to the actors in the market. How does regulation constrain the options available for both producers and consumers? I will argue that *regulation restricts competition by changing the incentives and opportunities for religious producers (churches, preachers, revivalists, etc.) and the viable options for religious consumers (church members)* (Finke, 1990).

For religious economies there are two common forms of regulation: suppression and subsidy. Although suppression is the more obvious form of regulation, subsidy is equally powerful. Both forms of regulation restrict competition in the market by defining the rules governing the operation of the religious economy. Subsidy rewards only selected religious groups, and suppression penalizes unauthorized groups. Each form of regulation changes the incentives and opportunities for producers and the options for consumers.

Suppression offers the most obvious examples of changing opportunities and incentives. Laws that place restrictions on the practice of religion deny opportunities to religions not authorized by the state. History has repeatedly shown that new religions are the most frequent targets of suppression, as is clearly evident in the examples of Japan and the U.S. offered earlier (Mead, 1963; McLoughlin, 1971; Beckford, 1985; Robbins and Beckford, 1993). The incentives and opportunities for starting a new religion in Japan were low before World War II. Religious leaders (producers) faced a battle for official acceptance and, once accepted, they still faced possible persecution from the state. And for the followers (consumers), the cost of membership included the usual demands of religious practice, along with the additional costs of concealing their membership or facing public harassment. Similarly, North America's colonial sects often struggled for acceptance, itinerant revivalists were denied preaching opportunities, and members faced persecution. In each case, suppression reduced the opportunities and the incentives for starting or maintaining an unauthorized religion, especially a new or "deviant" one.

The effects of suppression, however, reach far beyond the immediate repression of a few small and powerless religious groups. Suppression changes the incentives for *all* religions, as well as the long-term growth of the religious economy. First, consider how the incentives change for dominant religions when they can restrict competition through suppression. In North America, the colonial establishments found it far easier to suppress the activities of itinerants than to compete with them. Incentives for institutional change or popular appeal soon fade when churches find they can restrict their competition through suppression.

Second, the new religions so frequently suppressed by state regulations are a source of innovation and growth for any religious economy. Not only do they appeal to a segment of the population not reached by the more "refined" religions authorized by the state,[5] they also serve as a testing ground for religious innovation. Although most fail, a few succeed (Stark and Bainbridge, 1985). Soka Gakkai, the most successful new religion in Japan, went from 60 members in 1937 to 8 million in 1972 and is currently a powerful religious and political force in Japan. The struggling American Methodist sect went from 2.5 percent of all religious adherents in 1776 to 34.2 percent in 1850. For unregulated markets, today's religious majority is formed from yesterday's minority.

When compared to the open suppression of religion, the regulatory effects of subsidy are far more subtle. Indeed, at first glance subsidy would appear to stimulate activity by supporting religious institutions and reducing the cost of involvement for the individual. But closer inspection reveals that subsidy reduces the incentives of religious producers to gain popular support and limits competition by restricting the subsidy to a few select religions.

Church subsidies, for example, dramatically change the incentives of the clergy. A religious dissenter from Connecticut offered this biting assessment in 1791:

> Preachers that will not preach without a salary found for them by law are hirelings who seek the fleece and not the flock (as quoted in McLoughlin, 1971: 927.)

Dissenters offer similar assessments of the subsidized clergy in contemporary Sweden. The clergy receive generous salaries from the state, and 95 percent of all Swedes are registered as members of the Church of Sweden, yet only 2 percent of the population report attending church on any given Sunday. When asked to explain this discrepancy, the Bishop of Stockholm replied: "The Established Church is like a post office...people don't rush to it when it opens...They are just happy it's there" (Lamont, 1989: 164). When the state pays the clergy's salaries, the clergy have little incentive to mobilize popular support.

In sharp contrast, clergy without subsidies are forced to rely entirely on voluntary contributions from the people. Churches must elevate membership commitment to a level that generates adequate resources of time and money. In 1837 Francis Grund of Austria offered this pithy evaluation of American clergy:

> In America, every clergyman may be said to do business on his own account, and under his own firm...He always acts as principal, and is therefore more anxious, and will make greater efforts to obtain popularity, than one who serves for wages (in Powell, 1967: 77.)

He contrasted these clergy with the "indolent and lazy" clergy of Europe's established churches and explained that "a person provided for cannot, by the rules of common sense, be supposed to work as hard as one who has to exert himself for a living" (in Powell, 1967: 77). Historians have frequently marveled at the rise of popular religious movements in the nineteenth century, but the loss of subsidies mandated this change. When the market is unregulated, popular movements are the only groups that survive.

Finally, subsidies also change the incentives for religious consumers. When the state subsidizes only a few religions, this subsidy inflates the cost of joining an alternative religion. This inflated cost may be compared to the situation faced by American consumers of elementary and high school education. When parents choose a private school, they pay the full cost of the education, foregoing the option of a "free" education, although still "contributing" taxes to support public schools. Therefore, even if the public school provides a comparable education at a lower cost, the parents pay a far higher price for private education. In similar fashion, the state's preference (subsidy) for one religion increases the cost of joining another. For the religious consumer, the subsidy for one church reduces the incentive to seek out or join another.

Whether the regulations involve subsidy or suppression, the result is restricted competition. Subtle revisions in regulation can change incentives for gaining popular support, or increase the start-up and maintenance costs of new religions. But all forms of regulation reduce the number and diversity of religious options available for consumers.

LOCAL RELIGIOUS MARKETS

When religious regulations are absent, competition and pluralism soon emerge throughout the religious economy. Because a single faith cannot shape its appeal precisely to suit the needs of one market segment without sacrificing its appeal to another, the supply and diversity of religion rises as regulations are removed. The segmentation of any religious market leads to a diversity of faiths, each vying for popular support. The argument is a simple one: *Because of the underlying differentiation of consumer preferences, religious competition and pluralism will thrive unless regulated by the state.*[6]

But how do competition and pluralism affect the local religious market, at the level of communities and neighborhoods within a nation, where people make their decisions to join? Below I review three propositions that extend and clarify previous work on competition and pluralism in local markets. I begin with a proposition about the local church.

1. *To the degree that a religious market is competitive and pluralistic, religious organizations will be more efficient.*

Another way of stating this proposition is that a competitive and pluralistic market will provide churches that give a high ratio of return to investment. Regardless of the amount of time, money, or commitment invested in the church, people seek a church where the ratio of investment to desired outcomes is high. When competition is high, churches must provide a good ratio of return or face the declining support of the people.

Thus, efficiency refers to the ratio of total production to total costs. Churches produce a wide spectrum of social, spiritual, psychological, and even physical benefits for their members—ranging from soup suppers and social groups to uplifting worship and moral guidance. But churches also impose costs on their members, including money, time, strict behavioral demands, or confessing support for "rigid" beliefs. More efficient churches provide a higher ratio of benefits to costs.

This simple ratio offers religious organizations two alternatives for increasing efficiency. One, they can increase the services they provide for members; or, two, they can decrease the requirements (costs) of membership. The most seductive alternative—the choice selected by groups passing through the sect-church process—is to lower membership requirements. For sects with rigorous membership standards, this initial reduction might succeed in increasing their appeal to a broader segment of the market. Yet for most major denominations the story of relaxing membership standards ends in a sharply reduced ability to produce religious goods.

The Methodists' transformation from sect to church serves as one example. When Bishop Francis Asbury rode from circuit to circuit in the early nineteenth century, camp meeting revivals were "the battle ax and weapon of war" for converting sinners (Asbury, 1958: 453), the weekly class meeting challenged members on matters of faith and conduct, and lay ministers directed the affairs of local congregations, as the circuit riders served as traveling evangelists. But in 1855 the famous circuit rider Peter Cartwright (1856: 523) was lamenting that his Methodists had "almost let camp meetings die out," the class meetings were now neglected, and the circuit riders were dismounting and replacing the local lay preachers. By the end of the century, many suggested that the official standards for membership should not be enforced because the church "succeeds, not by casting out [members], but by getting them in and developing all their capabilities for good" (Carroll, 1898).

But the Methodist attempt to attract more by asking for less was a failure. When the membership standards were high, the Methodists skyrocketed from 2.5 percent of all church adherents in 1776 to 34.2 percent in 1850—and then the long decline began. Since 1850 the rate has fallen steadily to the current low of 8.1 percent of all church adherents (and still falling).[7] When members were no longer obligated to attend class or camp meetings, and weren't called to lead the local congregation, the organization was robbed of its ability to produce the collective goods sought by the membership. Camp meetings were more than a source of new members;

they were a social and spiritual revival for existing members. Class meetings were more than small groups enforcing membership standards; they were intimate groups committed to the welfare of their members and supportive of members' religious faith and lifestyle. The enforcement of membership standards in class meetings assured members that all would contribute to the collective goods of membership. Free-riding was not an option. Finally, the volunteer time of the lay ministers and class leaders gave local congregations a low overhead as well as greater control over the goods produced and the leaders selected. The Methodists failed to recognize that membership demands were producing resources of time, money, commitment, and group solidarity—resources that generated more benefits for the members.

At first glance, it seems paradoxical that decreasing the cost of membership could decrease the net gains of membership. Yet when the commodity involved is collectively produced and when lowering costs decreases collective action, this is necessarily the case. Michael Hechter (1987: 43) has argued that for any group, "the extensiveness of group obligations ought to be determined in part by the cost of producing the good in question." Religious organizations are no exception. Groups with low membership costs generate fewer resources, elicit lower levels of commitment from their membership, and host more free-riders (Kelley, 1972; Kanter, 1972; Finke and Stark, 1992; Iannaccone, Stark, and Olson, forthcoming; Iannaccone, 1992, 1994; Finke 1994). Because most religious goods (such as enthusiastic worship, fervent testimonials, and social support) are collectively produced, any reduction in membership requirements threatens the effective production of these goods.

But the other extreme is just as threatening. When organizations raise membership costs too high, the costs of joining exclude all but a few. Many sects and cults hold such high standards for membership that few will join even if the production of collective goods is high. Thus when religious markets are competitive, organizations must produce high levels of religious goods without making the costs prohibitive.

One alternative for lowering costs without changing membership requirements is the use of substitution. When a group asks members to give up secular opportunities or rewards, the group offers substitutes to reduce the cost of this sacrifice. Indeed, the more the organization demands, the more it must give in return. The extreme example is communes, where one must give all to get all. But many other groups depend on substitution. When local churches preach against the secular evils of bars, drinking, and dancing, they must provide a variety of social alternatives. Today's "evangelical subculture" promotes "Christian" radio stations, music, novels, video games, and news magazines that provide alternatives to secular products. Similarly, the Catholic subculture of the early twentieth century provided schools, professional organizations, publications, and social clubs that served as

alternatives to the dominant culture. To the extent that churches find valued substitutes, the costs of demanding membership requirements are reduced.

Even with effective substitution, however, the production of collective commodities requires the resources of time and money. Since financial resources are
often difficult to generate in new markets, economically depressed areas, or the
sparsely settled countryside, growing churches find ways to generate religious
goods with little financial support. Numerous examples can be offered from
American churches alone. Frontier settlers could never escape the Baptists or the
Methodists, because these groups could support a church with an unpaid lay
preacher and a handful of members. And Jehovah's Witnesses and Mormons operate without paid clergy by producing legions of volunteers that support the local
church and show up on doorsteps around the world.[8] Even the growing number
of meta- and mega-churches deliver many services at a low cost. Despite expensive facilities and sizeable staffs, their members receive many benefits in small
lay-led groups called "cells" or "home churches" (George, 1992). The larger church
provides the collective goods that no single group can offer, e.g., concerts, large-
scale worship events, special interest groups, etc., but the small lay-led groups
provide members with support and a sense of belonging. Churches operating in
competitive markets with no subsidy make efficient use of existing resources
(Finke, 1994).

Finally, although the competitive market will force all churches to be more efficient, the diversity of the market will require a variety of efficient churches. It is
important to realize that the ratio between costs and benefits might be identical for
two churches even if the level of costs and benefits vary. Some consumers are willing to tolerate fewer benefits if they can contribute less. Others want a wide range
of benefits from their church and are willing to invest heavily to get it. The various segments of the market will also differ on the types of benefits they seek and
the costs they avoid. Prohibitive costs and unacceptable benefits for one segment
might be highly appropriate for another segment. But regardless of the benefits
they seek, the costs they avoid, or the level of benefits they desire, all members seek
an efficient church—one where they get a good return for their investment.

But this raises yet another question. If the segmentation of any market requires
a diversity of efficient churches, why have the most rapidly growing churches
throughout American history been upstart sects? This leads to the second proposition.

2. *As major religious firms accommodate themselves to the secular culture (secularize),
growth will be concentrated among the less accommodated firms. In market terms, growth
occurs in areas with market openings.*

This is the basis for the sect–church cycle. Sects begin in sharp opposition to the
secular culture, but if they are successful, they gradually begin to reduce their ten-

sion with the host culture and reduce the demands they place on their membership (Niebuhr, 1929; Stark and Bainbridge, 1985; Finke and Stark, 1992).[9] This places them in competition with other accommodating churches and provides market openings for new upstart sects. Thus growth occurs in areas with market openings.

Notice that this explanation assumes a stable system of preferences for sects *and* churches. The rise of sectarian groups and the fall of mainline denominations are explained by changes in supply, not demand. As former sects drift into the mainline, the supply for sectarian religion decreases and the supply for accommodating religions increases. When this cycle occurs for several denominations, the inevitable result is an overabundance of accommodating religions and market openings for new sects.

Historically, this has given successful upstarts two advantages: a market opening and greater operating efficiency. The Methodists found a vast market opening in the early nineteenth century and used an effective organizational design for reaching this market. When the Methodists began to accommodate to the culture and change their organizational design, they lost their dominance of the South to a sectarian competitor. Between 1850 and 1926, the Baptists went from 30 to 43 percent of all religious adherents in the South, as the Methodists plummeted from 42 to 28 percent. Today, as the process of accommodation continues for Methodists, Baptists, and other mainstream denominations, market openings continue to show for a variety of sectarian groups, including Pentecostals, Jehovah Witnesses, Mormons, and new groups such as the Vineyards. This process could (hypothetically) reverse itself: mainstream churches could increase their tension with the dominant culture, and market openings would then occur for more mainline denominations. However, the weight of historical evidence suggests the contrary: churches will continue to accommodate and market openings will continue for the revivalistic, high-tension upstarts.

Thus, in an unregulated market, new groups arise in response to market openings. New sects grow as former sects drift into the mainline, and immigrant faiths flourish as the immigrant population grows. The diversity of the religious landscape reflects the diversity of the population. This leads to the third proposition.

3. *To the degree that a local religious market is competitive and pluralistic, the level of religious participation will tend to be high.*

This proposition parts company with a long sociological tradition holding that religion's power comes from its ability to monopolize all aspects of the culture—in other words, from its universality (Durkheim, 1951). The most respected proponent of this tradition, Peter Berger, has explained that a diversity of faiths shatters the sacred canopy and reduces the plausibility of all religions (Berger, 1967, 1979).[10] In sharp contrast, this proposition holds that the vitality of any religious market relies on its ability to generate pluralistic competition (Finke and Stark, 1988, 1992; Finke, 1990).[11]

Briefly, the argument is as follows. A variety of religious groups, each catering to the unique demands of specific market segments, can mobilize the population to higher rates of membership and commitment. This arises because of the inherent inability of a single religious organization to be at once worldly and otherworldly, while the market will always contain distinct consumer segments seeking more and less worldly versions of faith. The social markers of ethnicity, race, social class, and region will further divide the population into consumer segments with unique demands for their religion. It follows that many religious bodies will, together, be able to meet the demands of a much larger proportion of a population than can be the case when only one or very few faiths have free access.

This proposition has provoked a wide range of responses and a growing body of research. A series of recent studies illustrate how restricting competition can change the level of religious participation in national religious economies (Iannaccone, 1991; Chaves and Cann, 1992; Finke and Iannaccone, 1993; Stark, 1992; Duke, Johnson, and Duke, 1992; Iannaccone, Finke, and Stark, forthcoming; Stark and Iannaccone, 1994; Chaves, Schraeder, and Sprindys, forthcoming). But, for now, I want to restrict attention to the local religious markets where it is easier to separate the effects of pluralistic competition and state regulation. The study of local markets allows us to isolate the effects of pluralistic competition by holding formal state regulations constant. For local markets, religious pluralism becomes a measure of the religious options and the competition experienced by consumers.

Initial attempts to test the pluralism thesis using local markets offered uniform support. When controlling for the percentage of Catholics in the population, religious diversity consistently increased the rate of adherence in American cities in 1890, 1906, and 1926 (Finke, 1984; Christiano, 1987; Finke and Stark, 1988; Finke, 1992). Despite expecting support for the secularization model, Kevin Christiano found that "contrary to the theory…Protestant denominations may have grown *in conjunction with,* and not in spite of, increases in internal differentiation" (1987: 128–129).[12] More recently, Land, Blau, and Deane (1991) report that the positive effect of pluralism remains for urban counties, but switches to a strong negative for rural counties. In a future essay, we explain in detail why the use of rural counties, often several merged counties, causes a problem for the measure of diversity (Finke, Guest, and Stark, in preparation). For now, let me simply note that rural counties do not represent a single religious market and thus distort the probability equation used to measure diversity.

Meanwhile, evidence is mounting from a variety of sources supporting the competition and pluralism thesis. When Edmund des Brunner studied 138 agricultural villages in 1927, he vehemently opposed religious competition and sectarian groups, yet he reluctantly conceded that (based on his own data) rates of church membership and Sunday School enrollment increased through competition

(Brunner, 1927: 73; Finke and Stark, 1992). Using the 1865 New York state census on 942 towns, I have found that religious pluralism is a powerful predictor of all forms of religious activities—regardless of the controls entered (Finke, Guest, and Stark, 1994). And Eva Hamberg and Thorleif Pettersson's (1994) recent study of 284 municipalities in Sweden reports strong support for the pluralism thesis. Working with the diversity index and a measure of worship service alternatives offered by the Church of Sweden, Hamberg and Pettersson conclude: "[E]ven on the nearly monopolistic Swedish religious market, competition…[has] the effects we would expect."

Sociologists found out firsthand how important the "minutiae of creed" could be when they led a movement to consolidate rural churches in the early twentieth century (Madison, 1986). Writing in the *American Journal of Sociology* in 1914, John Hargreaves confidently predicted that within a decade rural churches would follow a trend of consolidation similar to that of rural schools. A decade later, however, the 1926 religious census reported only 301 federated churches out of a total of 167,864 rural churches. Rural Americans refused to let their churches merge. Even small, homogeneous, rural communities could not be satisfied by a single religious faith.

DISCUSSION

Over the last several years, rational choice theories of religion have addressed old questions with new answers. Existing questions about the sect–church cycle, the persistence of religion, patterns of religious switching, and explanations for the commitment and growth of the more demanding religions have all received new insights from the rational choice approach. As argued earlier, the answers have often shifted from demand-side to supply-side explanations. But many questions remain, and research is only beginning to explore some of the challenges posed by the new approach.

This essay has focused on the regulation of religious organizations and individual religious freedoms, but questions remain about how state regulations alter religion in the public arena. In his recent book, *The Culture of Disbelief*, Stephen L. Carter (1993) argues that recent American court decisions have not only separated church and state, but have also excluded the voice of religion from public dialogue. Supply-side arguments suggest that state regulations, whether in public discourse or private practice, constrain the options available for religious producers and consumers.

Recent work has also suggested that questions about regulation and constraining religious choices must move beyond state regulations. Just as states can subsidize some local religions and suppress others, local subcultures can effectively restrict the choices and alter religious preferences for local religious consumers. Ellison and Sherkat (1993: 2–3) have argued that because of normative constraints, "individuals may not be free to choose the type of religion they prefer, and they may be induced to consume types or levels of religious goods that conflict with their preferences." They demonstrate that these constraints exist for African Americans in the rural South. In earlier work, Stark and Bainbridge (1985) found less tolerance of religious deviance by all Southerners. But clearly similar restraints operate in many other religious markets—especially when one or two religions dominate a local market. American religious history is filled with examples of religious cartels attempting to regulate religious competition without state support (Finke and Stark, 1992).

This leads to another important question. If the state is not restricting competition in the United States, how do denominations such as the Roman Catholics and Latter-day Saints hold large segments of many local markets? One possible answer is that the population is homogeneous and doesn't require diversity. But even a cursory examination of the markets dominated by the Catholic and LDS churches refutes this argument. Instead, I would suggest that these groups effectively dominate local markets because they tolerate diversity within their organization.

When denominations dominate local religious markets, they find effective ways to allow for competition and pluralism within the organization. In the late nineteenth and early twentieth century, for example, the ethnic and social class homogeneity of Catholic parishes allowed the Church to serve the specific needs of each ethnic group, while the diversity across the parishes allowed specialized appeals to the broad spectrum of immigrants (Finke, 1992; Finke and Stark, 1992). In addition, the religious orders provided a source of innovation and pluralism that was lacking in Protestant organizations. Though Mormons do not share the ethnic pluralism or the religious orders of Catholics, they are equally effective at meeting the special needs of specific market segments. Because the local wards are territorially bound and limited in size, the membership tends to be homogeneous by social class and ethnicity (Mauss, 1994). Like the Catholic parishes, the local Mormon wards can serve the specific needs of individual market segments as the diversity of wards serves a broad spectrum of the market. Moreover, the use of local lay ministers ensures that clergy will be in touch with the specific needs of their local ward. Finally, the more traditional factions of Mormons, in common with the Roman Catholics, find it difficult to splinter off from the main body. Loyalty to traditional teachings on church hierarchy, the temple, and the prophet requires members to stay within the fold. Competing factions remain within the Church, because leaving carries a severe loss of religious heritage and legitimacy. Hence, both Roman Catholics and Latter-day Saints can tolerate pluralism and competition without frequent schisms.

Finally, a series of important questions about religious preferences remain: what explains the diversity of preferences in a religious market, how are preferences changed, and why are some preferences resistant to change? Extending the work of Gary Becker (1964) and George Homans (1974), an elite group of scholars is beginning to explain why status, power, ethnicity, and past religious consumption should predict current religious preferences (Stark and Bainbridge, 1985, 1987; Greeley, 1989; Iannaccone, 1988, 1990; Durkin and Greeley, 1991; Warner, 1993; Sherkat and Wilson, forthcoming). Social status and mobility not only change the religious goods individuals will seek, they change the social networks shaping these preferences. And past consumption of specific religious goods provides a familiarity with religious beliefs, rituals, and traditions that can make future practice of the same religion more satisfying. This work helps to explain why consumers hold specific preferences, and why they might retain a religious preference when it appears they receive little return on their investment. This new theoretical approach is rapidly generating a series of wide ranging propositions in need of further testing.

For this essay, I have confined my attention to only a few propositions on religious regulation and the consequences of a competitive pluralistic market. I have argued that decreasing religious regulation generates higher levels of pluralism and competition by changing the incentives of religious producers and consumers. Freed of regulation, upstart sects can appeal to new market openings, and the unbridled competition forces all churches to vie for popular support to survive. The result is an abundance of religious suppliers generating a high level of religious participation. Writing in 1855 about the separation of church and state, Philip Schaff (1961: 99) noted that "America is the classic land of sects." I would revise his assessment only slightly: America is a classic land of efficient sects.

NOTES

[1] I owe my use of the terms "supply-side" and "demand-side" to private conversations with Stephen Warner.

[2] Many of these explanations border on tautologies as cultural changes result in new cultural demands leading to cultural changes—including religious change.

[3] Overall, membership in non-traditional religions rose from about 2 million (4.5% of the population) at the turn of the century, to more than 21 million (20%) in 1975 (Barrett, 1982: 419–420).

[4] The Government-General of Korea reported 67 new religions in 1945; by 1982 the Cultural Research Centre reported 303 (Choi, 1986). A portion of this growth resulted from the missionary efforts of western nations, but the most substantial growth came from indigenous Protestant groups and the sects splitting off from the missionary churches.

[5] Michael Hechter, Debra Friedman, and Satoshi Kanazawa (1992: 82) extend this argument to the area of social control. Using the examples of Hare Krishna and Nation of Islam, they argue: "[G]roups that mobilize members who occupy the margin of society provide an even greater—albeit an unintended—service to the larger society."

[6] Adam Smith made similar claims over two hundred years ago: "[I]f the government was perfectly decided both to let them [religious sects] all alone, and to oblige them all to let alone one another, there is little danger that they would not of their own accord subdivide themselves fast enough, so as soon to become sufficiently numerous" (1933: 746).

[7] The 1776 and 1850 rates are taken from Finke and Stark (1989b). The contemporary rate is based on the 1990 totals reported in *Churches and Church Membership 1990* (Bradley et al., 1992). Because *Churches and Church Membership 1990* does not report membership for all denominations, the 1990 8.1 percentage rate for Methodists is slightly inflated.

[8] The *Deseret News 1991–1992 Church Almanac* reports that 201,747 Latter-day Saint (Mormon) missionaries were sent out from 1980–1989. Even as early as 1916, the Mormons supported more foreign missionaries—despite operating with a minuscule budget and a total membership of only 403,388—than any other denomination except the Methodist Episcopal Church and the Presbyterian Church in the U.S.A. (Bureau of the Census, 1919: 96).

[9] James D. Montgomery (1994) recently developed a formal model that demonstrates the dynamics of the sect–church cycle.

[10] See Steve Warner (1993) for a discussion of the old paradigm and how it contrasts with the new paradigm.

[11] Claude S. Fischer's (1982: 202) subcultural theory offers a related argument on why urbanism and greater diversity might increase rates of involvement: "[U]rbanism bolsters ethnic and religious community, particularly if the group is small enough so that affiliation is difficult."

[12] Christiano refers to two types of religious diversity throughout his study of American cities. One is the measure of Protestant denominational diversity, the other is the measure of diversity across the major religious subcultures, i.e., Protestant, Catholic, and Jew. He writes that Protestant "diversity seems to have augmented Protestantism's support," but diversity across major religious subcultures "may, it seems, hamper church membership" (1987: 128).

[13] When they use all counties and enter no control for the percentage of population which is Catholic, Blau, Land, and Redding (1992: 329) conclude that "religious monopoly—not diversity—fuels religious expansion."

Kevin Breault (1989) has also challenged these findings using contemporary data and a "random sample" of counties. However, because the results could not be replicated by a neutral investigator and Breault has destroyed the output and the data files, we refuse to acknowledge his claims as a credible challenge (Finke and Stark, 1989a).

REFERENCES

Asbury, Francis. 1958 [1852]. *The Journal and Letters of Francis Asbury*. 3 vols. Epworth Press: London.

Barrett, David B. 1982. *World Christian Encyclopedia*. Nairobi, Kenya: Oxford University Press.

Becker, Gary. 1964. *Human Capital*. New York: National Bureau of Economic Research.

Beckford, James A. 1985. *Cult Controversies: The Societal Response to New Religious Movements*. London: Tavistock Publications.

Berger, Peter. 1967. *The Sacred Canopy*. New York: Doubleday.

————1979. *The Heretical Imperative: Contemporary Possibilities of Religious Affirmation*. New York: Doubleday.

Blau, Judith R., Kenneth C. Land, and Kent Redding. 1992. "The Expansion of Religious Affiliation." *Social Science Research* 21: 329–352.

Bradley, Martin B., Norman M. Green, Jr., Dale E. Jones, Mac Lynn, and Lou McNeil. 1992. *Churches and Church Membership in the United States 1990*. Atlanta: Glenmary Research Center.

Breault, Kevin D. 1989. "New Evidence on Religious Pluralism, Urbanism, and Religious Participation." *American Sociological Review* 54: 1048–1053.

Brunner, Edmund des. 1927. *Village Communities*. New York: George H. Doran Company.

Bureau of the Census. 1919. *Religious Bodies: 1916, Vol. I.* Washington: Government Printing Office.

Carroll, H.K. 1898. "Is Methodism Catholic?" *Methodist Review* 14: 177–186.

Carter, Stephen L. 1993. *The Culture of Disbelief: How American Law and Politics Trivialize Religious Devotion*. New York: Basic Books.

Cartwright, Peter. 1856. *Autobiography of Peter Cartwright, The Backwoods Preacher*. W.P. Strickland, ed. New York: Carlton & Porter.

Chaves, Mark, and David E. Cann. 1992. "Regulation, Pluralism, and Religious Market Structure: Explaining Religion's Vitality." *Rationality and Society* 4 (3): 272–290.

Chaves, Mark, Peter J. Schraeder, and Mario Sprindys. Forthcoming. "State Regulation of Religion and Muslim Religious Vitality in the Industrialized West." *Journal of Politics*.

Choi, Syn-Duk. 1986. "A Comparative Study of Two New Religious Movements in the Republic of Korea." In James A. Beckford, ed., *New Religious Movements and Rapid Social Change*. Beverly Hills, CA: Sage.

Christiano, Kevin. 1987. *Religious Diversity and Social Change: American Cities, 1890–1906*. New York: Cambridge University Press.

Duke, James T., L. Johnson, and James B. Duke. 1993. "Rate of Religious Conversion: A Macrosociological Study." *Research in the Sociology of Religion* (JAI Press) 5: 89–121.

Durkheim, Emile. [1897] 1951. *Suicide*. Glencoe: Free Press.

Durkin, John Jr., and Andrew M. Greeley. 1991. "A Model of Religious Choice Under Uncertainty: On Responding Rational to the Nonrational." *Rationality and Society* 3: 178–196.

Ellison, Christopher, and Darren E. Sherkat. 1993. "The 'Semi-Involuntary' Institution Revisited: Regional Variations in Church Participation Among African Americans." Presented at the annual meeting of the Association for the Sociology of Religion, Miami Beach.

Finke, Roger. 1984. *The Churching of America.* Unpublished Dissertation.

———1989. "Demographics of Religious Participation: An Ecological Approach, 1850–1971." *Journal for the Scientific Study of Religion* 28: 45–58.

———1990. "Religious Deregulation: Origins and Consequences." *Journal of Church and State* 32: 609–626.

———1992. "An Unsecular America." In Steve Bruce, ed., *Religion and Modernization: Sociologists and Historians Debate the Secularization Thesis.* Oxford: Clarendon Press.

———1994. "The Quiet Transformation: Changes in Size and Leadership of Southern Baptist Churches. *Review of Religious Research* 36: 3–22.

Finke, Roger, Avery Guest, and Rodney Stark. 1994. "Mobilizing Local Religious Markets: Religious Pluralism in the Empire State, 1865. Presented at the annual meeting of the Society for the Scientific Study of Religion.

Finke, Roger, and Laurence R. Iannaccone. 1993. "Supply-Side Explanations for Religious Change." *Annals, AAPSS,* 527: 27–39.

Finke, Roger, and Rodney Stark. 1988. "Religious Economies and Sacred Canopies: Religious Mobilization in American Cities, 1906." *American Sociological Review* 53: 41–49.

———1989a. "Evaluating the Evidence: Religious Economies and Sacred Canopies." *American Sociological Review* 54: 1054–1056.

———1989b. "How the Upstart Sects Won America, 1776–1850." *Journal for the Scientific Study of Religion* 28: 27–44.

———1992. *The Churching of America, 1776–1990: Winners and Losers in our Religious Economy.* New Brunswick, NJ: Rutgers University Press.

Fischer, Claude S. 1982. *To Dwell Among Friends: Personal Networks in Town and City.* Chicago: University of Chicago Press.

George, Carl F. 1992. *Prepare Your Church for the Future.* Grand Rapids: Baker Book House.

Greeley, Andrew M. 1989. *Religious Change in America.* Cambridge: Harvard University Press.

Hadden, Jeffrey K. 1987. "Toward Desacralizing Secularization Theory." *Social Forces* 65: 587–611.

Hamberg, Eva M., and Thorleif Pettersson. 1994. "The Religious Market Denominational Competition and Religious Participation in Contemporary Sweden." *Journal for the Scientific Study of Religion* 33: 205–216.

Hardacre, Helen. 1989. *Shinto and the State, 1868–1988.* Princeton: Princeton University Press.

Hargreaves, Robert. 1914. "The Rural Community and Church Federation." *American Journal of Sociology* 20: 249–260.

Hechter, Michael. 1987. *Principles of Group Solidarity.* Berkeley: University of California Press.

Hechter, Michael, Debra Friedman, and Satoshi Kanazawa. 1992. "Advocacy for a Theory of Social Order." In James S. Coleman and Thomas J. Fararo, eds., *Rational Choice Theory: Advocacy and Critique.* Newbury Park: Sage Publications.

Homans, George C. 1974. *Social Behavior: Its Elementary Forms.* New York: Harcourt Brace Jovanovich.

Iannaccone, Laurence R. 1988. "A Formal Model of Church and Sect." *American Journal of Sociology* 94 (supplement): s241–s268.

———1990. "Religious Practice: A Human Capital Approach." *Journal for the Scientific Study of Religion* 29: 297–314.

Iannaccone, Laurence R. 1991. "The Consequences of Religious Market Regulation: Adam Smith and the Economics of Religion." *Rationality and Society* 3: 156–177.

———1992. "Sacrifice and Stigma: Reducing Free-Riding in Cults, Communes, and other Collectives." *Journal of Political Economy* 100: 271–292.

———1994. "Why Strict Churches are Strong." *American Journal of Sociology* 99: 1180–1211.

Iannaccone, Laurence R., Roger Finke, and Rodney Stark. Forthcoming. "Deregulating Religion: Supply-Side Stories of Trends and Change in the Religious Marketplace." *Economic Inquirer.*

Iannaccone, Laurence R., Rodney Stark, and Daniel V.A. Olson. Forthcoming. "Religious Resources and Church Growth." *Journal for the Scientific Study of Religion.*

Kanter, Rosabeth. 1972. *Commitment and Community: Communes and Utopias in Sociological Perspective.* Cambridge: Harvard University Press

Kelley, Dean. 1972. *Why Conservative Churches are Growing.* New York: Harper and Row.

Lambert, Frank. 1990. "'Pedlar in Divinity': George Whitefield and the Great Awakening, 1737–1745." *The Journal of American History* (December) 77: 812–837.

———1994. *Pedlar in Divinity.* Princeton: Princeton University Press.

Lamont, Stewart. 1989. *Church and State: Uneasy Alliances.* London: The Brodley Head.

Land, Kenneth C., Glenn Deane, and Judith R. Blau. 1991. "Religious Pluralism and Church Membership: A Spatial Diffusion Model." *American Sociological Review* 56: 237–249.

Madison, James H. 1986. "Reformers and the Rural Church, 1900–1950." *The Journal of American History,* 73: 645–668.

Mauss, Armand L. 1994. *The Angel and the Beehive: The Mormon Struggle with Assimilation.* Urbana: University of Illinois.

Mead, Sidney E. 1963. *The Lively Experiment.* New York: Harper and Row.

McFarland, H. Neill. 1967. *The Rush Hour of the Gods: A Study of New Religious Movements in Japan.* New York: Macmillan.

McLoughlin, William G. 1971. *New England Dissent, 1630–1833: The Baptists and the Separation of Church and State, Vol. I and II.* Cambridge: Harvard University Press.

———1978. *Revivals, Awakenings, and Reform.* Chicago: The University of Chicago Press.

Montgomery, James D. 1994. "The Dynamics of the Religious Economy: Exit, Voice, and Denominational Secularization." Working Paper.

Nakano, Tsuyoshi. 1987. "The American Occupation and Reform of Japan's Religious System: A Few Notes on the Secularization Process in Postwar Japan." *The Journal of Oriental Studies* 26 (1): 124–138.

Niebuhr, Richard H. 1929. *The Social Sources of Denominationalism.* New York: Henry Holt.

Powell, Milton B., ed. 1967. *The Voluntary Church: Religious Life, 1740–1860, Seen Through the Eyes of European Visitors.* New York: Macmillan.

Reed, Andrew. 1835. *A Narrative of the Visit to the American Churches.* London: Jackson and Walford.

Robbins, Thomas, and James A. Beckford. 1993. "Religious Movements and Church–State Issues." In D. Bromley and J. Hadden, eds., *Handbook of Cults and Sects.* 199–218. Greenwich, CT: JAI Press.

Schaff, Philip. 1961 [1855]. *America: A Sketch of Its Political, Social, and Religious Character.* Cambridge: The Belknap Press of Harvard University Press.

Sherkat, Darren E., and John Wilson. Forthcoming. "Preferences, Constraints, and Choices in Religious Markets." *Social Forces*.

Shupe, Anson David, Jr. 1973. "Toward a Structural Perspective of Modern Religious Movements." *Sociological Focus* 6 (3): 83–99.

Smith, Adam. 1933 [1776]. *The Wealth of Nations*. New York: The Modern Library.

Stark, Rodney. 1992. "Do Catholic Societies Really Exist?" *Rationality and Society* 4: 261–271.

Stark, Rodney, and William Sims Bainbridge. 1985. *The Future of Religion: Secularization, Revival, and Cult Formation*. Berkeley: University of California Press.

———1987. *A Theory of Religion*. New York and Bern: Peter Lang.

Stark, Rodney, and Laurence R. Iannaccone. 1994. "A Supply-Side Reinterpretation of the 'Secularization' of Europe." *Journal for the Scientific Study of Religion* 33: 230–252.

Stout, Harry S. 1991. *The Divine Dramatist: George Whitefield and the Rise of Modern Evangelism*. Grand Rapids, Michigan: Eerdmans Publishing Company.

Warner, R. Stephen. 1993. "Work in Progress toward a New Paradigm for the Sociological Study of Religion in the United States." *American Journal of Sociology* 98: 1044–1093.

Wilson, Bryan. 1966. *Religion in Secular Society*. London: C.A. Watts.

———1982. *Religion in Sociological Perspective*. Oxford: Oxford University Press.

EMBEDDING RELIGIOUS CHOICES

Preferences and Social Constraints into Rational Choice Theories of Religious Behavior[1]

Darren E. Sherkat

chapter 4

ABSTRACT

IN THIS paper I outline a theory of religious choice which focuses on individual preferences. Following Elster (1983), I propose that religious preferences are primarily adaptive, in that they become stronger with consumption (a notion similar to Iannaccone's (1990) human capital perspective). Yet, preferences can also respond to new information acquired through learning and seduction, and they can also be counteradaptive, with novel goods being typically valued over more traditional fare. But explanations which focus on egoistic preferences leave us wanting. Individual preferences are not the only factors which motivate religious choices, and the individual focus and voluntarism assumption in most presentations of rational models of religious behavior fails to capture social influences on religious choices. I identify three types of social influences: (1) sympathetic and antipathetic consumption; (2)

consumption for example setting; and, (3) consumption resulting from positive or negative social sanctions. In each case, consumption is not related to preferences for the religious good itself, but to desired social outcomes of potentially dubious religious value.

INTRODUCTION

Most applications of rational choice theory to religious behavior have avoided the question of where preferences for religious goods come from and what consequence this may have for the operation of religious markets. For some, the neglect of preferences comes (in part) from a concern to distance rational choice theories from "oversocialized" views of religious behavior which consider normative influences paramount (cf. Granovetter, 1985, 1993), however, most view preferences as exogenous to rational models of economic behavior merely to hold to the conventions of mainstream economic theories (e.g., Becker and Murphy, 1988; Stigler and Becker, 1977). Further, most rational choice applications in the sociology of religion have avoided discussing normative influences on choice, despite a growing rational choice literature on compliance norms and social influence (cf. Coleman, 1990; Heckathorn, 1990, 1993; Macy, 1993; Marsden, 1981). In this paper I develop a model of religious markets which begins with the preferences of individuals making choices in the market, and which explicitly considers both normative constraints and other social influences on religious choice. In contrast to economists of the revealed preference tradition (cf. Hicks, 1956: 6; Samuelson, 1938, 1948), I think that what is going on inside people heads is precisely what social scientists need to know in order to explain market behavior, and I do not think that such insights are beyond the scope of modern social scientific inquiry. While it may be difficult to discern the preferences which drive particular choices, it is not impossible.[2] What is lost in my formulation is the elegant parsimony of economic models of choice and rational choice theories of compliance. What is gained is an expansive scope which allows the model to integrate rational choice insights from the utilitarian and normative traditions and which provides a link to "supply-side" theories of religious markets.

First I will present a general statement on the social embeddedness of religious markets, and I will discuss how religious value is constructed in religious communities, and how choices are influenced in a general way by social relations. Second, I will construct an individual-level perspective on religious markets, looking at endogenous changes in preferences and preference formation, and linking such changes and continuities in preferences to broader social environments. Third, I will discuss how social influences on choice constrain individual options and create a gap between individual preferences and revealed choices. Finally, I will present a preliminary formulation of a general model of religious choice. Where possible, I link my perspective with the supply-side theories of Roger Finke, Laurence Iannaccone, and Rodney Stark; and though a formal integration of the demand- and supply-side models is beyond the scope of this paper, the relationship will be readily apparent in the model I propose.

MARKET EMBEDDEDNESS AND RELIGIOUS CHOICES

An integrated perspective on religious markets must focus on the reciprocal relationship between individual preferences and social options. Religious markets exhibit a "duality of structure" similar to that suggested by Anthony Giddens (1984) and William H. Sewell, Jr. (1992), such that individuals influence and are influenced by religious institutions. Individual religious schemas, or preferences, motivate participation in religious organizations, which are dependent resources acquired from constituents. Yet, religious organizations also influence individuals' religious schemas, and also control resources which make it difficult for individuals to exert control over their own choices or the quality and quantity of the resources meted out by organizations.

From this view, it becomes evident that markets are not comprised of freely choosing independent actors and competitive firms, but are instead embedded in social relations which flavor individual desires and limit both personal choices and market options. A sociological perspective seeks to define individuals' preferences in terms of their social context by analyzing: (1) the social configurations which produce preferences; (2) the social processes which alter or crystallize preferences; and (3) the social construction of the value of goods. Hence, for the sociologist, religious markets are fraught with social influences on the values which motivate market decisions. Individuals' choices are not simply a function of their preferences, but also of constraints on choices coming from two distinct sources: (1) social involvements which promote or prohibit particular choices, and (2) the goods provided in the marketplace. To date, investigations of religious markets have focused almost exclusively on the latter problem.

Like all markets, religious markets are social creations, and transactions which take place in these markets are governed by social forces. Social relations determine the choices individual's can make, the preferences individuals have, the types of religious goods offered, and changes in religious products over time. Indeed, the value we derive from religion is grounded in the participatory communities which sustain religious practice and meaning. Not only is religion a collectively produced good (cf. Iannaccone, 1992a, 1994; Wallis, 1991), the value of what is produced is very difficult to assess by those outside of the group.

My position on the social grounding of religious economies resonates with recent sociological investigations of market embeddedness (e.g., Granovetter, 1985, 1993) which attempt to mediate between the substantivist school associated with Karl Polanyi (1947, 1957, 1977) and Marshall Sahlins (1972) and formalist explanations based on classical and neoclassical economics. It is my contention that religious markets are much more thoroughly embedded in social relationships than are other markets. While religious markets bear some resemblance to markets for automobiles, textiles, and gasoline, they are more profoundly influenced by preexisting social relationships than are markets for such non-cultural goods or for cultural goods of less social import (such as art, music, or fashion). Central to this contention is my view that to some extent the intrinsic qualities of non-cultural goods determine their value on the market (either because of use value or material value based on labor-capital inputs), while valuations of cultural goods are much more arbitrary and require communities of likeminded individuals to support claims of quality. Religious goods are not simply "experience goods" which must be consumed in order to be evaluated (Iannaccone, 1992b); rather, these goods must be experienced within communities which direct us on how to evaluate them. My position on the social creation of religious value is somewhat similar to Iannaccone's (1988) specification of joint production functions for religious and secular goods. For Iannaccone, secular and sectarian religious value cannot be jointly produced, since what is considered exceptional and valuable in the secular world is considered tainted by sectarians. In contrast to Iannaccone (1988), I do not see joint production possibilities to be the primary feature of the social embeddedness of religious markets—though it certainly is a consequential feature. Religious value is not only created through collective production efforts (through singing, praying, greeting, and the like), but also through socially-conditioned endogenous preferences for specific varieties of religious goods.

PREFERENCE AND CHOICE

The starting point of any rational choice theory of human behavior is that actors choose options which maximize their benefits as determined by the actors' preferences (Stark and Bainbridge, 1987). In the sociology of religion, these preferences must be for goods with demonstrable religious content: preferences must be related to supernatural compensators (rewards in the afterlife, release from suffering, experience of total inner-bliss), or at least to correlatives of such compensators (such as sacred rituals or divinely ordained patterns of relations). When I speak of preferences for religious goods, I mean individuals' evaluations of competing religious goods. Unfortunately, "religious preference" has come to mean something quite different in colloquial speech and even in the sociology of religion. Following the fallacious reasoning of revealed preference theories in economics, most sociologists of religion equate "religious preference" with religious affiliation. This is a mistake. Affiliation is a choice, not a preference, and the two need never meet. Thus one should never be taken as evidence for the other.

Economists have contended that there is no accounting for taste (cf. Stigler and Becker, 1977), yet this contention ignores the fact that sociological processes can elaborate how individuals come to have the preferences they hold. In general, we learn our preferences through socialization and past experiences. For the most part, what we come to prefer is linear and complementary. Through participation and immersion in religious communities, individuals come to have particular religious understandings which give religion value. These meaning systems provide us with a number of distinctively religious benefits which we come to appreciate, such as existential certainty, explanations for stressful life events, internal coping resources, attachments to divine others, or examples for role taking (Ellison, 1991, 1993; Ellison and Sherkat, 1995b; Pollner, 1989). Jon Elster (1983; see also Veyne, 1990 and Gorman, 1967) implies that, in general, these meaning systems, or preferences, are "adaptive," indicating that they get stronger and stronger with additional consumption. Individuals come to prefer the familiar, and indeed, people tend to adjust their preferences to the feasible options available (see Elster, 1983; Darnell, 1994). Hence, religious experiences in childhood shape what individuals desire from religion, and this socialization continues through adulthood, as individuals continue familiar religious practices. Adaptive preferences can be used to explain a number of findings in the sociology of religion, such as (1) the tendency of individuals to remain in their denomination of origin (Newport, 1979; Kluegel, 1980; Sherkat and Wilson, 1995; Sherkat, Sorensen, and Chang, 1994), (2) the tendency, if they do leave, to switch to denominations similar to their original (Ellison and Sherkat, 1990; Sherkat, 1993; Sherkat and Wilson, 1995; Sherkat, Sorensen, and Chang, 1994; Sullins, 1993), (3) a negative relationship between past consumption and religious switching (Sherkat, 1991a; Sherkat and Wilson, 1995), (4) higher participation rates for females (Argyle and Beit-Hallahmi, 1975; De Vaus and McAllister, 1987; Nelsen and Potvin, 1981), and (5) the strong influence of past religious consumption on future religious consumption (Cornwall, 1989; Himmelfarb, 1979; Hoge et al., 1993; Sherkat, 1991b).

This view of religious preferences is similar to Iannaccone's (1990) human capital approach; it differs, however, in that I do not think of household production of religious value as the central stabilizing force for religious value. In Iannaccone's (1990) view, religious practice makes us better able to create value from our religion, whereas the notion of adaptive preference implies only that we come to desire particular goods. The difference is a philosophical point to some extent, and formal expositions of adaptive preferences may be made identical to those of human capital theory. The difference is that human capital theories view preferences as stable, assuming that current value depends on consumption capital developed through prior consumption (Becker and Murphy, 1988). Thus, rather than see preferences changing, human capital theorists conceive of production as changing with increases in capital. It is likely that both consumption capital and adaptive preferences have independent effects on choices.

If adaptive preferences or human capital were the only explanation for religious behavior there would be very little religious change. In fact, change can come from endogenous shifts in preferences, with shifts resulting from (1) counteradaptivity, (2) learning, or (3) seduction. First, preferences may be counteradaptive in nature, meaning that some people—or people sometimes—prefer the novel over the familiar (Elster, 1983: 111–112). Such rejection of the familiar is not typically a function of overt desires to overcome the everyday (as in Jon Elster's "character planning"), but is more likely the result of long-term burnout on what was once preferred. It differs from satiation in its much longer duration: counteradaptivity does not reverse itself in the short run, nor even necessarily in the long-run. Religious seekership fits this pattern. Some people try many different religious goods, always looking for more novel approaches. For others, seekership may end when one stumbles on the "right" goods. The termination of a seekership pattern is clearly evident in the example of "Devi" in E. Burke Rochford's work on conversion to ISKON (1985: 87–122).

Second, and more common, people learn new religious preferences through contact with others, or through experience with or information about new goods (Bikhchandani et al. 1992; Elster, 1979, 1983; Von Weizsacker, 1971). Our social relations provide us with a constant barrage of information about a variety of products, and religion is no exception. While uncertainty associated with religious goods makes us somewhat timid comparison-shoppers, we might be prone to try goods when recommended by trusted others. Having learned of and tried these new goods, we may find that we prefer them to those we once enjoyed. Hence, when John Lofland and Rodney Stark (1965: 871) report that final conversion amounts to the acceptance of "the opinions of one's friends," they are providing an example of learning new preferences. Indeed, many studies of religious conversion through social networks point to findings quite consistent with preference learning (cf. Rochford, 1985; Snow et al., 1980, 1986; Stark and Bainbridge, 1980, 1985). Similarly, effects of education on religious beliefs may be explained in this fashion (Sherkat and Wilson, 1995; Roof and McKinney, 1987; Wuthnow and Glock, 1973; Wuthnow and Mellinger, 1978), as may the influence of geographic mobility and family ties on religious switching or conversion (Sherkat, 1991a; Sherkat and Ellison, 1991; Stark and Bainbridge, 1980, 1985).

Third, Elster's (1979) notion of seduction is a preference changing process different from learning, and religious seduction is an important source of interreligious conflict. Seduction differs from learning in that it originates out of coercion. Once enticed to try something, individuals may come to prefer that which they at first found objectionable. Fundamentalists' objections to public school curricula rests on this seduction process: once their children have been forced to engage modernist thinking in the classroom, they may come to prefer it. Hence, the seduction of humanist education is actively opposed by fundamentalist writers, and opposition to the seductive influences of forced education drives political conflicts (Page and Clelland, 1978; Provenzo, 1990), as well as influencing the educational attainment of fundamentalist children (Darnell and Sherkat, 1995).

In a recent empirical examination of the theory of adaptive preferences and preferences learning, John Wilson and I (Sherkat and Wilson, 1995) have shown how people are socialized into particular religious beliefs by their parents and denominations of origins. Religious participation is shown to foster strong religious beliefs, or, in more specific terms, to foster preferences for particular religious meaning systems. Those who participated often as youths, and those who had strong religious beliefs, were unlikely to become apostates, and less likely to join less demanding, theologically liberal denominations. If they did switch, those who were frequent consumers of religious goods as youths and who had developed preferences for demanding religion (evidenced by agreement with a literal interpretation of the Bible) were more likely to join conservative Protestant denominations. Compared to their liberal counterparts, youths who originated in conservative groups were more frequent religious consumers, and developed stronger religious beliefs—or preferences, to use my terminology. Hence, while the liberals and conservatives each lose about as many members as they gain in the religious market, the liberals gain the least committed, while the more committed choose the conservative denominations.

This notion of individual preferences generates a number of additional insights when theories of affective attachment to groups are also taken into account. First, following Edward Lawler (1992), we may reason that, *groups which are more proximal in terms of social relations—those that place individuals in constant contact with institutional representatives—will have more of an influence on preferences either through adaptivity or learning.* Simply put, we are more likely to be influenced by participation in local congregations than by the pronouncements of denominational leaders. Further, people will be more likely to follow the teachings of their parents than their ministers. Second, *a person is more likely to learn preferences from those whom she feels close to.* Hence, those who feel close to parents will be more likely to accept their religious teachings (Sherkat and Wilson, 1995). Third, *ties to likeminded others will have more of an impact on preferences and choices than ties to discordant relations.* Hence, parents who share the same faith are more likely than mixed-faith parents to pass on a religious affiliation to a child (Nelsen, 1991; Sandomirsky and Wilson, 1990; Sherkat, 1991a).

My view of preferences is more nuanced than formalist treatments which assume that preferences are stable and exogenous to market forces, since I view preferences as responsive to social institutions which produce religious products. The reciprocal influences between individuals' schemas and institutional resources in the marketplace elucidates how markets are embedded in social relations. Rather than being exogenous to explanations of market operations, preferences are influenced by market offerings and social relations that disseminate information about religious products. So far I have presented the case that religious preferences direct religious choices. This assumes that individuals make choices about products because preferences for commodities allow consumption to maximize utility. But markets are also embedded in social contexts which make choices diverge from egoistic preferences for particular commodities, and below I examine some of these social influences on choice.

MAKING CHOICES SOCIAL:
SYMPATHY, EXAMPLE-SETTING, AND SANCTIONS

Discussing the nature of individual choices, Amartya Sen (1973: 252–253) writes: "[M]an is a social animal and his choices are not rigidly bound to his own preferences only…An act of choice for this social animal is, in a fundamental sense, always a social act…[H]is behavior is something more than a mere translation of his personal preferences." Indeed, religious choices are always social choices, and we should not confuse utility individuals receive from religious goods because they desire those religious goods with utility derived as an externality of making certain choices in the religious marketplace. In the forgoing section I have shown how the social embeddedness of religious markets influences individual choices by altering preferences; in this section I will discuss how social embeddedness influences religious choices *in spite of* individual preferences. Social influences on religious choices are manifest in three distinct ways: (1) choices are influenced by sympathy or antipathy; (2) choices are made for the purpose of example setting; and (3) choices are influenced by rewards or punishments.

Sympathy and Antipathy

Consumers often make choices because of the effect their choices may have on other peoples' satisfaction. Choices may be influenced by sympathy when individuals believe that others they feel close to will be happy if they make certain choices. Sen (1993) writes of how the choice of an apple versus an orange in the fruit bowl of a friend's house would vary depending on the number of oranges and apples. A person may strongly prefer oranges to apples, but would not take the last orange and deny the host her preferred commodity—even though the host might rather the guest take the last orange. This example illustrates the crucial difference between sympathetic choices and choices made because of sanctions: were sanctions operative, the host would give some incentive for choosing apples or punishment for taking an orange. The flip side of sympathy is antipathy. A choice is influenced by antipathy when a primary motive for choice is to hurt a person or people held in disdain (Sen 1977: 327). For example, parent–child conflict may drive adolescents and young adults to make cultural choices simply to spite their parents, or to clearly distinguish themselves from the older generation. Young people may get mohawk haircuts, listen to rap music, pierce their noses, or join new religious movements not because they find them aesthetically pleasing or philosophically unassailable, but because making such choices offends those they dislike. As one subject in an ethnography of body piercers put it, "I love it when they stare at me and their eyes scream 'Deviant!'" (Myers, 1992: 295). Examples of consumption for reasons of sympathy abound in the sociology of religion. Children who feel close to their parents have been shown to be more likely to follow their parents' religious choices (Nelsen, 1981; Sherkat and Wilson, 1995) and less likely to join new religious movements (Rochford, 1985). What is important to remember is that consumption for sympathetic reasons is not the same as making a choice because of social sanctions. Sympathetic (or antipathetic) consumption seeks to make others feel good (or bad), which differs from making choices to gain rewards or avoid punishments.

Example-setting

The second important social influence on choice comes from example-setting motivations (Sen, 1973, 1977). We may do things not because we want to, but because we wish to show others a particular image of ourselves or provide an example for them. Many studies have found that often individuals reaffirm religious affiliations and memberships when they have children (Sandomirsky and Wilson, 1990; Sherkat and Wilson, 1995; Stolzenberg, Blair-Loy, and Waite, 1994; Wilson and Sherkat, 1994), or increase their religious participation when children are in their formative years (Anders, 1955; Hoge and Carroll, 1978; Lazerwitz, 1961, 1964; Mueller and Johnson, 1975; Nash, 1968; Nash and Berger, 1962; Wilson, 1978: 262). These studies suggest that many parents participate for the sake of their children. Hence, rather than choosing religious options because they desire religious solace, enjoy religious demands, or find religious rituals meaningful, parents may participate to demonstrate a particular behavior to their children. Egoistic preferences for religious goods may have nothing to do with the choices made.

Social Sanctions

No general overview of the social embeddedness of religious choices would be complete without a discussion of what is perhaps most pervasive and certainly the most well studied of social influences on choice: social sanctions. Incentives have been cited as motivators for participation in a number of voluntary organizations, and religion is no exception (cf. McCarthy and Zald, 1977; Stark and Bainbridge, 1985, 1987; Wallis, 1991). Indeed, Mancur Olson (1965) views selective incentives as necessary to entice participation in any voluntary organization. In my estimation, what is important to remember here is that such rewards or punishments are absolutely *not* related to the intrinsic qualities of the goods being evaluated for choice. Sanctions are externalities of our consumption choices produced by the reactions of those around us. While sanctions alter the choices we make, they do not change our preferences. The social context in which religious markets are embedded divorces an individual's preferences from the choices she makes (in contrast to the revealed preference assumptions in neoclassical economics). Further, the presence and pervasiveness of sanction-driven choices violates one of the sacred assumptions of the utilitarian tradition in rational choice (which has unnecessarily dominated rational choice theories of religious behavior): the assumption of voluntarism (Warner, 1993).

Sanction-based rational choice models argue that social constraints, and not individual preferences, are the key to understanding involvement in collective action. Individuals engage in particular collective pursuits not because these activities *themselves* generate or provide value and thereby maximize utility, but because performing these duties allows us to gain rewards or avoid penalties. Rational choice theory is useful for analyzing constraints on choice at the individual level, though few sociologists of religion have used it for this purpose. Recent contributions by Heckathorn (1988, 1990, 1993), Macy (1993), and others (cf. Coleman, 1990; Marsden, 1981) have shown how collective action can be modeled as a function of constraints on behavior. Sanctions prevent people from defecting, from choosing not to participate. Rather than viewing behavior as a reflection of agreed-upon and internalized norms, as implied by functionalist theories, norms can be seen as being in conflict with individual desires (see especially Heckathorn, 1993).

So how do sanctions work for religious groups? A person may participate in a religious group and receive no substantial or plausible supernatural compensators, but may receive valuable "in process" benefits, solidarity incentives, or other selective incentives for participation (Buchanan, 1979; McCarthy and Zald, 1977; Wallis, 1991). Another motivation for making religious choices is the avoidance of punishment. If a person fails to participate and gains individual benefit from defection (she prefers to sleep rather than go to church), she will be ridiculed and excluded from the group in the future (and thus suffer costs as a consequence of defection). I may get nothing from the sermons or the religious ideology of a particular group (the plausibility of the religious meaning system may be nil for me, despite a committed community of believers), however I may garner a number of benefits from participation—friendships, access to mating markets, a place on the basketball team, confirmation of social legitimacy, insider information which benefits my research, and the like.

In our study of religious participation among African Americans, Christopher G. Ellison and I (Ellison and Sherkat, 1995a) characterized the participation choices of African Americans as semi-involuntary (see also, Nelsen and Nelsen, 1975; Ellison and Gay, 1990). The central and *multifunctional* role of the churches in the African American community, together with African Americans' lack of opportunities for social participation and legitimation, especially in the rural south, makes it very difficult for blacks to leave the church or to cease participating in church activities, even if they do not get much in the way of *religious* value through participation. Hence, we found that religious benefits are much more strongly predictive of religious participation outside of the South than they are in the South, especially the rural South. And consequently, preferences are more strongly related to choices in the non-South, where the *non-religious* benefits provided by the church are also available from secular institutions. There is nothing religious about the benefits of having access to mating markets, having a social group to provide you with legitimacy, getting financial assistance to help bury your relatives, and the like. The link between sanction-based rational choice theories and power-dependency theories (cf. Emerson, 1962) is clear. Since people desire a range of social benefits, and since these benefits are only available to African Americans through participation in religious institutions (especially in the rural South), African Americans must attend a church to get the benefits. One important implication of our study is that it presents a case where religious monopolies can actually increase religious partic- ipation. Baptists in the South, Mormons in Utah, Catholics in Ireland, Moslems in Iran, and so on, may participate because they have no viable alternatives to reli- gious participation if they want to enjoy non-religious social benefits. This is not to say that religious choices are coercive or pathological, only that they are not necessarily made for religious reasons. Indeed, in our study we found that prefer- ences for religious benefits are the strongest predictors of participatory choices, even for African Americans in the rural South.

Finally, sanctions are not simply external; internalized social norms must play a role in any comprehensive theory of religious behavior. In an important recent paper on the economics of religious participation, Joe Wallis (1991: 189) draws on contemporary considerations of preferences to speculate that the free-rider prob- lem in religious organizations is overcome in large part through the development of second- and higher-order volitions and desires: "Where a person identifies strongly with the purpose or function of a collective action group, it is likely to be a second order volition of this person to actively participate in the group enter- prise although the benefits of participation may even be derived free of charge." This is similar to the argument that internalized norms generate shame in those who break with their conscience (Grasmick et al, 1990). At the egoistic level a per- son may gain by cheating on her taxes or sleeping late on Sunday; however, this same person will suffer from the consequences of violating her principles. I con- tend that "second-order" preferences or "character planning" (Elster, 1983) should be seen as an internal sanctioning system.

A number of corollary propositions follow from the general specification of social influences on choice. First, *people with strong affective ties to others will be more careful in their religious choices.* These affective attachments may be positive or nega- tive, and they may be directed towards groups or individuals. A person may, for instance, join the Nation of Islam because of a general antipathy towards Jews, not to spite a particular Jew, or to horrify her Baptist grandmother. Second, *example- setting motivations for choices will be more prevalent among those in positions of authority or power.* This certainly applies to parents, but one can think of other applications, such as attendance at chapel by administrators and faculty of religious schools.

Third, *sanctions will be more influential on choices where social ties are consolidated.* When a number of social positions are interwoven—when family, religion, employment, ethnicity, neighborhood, and the like are entangled—decisions in one realm will often have an impact on another area of life (Blau, 1993; Blau and Schwartz, 1984; Blau et al., 1984). If we leave our religion, we may be subject to sanctions by those in the neighborhood, or on the job, or in the family. But if we live in a neighborhood with religious diversity, community sanctions will not be effective. The same is true for the workplace or the family. For example, spouses who have disparate religious affiliations will find it hard to sanction a child taking up an affiliation different from that of either parent. Another way of putting this is that cross-cutting ties reduce the effectiveness of social sanctions.

Fourth, *when other goods are tied up with church participation, monopolies may foster high rates of religious participation.* Even though monopolies tend to provide inferior religious products at higher prices and thereby lower overall levels of participation where they exist (cf. Finke and Stark, 1988; Iannaccone, 1991), when the consolidation of social ties causes other goods to be linked to religious participation, monopolies may be quite successful in generating participation (which could explain the findings of Blau et al. 1992, 1993, and Land et al. 1991). Fifth, *the stronger the second-order preferences for religious goods, the greater the character planning sanctions of shame and guilt directed against nonparticipation in religious groups and rituals.* Contradictory first-order preferences can result in sanctions generated by second-order preferences for character planning. For example, those with strong preferences for piety (a second-order preference) will feel guilty when they prefer to sleep in on Sunday (a first-order preference).

Sixth, *sanctions meted out by groups and individuals to whom one has affective attachments will be more influential on religious choices.* Approbation and disapprobation mean more when they come from people we feel close to. Loss of standing in a group we care about is more of a blow than outright excommunication from a group to which we are marginally attached. Again, since we tend to feel closer to groups which are more proximal—those which are characterized by more face-to-face interactions—sanctions coming from proximal groups will tend to have more of an impact on religious choices. For instance, individuals may avoid engaging in ecstatic worship if members of their Sunday school class disdain such behavioral choices. However, castigating glances or even formal sanctions from denominational officials will have less of an impact on people's choices. Finally, *when religious groups offer a wide variety of goods unavailable in secular society, the efficacy of control efforts by these groups on individuals' choices will be high.* In the case of the multifunctional rural southern Black Church this was clearly the case, and other examples are commonplace. Where the Catholic Church serves as an ethnic enclave or political force, for instance, it is providing not only supernatural compensators, but also a range of secular goods which may not be available elsewhere. In places where churches have this multifunctionality, individuals may participate not for religious reasons, but to gain other benefits or avoid costs.

Of course, a number of other implications could be generated from these three different types of social influences on choice. I have focused on establishing a number of important social considerations for rational choice theories and have discussed these social influences on religious markets using rational choice theories (though not always the theories which others have applied to religious choices). In the following section is my proposal for constructing an encompassing rational choice theory of religious markets.

TOWARD A GENERAL MODEL OF RELIGIOUS CHOICE

In my attempt to create a more formal statement of the theory presented in prose above, I will not propose a formal mathematical statement of the model, and a functional explication may not be possible. Instead, I will sketch an outline for a stochastic model which could be examined using empirical analyses of religious choices given preferences and constraints. Generalizations of this model could allow the introduction of market constraints and multimarket relations.[3]

A religious choice is a function of the utility derived from preferences at both the individual and social levels, and an individual will choose commodity 1 over commodity x when:

Equation 1: $\quad u(E_{1ik}) + u(S_{1il}) > u(E_{xik}) + u(S_{xil})$

where $u(E_{\star ik})$ is the utility associated with satisfaction of egoistic preferences for individual i and for the k dimensions of egoistic value produced by a commodity. $U(S_{\star il})$ is the utility associated with pressures from family relations, social ties, normative expectations, or internalized norms for individual i and for the l possible relational pressures of sympathy or antipathy, example setting, or sanctions. This should hold between all pairs of comparisons in the religious market, with x defining the number of products being evaluated for choice, the feasible set of options available to actors in the market, which is itself subject to constraints both from the supply side directly (Finke and Iannaccone, 1993; Finke and Stark, 1988, 1992; Iannaccone, 1991) and also from cultural barriers which prevent particular goods from being considered as part of the feasible set (cf. Elster, 1979; Darnell, 1994). Who, for instance, seriously considers Aztecan religion as a viable choice in the American religious market? If there was considerable demand for such "deviant" religious goods, there would likely be macro-level market restrictions on the supply of these goods, as is evidenced by the consistently hostile stance of various nations to sectarian and cult movements.

Each element of equation 1 implies another equation. Religious choices are usually made across a basket of goods, and there is a good deal of uncertainty about the costs and benefits associated with unfamiliar choices. For each element in the basket, individuals have some preference related to individual utility as well as utility generated by social influences. The utility associated with a particular choice of denomination can be specified at the individual level as a function of:

Equation 2: $\quad u(E_1) = b_k(\text{Theology}) + b_l(\text{Ritual}) + b_m(\text{Polity}) + b_n(\text{Demands})$

Where parameters b_k through b_n are weights associated with the k elements of a denomination's theology, l elements of ritual, m facets of its polity, and n types of demands placed on members. Hence, an individual will choose a denomination based on these multiple factors and will weigh each factor according to some parameter associated with her valuation of these aspects of the denomination or participatory act being considered for choice. Obviously, these weight parameters will be heavily influenced by past consumption and social learning, by adaptive preferences and preference learning. Indeed, they may respond noticeably to past consumption or information in a way very similar to Iannaccone's (1990, 1992) formulation of the human capital perspective. Notice that in the egoistic utility function I specify, there is no room for the rewards of a church basketball league, access to mating markets, pressure from grandma, ostracism by coworkers, and other important factors which have no natural connection to the intrinsic qualities of the basket of *religious* goods a denomination is pushing. Unless basketball is an integral part of the religious ritual or beliefs of a group, it isn't a part of individual-level evaluations of a denomination. While it may seem unconventional to discuss preferences for demands, I argue that such preferences reflect the strength of aversion to demands (though I also contend that many may enjoy what others think of as discomforting strictures). Hence, preferences for demands determine who will and will not be dissuaded from participating in strict religious groups and thereby allow these groups to have strong collective production of religious value (see Iannaccone, 1992, 1994).

Next I consider social influences on choice that make up the other half of the choice function. This specifies the utility derived from a choice through family, friends, community, and the like. Here, the utility function is defined as:

Equation 3: $u(S_1) = b_k(\text{sympathies}) + b_l(\text{example-setting}) + b_m(\text{sanctions}) + b_c(\text{character planning})$

where b_k represent parameter weights for rewards associated with sympathetic or antipathetic results of choices across k ties, be they friends, family, neighbors, coworkers, or others in the social environment. If an individual feels close to social ties, she will make choices which make significant others feel comfortable, while she may choose goods to anger those whom she despises. B_l presents weights for benefits or costs associated with example-setting for l targets. Presumably, individuals will place more weight on examples set for their own children than on examples set for neighbors' children or coworkers. B_m is the vector of parameters denoting benefits and costs associated with social ties (with m ties, or possible ties). Legitimacy and ostracism in the eyes of the individuals and communities to which individuals are linked constitute the essence of these influences on choices. Finally, b_c weights the influence of internalized norms or character planning on individual choices. I note that this view of the self as sanctioner corresponds somewhat to the Meadian distinction between the "I" as actor, and "me" as a reflective component responsible for self-monitoring. It is also notable that this provides an integration between the two levels: only through inculcating strong first level preferences for a particular style of piety is it possible to be subject to self-sanctioning through guilt or shame.

Different denominations may provide varying levels of social support and community ties (positive social rewards such as help when people are sick or bereaved, basketball leagues, access to mating markets, friendship opportunities), yet such choices may also generate hostility from other social groups to which individuals are bound, such as family, friends, occupational groups, political organizations, or whatever. The joint production of religious and secular value and the relative influence of these factors could be identified in a model which specifies how demand and supply in one area of a market influence market choices in another area, as in general models of multimarket disequilibrium (Maddala, 1983). Notice also that rewards emanate from different levels, from binary ties to friends and family to multiplex ties to occupation and community. Clearly, these affiliations are often nested, as the family resides in a congregation, which is a part of a community. Other ties may not fall into such a clear pattern of nesting, such as when an occupational group falls outside of any clear religious order and has no real ties to a particular community. The degree to which such ties are nested consolidates social pressures, while non-nested ties represent cross-cutting social pressures (Blau, 1993). Here, cross-cutting pressures would be formally identifiable by the signs of the weights associated with influence on consumption of particular religious goods. A family may reward a member for one type of religious choice (b would be positive), while the individual's friends are indifferent to this choice (b would be 0), and her coworkers are hostile to the choice (b would be negative). Further, these social pressures on our religious choices may be directed to particular aspects of the choice. It is not so much the Hindu ritual or theology which creates immense social sanctions against becoming a Hare Krishna, it is the demands they place on their members, and the guru-led nature of their polity which causes friends and family to pressure individuals not to make such a choice, even if the individual prefers the very same religious goods her relations despise. This differs from sympathy or antipathy, since tangible social pressures are being exerted by friends, relatives, and people in the community.

The model can be expanded to incorporate macro-level market conditions by considering them as being the determinants of the number and type of choices offered in the market. Hence, the set of market options is restricted by market regulation, the presence of monopolies, cartel arrangements, and the like. Regulation could affect denominations which offer particular types of religious goods in terms of theologies, ritual, polity structure, or demands on adherents. Restricting market offerings in such a fashion could have a profound effect on the overall levels of consumption, since competing pressures on choices could make it rational for individuals to exit the market rather than consume goods which give them limited utility.

In conclusion, I must admit to having only made a first step toward specifying a more realistic model of religious action. Getting beyond the minimalist conception of the actor is a tall order, but one I think will be rewarding. Integrating macro- and micro-level rational choice theories will be even more difficult, requiring multi-level, multi-equation models, and high quality data at each level. Despite the difficulties, it is clear that only rational choice theories provide a systematic framework for such an undertaking.

NOTES

[1] Direct correspondence to: Darren E. Sherkat, Department of Sociology, Vanderbilt University, Nashville, TN 37235. A version of this paper was presented at the Assessing Rational Choice Theories of Religion Conference, Sundance, Utah, April 9, 1994. This paper extends and benefits from collaborative work with Alfred Darnell, Christopher G. Ellison, and John Wilson, and also from the insightful comments and discussions from participants in the conference. A grant from the Vanderbilt University Research Council facilitated the development of the general model.

[2] Michael Hechter (1992, 1994) has pointed out the difficulty of determining the values that drive individual choices, and is quite skeptical about the payoffs from such an enterprise, particularly when there are constraints and conflicts involved with choices. While I agree that caution is warranted, I think that particular values can be linked directly to specific choices. I do not think that the minimalist view of the actor—preferred by structural social psychologists and rational choice theorists alike (see Lawler, Ridgeway, and Markovsky, 1993)—allows for the development of powerful theories. First, many "structural" influences on behavior may instead result from endogenous traits. Behaviors are assumed to be linked to influence processes or social constraints, while alternative explanations are ignored. Further, structural influences are most likely strongest on actor orientations (values, beliefs, and preferences), hence to view the actor as having a minimal range of experiences is to limit theoretical scope needlessly.

[3] See Maddala's (1983: 291–345) discussion of disequilibrium models with price controls and multimarket disequilibrium models for a much more formal treatment.

REFERENCES

Anders, Sarah. 1955. "Religious Behavior of Church Families." *Journal of Marriage and the Family* 17: 54–57.

Argyle, Michael, and B. Beit-Hallahmi. 1975. *The Social Psychology of Religion*. London: Routledge and Kegan Paul.

Becker, Gary S., and Kevin M. Murphy. 1988. "A Theory of Rational Addiction." *Journal of Political Economy* 96: 675–700.

Bikhchandani, Sushil, David Hirshleifer, and Ivo Welch. 1992. "A Theory of Fads, Fashion, Custom, and Cultural Change as Information Cascades." *Journal of Political Economy* 100: 992–1026.

Blau, Judith R., Kenneth C. Land, and Kent Redding. 1992. "The Expansion of Religious Affiliation: An Explanation of the Growth of Church Participation in the U.S., 1850–1930." *Social Science Research* 21: 329–352.

Blau, Judith R., Kenneth C. Land, and Kent Redding. 1993. "Ethnocultural Cleavages and the Growth of Church Membership in the United States." *Sociological Forum.*

Blau, Peter M. 1993. "Multilevel Structural Analysis." *Social Networks* 15: 201–215.

Blau, Peter M., Carolyn Beeker, and Kevin M. Fitzpatrick. 1984. "Intersecting Social Affiliations and Intermarriage." *Social Forces* 62: 3: 585–606.

Blau, Peter M., and Joseph Schwartz. 1984. *Crosscutting Social Circles.* New York: Academic Press.

Buchanan, Allen. 1979. "Revolutionary Motivation and Rationality." *Philosophy and Public Affairs* 9: 59–82.

Coleman, James Samuel. 1990. *Foundations of Social Theory.* Cambridge: Belknap.

Cornwall, Marie. 1989. "The Determinants of Religious Behavior: A Theoretical Model and Empirical Test." *Social Forces* 68: 2: 572–592.

Darnell, Alfred T. 1994. "Refining the Feasible Set: The Significance of Cultural and Historical Constraints." Unpublished Manuscript, Department of Sociology, Vanderbilt University.

Darnell, Alfred T., and Darren E. Sherkat. 1995. "Fortunes and Feasible Sets: Culturally Shaped Opportunities and Choices Among Biblical Literalists in Pursuit of Educational Attainment." Paper presented at the annual meetings of the Public Choice Society. Long Beach, CA.

De Vaus, David, and Ian McAllister. 1987. "Gender Differences in Religion." *American Sociological Review* 52: 472–481.

Ellison, Christopher G. 1991. "Religious Involvement and Subjective Well-Being." *Journal of Health and Social Behavior* 32: 80–99.

————1993. "Religion, The Life Stress Paradigm, and the Study of Depression." In Jeffrey S. Levin, ed., *Religious Factors in Aging and Health: Theoretical Foundations and Methodological Frontiers.* Newbury Park, CA: Sage.

Ellison, Christopher G., and David Gay. 1990. "Region, Religious Commitment, and Life Satisfaction." *Sociological Quarterly* 31: 123–147.

Ellison, Christopher G., and Darren E. Sherkat. 1990. "Patterns of Religious Mobility Among Black Americans." *The Sociological Quarterly* 31: 4: 551–568.

————1993a. "Conservative Protestantism and Support for Corporal Punishment." *American Sociological Review* 58: 131–144.

————1993b. "Obedience and Autonomy: Religion and Parental Values Reconsidered." *Journal for the Scientific Study of Religion* 32: 313–329.

————1995a. "The Semi-Involuntary Institution Revisited: Regional Variations in Church Participation Among Black Americans." Forthcoming, *Social Forces.*

————1995b. "Is Sociology the Core Discipline for the Scientific Study of Religion?" Forthcoming, *Social Forces.*

Elster, Jon. 1979. *Ulysses and the Sirens: Studies in Rationality and Irrationality.* Cambridge: Cambridge University Press.

————1983. *Sour Grapes: Studies in the Subversion of Rationality.* Cambridge: Cambridge University Press.

Emerson, Richard. 1962. "Power-Dependence Relations." *American Sociological Review* 27: 31–41.

Finke, Roger, and Laurence R. Iannaccone. 1993. "Supply Side Explanations for Religious Change." *The Annals of the American Academy of Political and Social Science* Vol. 527.

Finke, Roger, and Rodney Stark. 1988. "Religious Economies and Sacred Canopies: Religious Mobilization in American Cities." *American Sociological Review* 53: 41–49.

———1992. *The Churching of America: Winners and Losers in Our Religious Economy.* New Brunswick, NJ: Rutgers University Press.

Giddens, Anthony. 1984. *The Constitution of Society: Outline of the Theory of Structuration.* Berkeley: University of California Press.

Gorman, W.M. 1967. "Tastes, Habits and Choices." *International Economic Review* 8: 218–222.

Granovetter, Mark. 1985. "Economic Action and Social Structure: The Problem of Embeddedness." *American Journal of Sociology* 91: 481–510.

———1993. "The Nature of Economic Relationships." In Richard Swedberg, ed., *Explorations in Economic Sociology.* New York: Russell Sage Foundation: 3–41.

Grasmick, Harold G., Robert J. Bursik, and John K. Cochran. 1991. "'Render unto Caesar what is Caesar's': Religiosity and Taxpayers' inclinations to Cheat." *The Sociological Quarterly* 32: 251–266.

Hechter, Michael. 1992. "Should Values be Written Out of the Social Scientist's Lexicon?" *Sociological Theory* 10: 214–230.

———1994. "The Role of Values in Rational Choice Theory." *Rationality and Society* 6: 318–333.

Heckathorn, Douglas D. 1988. "Collective Sanctions and the Emergence of Prisoner's Dilemma Norms." *American Journal of Sociology* 94: 535–562.

———1990. "Collective Sanctions and Compliance Norms: A Formal Theory of Group Mediated Social Control." *American Sociological Review* 55: 366–384.

———1993. "Collective Action and Group Heterogeneity: Voluntary Provision Versus Selective Incentives." *American Sociological Review* 58: 329–350.

Hicks, J.R. 1956. *A Revision of Demand Theory.* Oxford: Clarendon Press.

Himmelfarb, Harold. 1979. "Agents of Religious Socialization Among American Jews." *Sociological Quarterly* 20: 477–494.

Hoge, Dean R., Benton Johnson, and Donald A. Luidens. 1993. "Determinants of Church Involvement of Young Adults Who Grew Up in Presbyterian Churches." *Journal for the Scientific Study of Religion* 32: 242–255.

Hoge, Dean R., Gregory H. Petrillo, and Ella I. Smith. 1982. "Transmission of Religious and Social Values from Parents to Teenage Children." *Journal of Marriage and the Family* 44: 3: 569–580.

Hoge, Dean R. and David Roozen, eds. 1979. *Understanding Church Growth and Decline: 1950–1978.* New York: Pilgrim Press.

Hunsberger, Bruce E. 1983. "Apostasy: A Social Learning Perspective." *Review of Religious Research* 25: 1: 21–38.

———1980. "A Re-examination of the Antecedents of Apostasy." *Review of Religious Research* 21: 2: 158–170.

Hunsberger, Bruce E., and L. B. Brown. 1984. "Religious Socialization, Apostasy, and the Impact of Family Background." *Journal for the Scientific Study of Religion* 23: 3: 239–251.

Iannaccone, Laurence R. 1988. "A Formal Model of Church and Sect." *American Journal of Sociology* 94 (supplement): s241–268.

———1990. "Religious Practice: A Human Capital Approach." *Journal for the Scientific Study of Religion* 29: 297–314.

Iannaccone, Laurence R. 1991. "The Consequences of Religious Market Structure: Adam Smith and the Economics of Religion." *Rationality and Society* 3: 2: 156–177.

———1992a. "Sacrifice and Stigma: Reducing Freeriding in Cults, Communes, and Other Collectives." *Journal of Political Economy* 100: 271–291.

———1992b. "Religious Markets and the Economics of Religion." *Social Compass* 39: 123–131.

———1994. "Why Strict Churches are Strong." Forthcoming, *American Journal of Sociology*.

Kelley, Dean M. 1977. *Why Conservative Churches are Growing*. New York: Harper and Row.

Kluegel, James. 1980. "Denominational Mobility: Current Patterns and Recent Trends." *Journal for the Scientific Study of Religion* 19: 26–39.

Land, Kenneth C., Glenn Deane, and Judith R. Blau. 1991. "Religious Pluralism and Church Membership: A Spatial Diffusion Model." *American Sociological Review* 56: 237–249.

Lawler, Edward J. 1992. "Affective Attachments to Nested Groups: A Choice Process Theory." *American Sociological Review* 57: 327–339.

Lawler, Edward J., Cecelia Ridgeway, and Barry Markovsky. 1993. "Structural Social Psychology and the Micro-Macro Problem." *Sociological Theory* 11: 268–290.

Lazerwitz, Bernard. 1961. "Some Factors Associated with Variations in Church Attendance." *Social Forces* 39: 301–309.

———1964. "Religion and Social Structure in the United States." In *Religion, Culture, and Society*, Louis Schneider, ed. New York: Wiley: 426–439

Lofland, John and Rodney Stark. 1965. "Becoming a World Saver: A Theory of Conversion to a Deviant Perspective." *American Sociological Review* 30: 862–875.

Macy, Michael W. 1993. "Backward Looking Social Control." *American Sociological Review* 58: 819–836.

Maddala, G.S. 1983. *Limited Dependent and Qualitative Variables in Econometrics*. Cambridge: Cambridge University Press.

Marsden, Peter V. 1981. "Introducing Influence Processes into a System of Collective Decisions." *American Journal of Sociology* 86: 1203–1235.

McCarthy, John D., and Mayer N. Zald. 1977. "Resource Mobilization and Social Movements: A Partial Theory." *American Journal of Sociology* 82: 1212–1239.

Mueller, Charles W. and Weldon T. Johnson. 1975. "Socioeconomic Status and Religious Participation." *American Sociological Review* 40: 785–800.

Myers, James. 1992. "Nonmainstream Body Modification: Genital Piercing, Branding, Burning, and Cutting." *Journal of Contemporary Ethnography* 21: 267–306.

Nash, Dennison. 1968. "A Little Child Shall Lead Them: A Statistical Test of an Hypothesis that Children were the Source of the American 'Religious Revival.'" *Journal for the Scientific Study of Religion* 7: 238–240.

Nash, Dennison and Peter Berger. 1962. "The Child, the Family, and the 'Religious Revival' in the Suburbs." *Journal for the Scientific Study of Religion* 2: 85–93.

Nelsen, Hart M. and Anne K. Nelsen. 1975. *The Black Church in the Sixties*. Lexington: University Press of Kentucky.

Nelsen, Hart M. and R.H. Potvin. 1981. "Gender and Regional Differences in the Religiosity of Protestant Adolescents." *Review of Religious Research* 22: 278–285.

Nelsen, Hart M. and William E. Snizek. 1976. "Musical Pews: Rural and Urban Models of Occupational and Religious Mobility." *Sociology and Social Research* 60: 279–289.

Newport, Frank. 1979. "The Religious Switcher in the United States." *American Sociological Review* 44: 528–552.

Olson, Mancur. 1965. *The Logic of Collective Action.* Cambridge: Harvard University Press.

Page, Ann L., and Donald A. Clelland. 1978. "The Kanawha County Textbook Controversy: A Study of the Politics of Life Style Concern." *Social Forces* 57: 265–281.

Polanyi, Karl. 1947. "Our Obsolete Market Mentality: Civilization Must Find a New Thought Pattern." *Commentary* 3: 109–117.

———1957. "The Economy as Instituted Process." In Karl Polanyi, Conrad Arensberg, and Harry Pearson, eds., *Trade and Market in the Early Empires.* New York: Free Press.

———1977. *The Livelihood of Man.* New York: Academic Press.

Pollner, Melvin. 1989. "Divine Relations, Social Relations, and Well-Being." *Journal of Health and Social Behavior* 30: 92–104.

Provenzo, Eugene F. Jr. 1990. *Religious Fundamentalism and American Education.* Albany: State University of New York.

Rochford, E. Burke. 1985. *Hare Krishna in America.* New Brunswick, NJ: Rutgers University Press.

Roof, Wade Clark. 1989. "Multiple Religious Switching: A Research Note." *Journal for the Scientific Study of Religion* 28: 4: 530–535.

Roof, Wade Clark and William C. McKinney. 1987. *American Mainline Religion: Its Changing Shape and Future.* New Brunswick, NJ: Rutgers University Press.

Rossi, Alice S. and Peter H. Rossi. 1990. *Of Human Bonding: Parent-Child Relations Across the Life Course.* New York: Aldine de Gruyter.

Sahlins, Marshall. 1972. *Stone Age Economics.* New York: Aldine.

Samuelson, Paul Anthony. 1948. "Consumption Theory in Terms of Revealed Preference." *Economica* 15.

———1938. "A Note on the Pure Theory of Consumers' Behaviour." *Economica* 5: 61–71.

Sandomirsky, Sharon and John Wilson. 1990. "Processes of Disaffiliation: Religious Mobility Among Men and Women." *Social Forces* 68: 4: 1211–1229.

Sen, Amartya. 1973. "Behavior and the Concept of Preference." *Economica* 40: 241–259.

———1977. "Rational Fools: A Critique of the Behavioral Foundations of Economic Theory." *Philosophy and Public Affairs.* 317–344.

———1993. "Internal Consistency of Choice." *Econometrica* 61: 495–521.

———Sewell, William H. Jr. 1992. "A Theory of Structure: Duality, Agency, and Transformation." *American Journal of Sociology* 98: 1–29.

Sherkat, Darren E. 1993. "Theory and Method in Religious Mobility Research." *Social Science Research* 22: 208–227.

———1991a. "Leaving the Faith: Testing Sociological Theories of Religious Switching Using Survival Models." *Social Science Research* 20: 171–187.

———1991b. *Religious Socialization and the Family: An Examination of Religious Influence in the Family over the Life Course.* Unpublished PhD Dissertation. Department of Sociology, Duke University.

Sherkat, Darren E. and Christopher G. Ellison. 1991. "The Politics of Black Religious Change: Disaffiliation from Black Mainline Denominations." *Social Forces* 70: 431–454.

Sherkat, Darren E., Jesper Sorensen, and Patricia M.Y. Chang. 1994. "Twenty Years of Religious Mobility in the United States." Paper presented at the annual meetings of the Association for the Sociology of Religion. Los Angeles, CA.

Sherkat, Darren E. and John Wilson. 1995. "Preferences, Constraints, and Choices in Religious Markets: An Examination of Religious Switching and Apostasy." Forthcoming, *Social Forces.*

Snow, David A., E. Burke Rochford, Steven K. Worden, and Robert D. Benford. 1986. "Frame Alignment Processes, Micromobilization, and Movement Participation." *American Sociological Review* 51: 464–481.

Snow, David A., Louis A. Zurcher, and Sheldon Ekland-Olson. 1980. "Social Networks and Social Movements: A Microstructural Approach to Differential Recruitment." *American Sociological Review* 45: 787–801.

Stark, Rodney and William Sims Bainbridge. 1987. *A Theory of Religion.* New York: Peter Lang.

———1985. *The Future of Religion: Secularization, Revival, and Cult Formation.* Berkeley: University of California Press.

———1980. "Networks of Faith: Interpersonal Bonds and Recruitment to Cults and Sects." *American Journal of Sociology* 85: 1376–1385.

Stigler, George G. and Gary S. Becker. 1977. "De Gustibus Non Est Disputandum." *American Economic Review* 67: 76–90.

Stolzenberg, Ross M., Mary Blair-Loy, and Linda J. Waite. 1994. "Religious Participation In Early Adulthood: Age and Family Life Cycle Effects on Church Membership." *American Sociological Review* 60: 84–103.

Veyne, Paul. 1990. *Bread and Circuses: Historical Sociology and Political Pluralism.* London: Penguin Press.

Von Weizsacker, Carl Christian. 1971. "Notes on Endogenous Change of Tastes." *Journal of Economic Theory* 3: 345–372.

Wallis, Joe L. 1991. "Church Ministry and the Free Rider Problem: Religious Liberty and Disestablishment." *American Journal of Economics and Sociology* 50: 183–196.

Warner, R. Stephen. 1993. "Work in Progress Toward a New Paradigm for the Sociological Study of Religion in the United States." *American Journal of Sociology* 98: 1044–1093.

Wilson, John. 1978. *Religion in American Society: The Effective Presence.* Englewood Cliffs, NJ: Prentice Hall.

Wilson, John and Darren E. Sherkat. 1994. "Returning to the Fold." *Journal for the Scientific Study of Religion* 33: 148–161.

Wuthnow, Robert and Charles Glock. 1973. "Religious Loyalty, Defection, and Experimentation Among College Youth." *Journal for the Scientific Study of Religion.*

Wuthnow, Robert and Glen Mellinger. 1978. "Religious Loyalty, Defection, and Experimentation: A Longitudinal Analysis of University Men." *Review of Religious Research* 19: 3: 234–245.

CONVERGENCE TOWARD THE NEW PARADIGM

A Case of Induction[1]

R. Stephen Warner

A YEAR before the Sundance conference, I published a long article in the *American Journal of Sociology,* the thesis of which was that a "new paradigm" was emerging in the field of sociology of religion. I deliberately chose a general journal in sociology to introduce this claim. Citing the work of many scores of scholars, I nonetheless singled out Theodore Caplow, Roger Finke, Andrew Greeley, Nathan Hatch, Laurence Iannaccone, Mary Jo Neitz, Daniel Olson, Rodney Stark, and myself as exemplars of a "loose school of thought" (Warner, 1993a: 1080), which, I claimed (and hoped), represented a scientific revolution in the making. Appropriately, most of those named were in attendance at the Sundance conference.[2]

Anyone who has read that article (a considerable number, since the article has been discussed at two "author meets critics" sessions[3] and has been included on required reading lists in several graduate seminars) will know that my statement of the "new paradigm" is deeply indebted to the work of the three men who spoke first on the Sundance program: Rodney Stark, Laurence Iannaccone, and Roger Finke. I think each of them knows from my published and private testimony how much I value his work, and how much I stand in basic agreement with it.[4]

Yet in this chapter I want to stress some differences I have with what has come to be called the "Rational Choice Model of Religion," that these men have developed. The differences are of two sorts. One is a substantive difference, above all a difference regarding the scope to which the new approach—whether it be called a "paradigm" or "model"—properly applies. The other is a methodological difference, specifically the inductive rather than deductive path that I traversed on the way to my statement of the new approach. These differences are related, and I will interweave the two in this paper. In rehearsing these differences, my purpose is not to break ranks with my co-workers. Quite the contrary, my purpose is to broaden our flanks. I want to suggest to fencesitters that one can join us in our new approach (and abandon our bankrupt competitors) without embracing the individualistic presuppositions and deductive logic of rational choice theorizing. I make this suggestion because, in my statement of the new paradigm, I claim to have grounds for it independent of the assumptions of rational choice theory; these independent grounds, I believe, add confirmation to our perspective.

I will begin by citing from my overview (Warner, 1993a: 1045) of the new paradigm:

> The presuppositional key to the new paradigm [is] the idea that religious institutions in the United States operate within an open market....[C]orollaries to this idea [are] that institutional religion in the United States is constitutively pluralistic,...that American religious institutions are structurally flexible,...that they can serve as vehicles of empowerment for minorities and otherwise subjugated people, and...that recent individualistic tendencies in American religion are consistent with its history.

The 1993 article gives extensive examples, documented in a massive bibliography (1082–1093), illustrating these claims; the present chapter focuses on the key "open market" presupposition and the first two corollaries, those concerning "pluralism" and "flexibility." In contrast to the "old paradigm" view that religion is most viable under societal conditions of monolithic consensus and unquestioned stability, the "new paradigm" draws on American history to argue that religion can flourish under conditions of societal diversity and change.

The first item I want to call attention to is that in my formulation, as the title to my 1993 article indicates, the new paradigm applies explicitly to religion *in the United States*. The paper is not a general theory of religion,[5] and only the very last paragraph of the article (1081–1082) hints that the American pattern might be useful as a general model. This cautious restriction of the new approach's scope is the *substantive* difference I have with the general "rational choice" formulation we discussed at Sundance. The basic substantive issue is my suspicion that the dynamics modeled by the general theorists may operate particularly within the "distinctive institutional parameters of the U.S. religious system" (Warner, 1993a: 1080), rather than in every society. I will return frequently to aspects of this suspicion.

My circumspection regarding the scope of the new approach stems not from lack of theoretical ambition, but from following a different path toward theory, an inductive rather than deductive one, in the footsteps of Carl Hempel rather than Karl Popper (cf. Warner, 1987: 37, with Stark's paper above [MS p. 1]). Thus, I understand "theory" to be an intellectual structure that bridges empirical observations instead of a thought process that produces hypotheses that are "refutable-in-principle."[6] In my own case, the new paradigm emerged from sustained reflection on what I and others had observed, particularly in our field research on American religious communities, rather than from working out the logical implications of first principles. This inductive process is the *methodological* issue that I will focus on in this paper, for it was an inductive process that led me to my circumscribed synthesis of the new paradigm.

My journey began in 1976 with the field research I started that year on the Presbyterian Church of Mendocino, California, a thriving, theologically conservative congregation in a highly cosmopolitan small town. I have detailed the process of that research before (Warner, 1988: 66–87; Warner, 1991b), but particularly relevant here is that the Mendocino project began as a study in political sociology. Despite being a product of the same PhD program as Stark, I was not trained in sociology of religion.[7] My assumptions about the Mendocino site proved erroneous, and to salvage the project, I had to master a new field, sociology of religion, years after leaving graduate school.

I was fortunate that my previous work in theory had earned me tenure and that my autodidactic project could therefore proceed at a leisurely pace,[8] because my initial reconnaissance of the literature in that new field in the late 1970s was frustrating. Whatever might be the shape of my eventual report on Mendocino Presbyterian Church, I knew that I had there encountered evangelicals who were young, educated, and sophisticated, while the literature told me that I should expect evangelicals to be old, ignorant, and otherworldly (Warner, 1979). Although the literature predicted accurately that evangelicalism would fare best among those with a small-town mindset (Roof, 1978), the evangelicals of Mendocino had *chosen* to live in a small town. It was not the case that their small-town circumstances provided the "plausibility structure" (cf. Berger, 1969) that constrained their imaginations and left them no alternative to Christian orthodoxy. They were "elective parochials" (Warner, 1988: 87), aware of alternatives. They had seen Paree. The prevailing notion that conservative religion could not survive in a mobile society soon became patently implausible to me.[9]

One of my fortunate meetings in Chicago in the late 1970s was with Mary Jo Neitz, who was similarly encountering conservative religion (in her case, the Catholic charismatic movement) among wide-awake people (in her case, affluent, respectably employed suburbanites; Neitz, 1987, 1990). Neitz's interviews disclosed a process by which comparison of religious options validated the eventual choice of the conservative alternative. Better acquaintance with the simultaneous religious variety and vitality of my adopted home, Chicago, led me to reject another expectation of the literature I was reading—namely that cultural pluralism was incompatible with conservative religion. I was being drawn toward the idea that conservative religion thrives precisely under the mobile, pluralist conditions of the modern United States, and simultaneously I was growing skeptical of theories (e.g., Hunter, 1983) that could grasp such vitality only as an exception to the rule.

Just when I was on the verge of confining my inductive theorizing to religious conservatism, one of my students insisted that our sociology of religion class take a field trip to a local congregation of the gay church, the Metropolitan Community Church, and there (the year was 1985) we experienced undeniable religious vitality without the conservatism that accompanied such vitality in either Mendocino or Neitz's suburban Chicago. So it occurred to me that the key to the vitality of the Mendocino church was not so much its evangelicalism, *per se*, as the fact that the message preached there spoke to the culture of the congregation, a proposition which was also true of the Metropolitan Community Church. In Mendocino, the pastor's evangelicalism made it possible for him to affirm what his flock had in common—their small-town values (see Warner, 1988: chapter 9)—just as the pastor's teaching at the Chicago M.C.C. congregation affirmed her flock's sexual orientation as the gift of a beneficent God.[10] The Mendocino and gay churches flourished in cultural niches of the members' own making.

As my class went on more field trips—to places ranging from Anglo-Catholic parishes and egalitarian synagogues through Indo-Pakistani mosques to African American and Korean immigrant Protestant churches—and as I read more in the literature, my thinking turned more self-consciously away from the phenomenologist's and survey sociologist's focus on *individual religiosity* and toward the historian's and ethnographer's focus on *religious institutions*.[11] Once I had cleared way the theoretical baggage of theologians' ethical objections to particularism, I came to see that the congregational form of American religion had long made room for the aspirations of subcultural communities, including different communities within the same denomination. A key correlate of the new paradigm ("The Master Function of Religion in the United States [is to provide] Social Space for Cultural Pluralism;" Warner, 1993a: 1058) began to fall into place.[12]

After I presented some rudiments of these ideas in a coda to the final chapter of the long-delayed book on my Mendocino project (Warner, 1988: 289–296), I thought I might have in them the germ of a new book, a book interpreting American religion generally from the point of view of the vitality and variety of congregational life. In 1987, I wrote a fellowship proposal to work on the new book, to be entitled *Communities of Faith*, and I was awarded a year's leave at the Institute for Advanced Study. When, during that fellowship year, I looked further into the history of the Metropolitan Community Churches (see Warner, 1995), I discovered that its founder, Troy Perry, not only had articulated the compelling religious vision that my class encountered in the Chicago congregation, he had also created an organization to promote this vision to what he thought might be an appreciative audience and to voice their common concerns to a broader public. In other words, the Metropolitan Community Churches were not only religio-cultural communities, groups of people coming together to celebrate and implement their values; they were also social organizations.

Troy Perry was, in short, a religious entrepreneur—an energetic salesman and tireless organizer—as well as a prophet. After reading Perry's autobiography (Perry, 1972) and hearing him preach, after reading books and articles about him and his church, after having met him and hugged him—nothing personal, you understand; he hugs everybody—it never occurred to me that he was anything other than sincere in his preaching and praying. Therefore, I was not inclined to see his entrepreneurship as being at all incompatible with the vibrant religion my class had encountered in the Chicago congregation of the M.C.C.; there was no necessary contradiction between sacred and economic modes of action. Indeed, I soon came to see Perry as the latest example of an American social type going back through Oral Roberts and Charles Grandison Finney to George Whitefield (see, respectively, Harrell, 1985; Hatch, 1989; and Stout, 1991), people who have been enormously successful *for* preaching from the heart. In Perry's founding of a new denomination, I sensed (but did not yet specify) that the energies of religious producers were as important a factor in the understanding of religious institutions as the demands of religious consumers. Later, I discovered "new paradigm" historians speaking of this factor, using the metaphor of "supply-side" analysis (Warner, 1993a: 1051).

Then, during my fellowship year (1988–89), I read the articles that Finke and Stark were turning out, and I quickly realized that they had seen some of the same things I had about American religion. They also thought that religious variety and vitality went hand-in-hand in the United States (Finke and Stark, 1988), and they had numbers to prove their point. They also saw the role in American religious mobilization of vigorous, often disreputable, leaders who stayed close to their grass roots (Finke and Stark, 1989). I have followed their work closely ever since, and I have borrowed economic imagery (above all, that of the religious market) from them.

Yet, with all due respect, I have never been particularly inspired by Stark's rational choice theorizing about religious compensators (Stark and Bainbridge, 1985, 1987). It's not that I think Stark is wrong; only that I see a different side of things. Yes, individuals get rewards from their religious involvements; yes, they are free to make religious choices; and yes, they can come and go from churches as they please—these features are fundamental to the American religious system as I see it. On this score I believe I am in agreement with Stark. But studying *congregations* as I do (Warner, 1983, 1988, 1990, 1992, 1994, 1995; Warner and Pappas, 1993; Wedam and Warner, 1994), I fail to see that *individuals* create religious alternatives (Yamane and Polzer, 1994). Unlike the pseudonymous Sheila,[13] most people do not define their own religions; instead, they respond to definitions offered (to real or imagined communities) by priests, prophets, entrepreneurs, and organizations.[14] Thus I have been most drawn to the rational choice theorists when they work in the "supply side" rather than "demand side" mode.[15]

Given the cultural pluralism of U.S. society and the pattern by which the energies of cultural entrepreneurs in the U.S. get channeled so typically into religious forms,[16] the alternatives proffered by religious suppliers come in staggering variety. They are not confined to the sectarian-versus-churchly choice that Finke and Stark (1992) and Iannaccone (1988) so compellingly model. The "structural flexibility" of American religious institutions, which I have designated as a correlate of the new paradigm, by which they can satisfy many needs, from cultural valorization through political mobilization to social support and emotional intimacy, pertains to far more than the strictness-lenience dimension.

Moreover, my observations of religious communities leave me unconvinced by the argument of Finke and Stark (1992) and Iannaccone (1994a) that strictness is the key to maintaining vitality of religious organizations. The charismatic group I followed in Mendocino in the mid-1970s—a *collegium pietatis* coexisting with the Presbyterian church—came to grief over the decision of their leaders to disfellowship a woman who was "living in sin" (Warner, 1988: 220–224). Similarly, Mendocino Presbyterian pastor Peter Hsu, another cohort leaning toward "strictness," and other liberal "new breed" pastors of the 1960s, could not readily mobilize their congregations to follow their demanding lead on civil rights (Warner, 1988: 98–107; Warner, 1985: 213). Also contradicting the strictness theory were Mary Jo Neitz's charismatics (Neitz, 1987), who did not draw strict boundaries between their own fellowship and those of the Catholic churches they continued to attend, and Nancy Ammerman's fundamentalists (Ammerman, 1987), who drew sharper lines in theory than in practice between themselves and their "unsaved" kinsmen. As I reflected on these findings, I remembered that the "strictness" aspect of Dean Kelley's theory (Kelley, 1977) did not stand up well to the empirical tests that the Hartford seminary people put it to (Hoge and Roozen, 1979). Somewhat later, I learned that the nineteenth-century southern Baptist growth that continued after the Methodists had run out of steam—the acid test of Finke and Stark's "winners and losers" narrative (Finke and Stark, 1992: chapter 5)—was accompanied, despite their strictness theory, by considerable relaxation of standards for membership in good standing (Holifield, 1994).

I suspect that there is very little popular taste for strictness, *per se*.[17] In my research, what is essential to religious vitality is for leadership to keep in touch with the grassroots, and insofar as "strictness" means adhering to prosaic rather than convoluted hermeneutics, it can promote such connection. Thus I think Finke and Stark are onto something when they insinuate that seminaries insulated from grassroots constituencies promote church decline. The people in the pews seem to have no interest in the rationalization and demystification that seminaries chronically promote. A taste for "strictness" appears to be more characteristic of elites, or what Weber calls religious "virtuosi," than of the religious masses, who provide the ultimate resource base for churches. What the masses seem to want in religious teachings are messages that speak to their needs instead of to the intellectual needs of elites. Insofar as religious masses are organized into pluralistic communities, they want their cultures, not the cultures of elites, upheld. But I see very little evidence that they are attracted to strictness.[18]

My year's leave in 1988–89 coincided with the appearance of my book on the Mendocino church, which brought me to the attention of religion scholars I had not previously known, particularly historians and religious educators whom I met through a variety of Lilly Endowment-sponsored projects.[19] Being at the Institute for Advanced Study, I had the time to read far more widely in the field than ever before. Plus, with the secretarial help, I was able to send off for scores of empirically-based conference papers, and had time to correspond with their authors. Such was the beginning of the literature review that underpins my new paradigm article. I gathered voluminous examples of variety, vitality, and flexibility in U.S. religious institutions—Protestant, Catholic, Jewish; evangelical, liberal, and feminist; white, black, and Asian—and incorporated them in drafts for chapters of my book.

But I also encountered confusion and bewilderment among their authors, many of them young scholars working on masters' theses, dissertations, or first books. They had been rightly admonished by their mentors to connect their discrete studies to wider theory, but the theory most of them had been taught, the "Sacred Canopy" theory of Peter Berger (1969), gave them little help (Warner, 1993a: 1048). Based on European notions of secularization, Berger's theory told them to expect religious particularism in the backwaters of society, but, like Ammerman, Neitz, and myself, they were finding it in midstream. Too many of them wasted valuable intellectual energy trying to create room for their observations within the basically inhospitable intellectual confines of the old theory; they reminded me in this respect of Copernicus grappling with Ptolemy.[20] Moreover, confronted with findings of flexibility and novelty in American religion—"me'n'Jesus" spirituality, home-based small groups, egalitarian minyans, women clergy, inclusive language, de-facto congregationalism—they were too inclined to interpret such innovation as evidence of the "accommodation" predicted by secularization theorists, for whom any deviation from elite-defined orthodoxy constitutes "worldliness."[21] I looked forward to the day that my book could become the source of the "wider theory" they'd use.

But that day seemed to recede further into the future as I found that the literature I was amassing provided me very little case material for an essential chapter of *Communities of Faith*, the chapter that was to cover the congregations of new ethnic and immigrant communities and without which the book would not be the breakthrough I had imagined. Scholars were just beginning to produce studies of the Korean-American religious experience, and a very few, mostly sketchy, studies of Muslim, Buddhist, and Hindu communities. There was a particularly glaring dearth of studies of the emerging religious institutions of Latinos, a highly religious constituency amounting to nine percent of the U.S. population. I have since made it my business to help fill these gaps (Warner, 1993c), thus postponing work on the book still further.

Since the book was taking longer than anticipated and I was anxious to provide younger scholars with an alternative to the older, unworkable, theory,[22] I spent most of the next year I had on leave (1991–92) revising for publication a lecture originally given at the Institute for Advanced Study. For the article, I planned to draw upon the literature I had mastered in the intervening years since 1988, but instead of portraying American communities of faith in the textured depth appropriate for a book, I would concentrate on a few propositions of the new approach that by then I recognized several of us were working on. And instead of writing for a general interest audience, I would address my sociological colleagues. The revised lecture became, halfway through the year, a 127-page manuscript which I nonetheless had the nerve to send off to a professional journal. Six months, one revise-and-resubmit, and 20 percent less bulk later, it was accepted for publication.

As I worked on the paper, I drew heavily on the economic imagery of Finke, Stark, and Iannaccone, as well as on the work of others who, with somewhat less assertiveness, indeed with diffidence, were groping their way toward a new theory. (In addition to those mentioned above, I refer to Mark Chaves, Kevin Christiano, Christopher Ellison, Jeffrey Hadden, Clark Roof and William McKinney, and Robert Wuthnow.) Because of my associations with historians, I was acquainted with new work in that field, especially books by Hatch (1989) and Butler (1990), and I was thrilled when I recognized that, despite the longstanding theoretical disagreement between those two men,[23] their work could be reconciled under the "supply side" concept (Warner, 1993a: 1054–1055).

Yet I shied away from making too much of economic thinking as the foundation of our efforts when I kept encountering citations, in the writings of the younger scholars whose work I was trying to redirect, to economic analogies in the work of my theoretical foil, Peter Berger. They quoted from the *Sacred Canopy* Berger's statement that in modern societies like the United States "religious institutions become marketing agencies and the religious traditions become consumer commodities" (Berger, 1969: 138). That this economic imagery seemed to function more as an excuse for cynicism than a tool for understanding did not diminish its prominence in their writing (Warner, 1993a: 1053). So what was to distinguish their economics from ours?

My conviction that the invisible college of scholars I was identifying was moving toward a unifying conception was rescued when, during a temporary strategic retreat, I reflected on another observation I had recently made during my first trip to Europe (reported in Warner, 1991a). When I drove through England, the prominence of grand medieval churches in the countryside but not in the industrial cities presented a sharp contrast to the skylines of the prairie and Chicago in the American Midwest. On this side of the Atlantic, the great churches rose in the cities and the grain elevators in the country, both the product of nineteenth-century efforts. Of course, I reflected, the Christianization of the United States was recent (Herberg 1960; Caplow et al., 1983: 29; Butler, 1990; Finke and Stark, 1992), whereas in Europe it was ancient. I suddenly realized why the secularization theory that fit the U.S. case so poorly had such visceral appeal to European-oriented social theorists.[24] In Europe, religion is quite tangibly a thing of the distant past, and in Europe, disestablishment *was* a degenerate state of religion. In the United States, by contrast, religious triumph was recent, and religious competition was constitutive.

That is when I decided that what unites us as new paradigm thinkers is not so much "rational choice theory" as the recognition that disestablishment (and the consequent release of religious energies) is the analytic norm for our theorizing. What I wanted to stress through the explicit delimitation of the scope of my "new paradigm" article (1993) is that that the *norm* is *institutionalized* particularly in the United States. In other words, what we new paradigm scholars had hit upon was not so much an economic theory of an unregulated religious market as the institutional secret of American religion as an open religious market, where barriers to entry were low but religion was a respected, popular, and, to a great extent, protected, idiom.[25] As Randall Collins pointed out at the Sundance conference, unregulated markets frequently fall prey to monopolistic control. What is remarkable in the U.S. is how open its religious market has continued to be despite monopolistic efforts (see Finke and Stark, 1992: chapter 6). This continued openness is one of the institutional parameters of the U.S. religious system. Whether the American recipe for religious vitality would work in other climates, however, is beyond my ken.[26]

I hope, in conclusion, that scholars of American religion with an ethnographic and historical bent might put aside their misgivings to join me in embracing a fundamental vision (a "paradigm") of their subject matter consonant with its distinguishing characteristics, even if that vision has been most forcefully articulated by rational choice theorists. Despite what I think may be a tendency to overreach and to be too confident about first principles, they are on to something.

NOTES

[1] I am indebted to Larry Young for his suggestions prior and subsequent to the presentation of the first draft of this paper, and for the creative and efficient way in which he brought the Sundance conference to fruition.

[2] The article also draws upon the work of Sundance participants Nancy Ammerman and Darren Sherkat, but at the time I wasn't sure that they would appreciate being included in the "new paradigm" company.

[3] The first occasion, prior to the article's publication, was the 1992 Fall Symposium of the Center for the Study of American Religion at Princeton University; the second was a session at the 1994 Annual Meeting of the Religious Research Association in Albuquerque.

[4] For example, see my review (Warner, 1993b) of Finke and Stark, 1992. Nine of Finke's publications, eight of Stark's, and four of Iannaccone's are cited in Warner, 1993a.

[5] Indeed, like the work of Weber, the new paradigm as I conceive it deals with religion primarily as a series of concrete institutions in particular historic societies rather than an analytic component of "societies" in general.

[6] I am sure that in this regard I differ with Stark and Iannaccone. On the grounds of my reading of his work, I am not so sure that I differ methodologically with Finke.

[7] My dissertation (Warner, 1972) was an exercise in sociological theory written under the direction of Neil Smelser and Guenther Roth and inspired by them and Reinhard Bendix. I took no courses with Robert Bellah, Charles Glock, or G.E. Swanson.

[8] I was also fortunate in the institutional, personal, and intellectual support I received in those years. My debts are recorded at length in Warner, 1988: 341–344, and Warner, 1993a: 1044–1045, and I am happy to acknowledge them again here.

[9] My first serious encounter with rational choice theory of religion came late in this protracted learning period (about 1986) when I refereed the article that was published as Iannaccone, 1988. At the time I appreciated Iannaccone's formulation for showing, among other things, that adherents of conservative religion could be aware of alternatives.

[10] It was in this stage of my theorizing that *New Wine in Old Wineskins* (Warner, 1988) went to press, and I turned to a proposal for my next book project, drafted in 1987, from which the ideas in the following paragraph are drawn.

[11] I was particularly inspired by Niebuhr, 1929; Herberg, 1960; Smith, 1971; Dolan, 1985; and Ammerman, 1987.

[12] This correlate was stated as a proposition in the 1987 fellowship proposal.

[13] "Sheila Larson" is the name given by Robert Bellah and his co-authors (1985: 221) to the young nurse whose religion was "Sheilaism": "I believe in God," she told the interviewer. "I'm not a religious fanatic. I can't remember the last time I went to church. My faith has carried me a long way. It's Sheilaism. Just my own little voice."

[14] In her studies of the Castro District of San Francisco and of Liberty Baptist Church of Lynchburg, Virginia, Fitzgerald (1986) made a major contribution to the understanding of the effect of geographic mobility on the creation of cultural niches and hence local markets—of gays and lesbians, on the one hand, and cultural conservatives, on the other—that could be exploited by entrepreneurs like Troy Perry and Jerry Falwell.

[15] Finke (1994: note 1 [MS]) says that he derived from me his own use of "supply side" language, whereas it is clear to me that supply side *thinking* was abundantly present in his own work before he began to employ the term. For a brief account of the term's intellectual history, see Warner, 1993a: 1051, 1057–1058.

[16] Some cultural minorities in the U.S.—e.g., Koreans and blacks—take greater advantage of religious forms than do others—e.g., Japanese and Arabs. Explaining why this is so is among the institutional parameters that new paradigm scholars have to specify.

[17] Surely Iannaccone, for whom strictness is a mechanism for producing goods that sect members desire, rather than a good in its own right, recognizes this much.

[18] They also want social support. The work of Olson (1989) and Marler and Hadaway (1992) together explains another reason why active religious suppliers—those executives who promote new church plantings—are conducive to church growth; see Warner, 1993a: 1064.

[19] Notable were the Congregational History Project at the University of Chicago, directed by James Wind and James Lewis, and projects directed by Edith Blumhofer through the Institute for the Study of American Evangelicals at Wheaton College.

[20] I engaged in correspondence with many younger scholars over these issues. Two who publically acknowledged the exchanges are Nancy Ammerman (reference to "anonymous person," 1987: viii) and Lynn Davidman (1991: x-xi).

[21] In other words, *pace* Stark (1994: 2 [MS]), the old paradigm had a theory, even if it wasn't a theory in Popper's sense. Perhaps it did not constrain scholars' *observations*, but it did constrain their *interpretations*. My response to their theorizing was the same as that Stark was scandalized to hear from Hanan Selvin: I ignored their interpretations so that I could use their observations.

[22] I was also motivated by the productivity of Finke, Stark, and Iannaccone to document whatever claim I had to scientific priority.

[23] Hatch had been long inclined to see consumer sovereignty operating in American religion, whereas Butler stressed leaders' authoritarianism with equal persistence.

[24] Secularization theory also appeals to those who grew up in religious enclaves, only to leave them for the world of the academy (Warner, 1993a: 1054). It may be a relevant biographical fact that I grew up in an unchurched family in an unchurched region of the country—the far west. Whereas the formerly churched feel alternately bewildered and vindicated to see the religious glass half empty, I have always been astonished to see it half full.

[25] Stephen Carter (1993) laments a recent loss of respect and protection for still-popular religious activities.

[26] Nonetheless, I am intrigued by the possibility that Iannaccone's (1994: 21–23 [MS]) extension of rational choice theory to the distinction between "collective" and "private" religious commodities may contribute to our understanding of the distinctiveness of typical Western, including American, religious organizational forms.

[27] I am grateful to Diego Gambetta and Federico Varese for comments.

[28] Principled action need not be considered to be irrational under this definition. If I place a high value on being a faithful husband, then this may enable me to resist the temptations of an affair at the office. Although I may be attracted to the promise of an affair, I can predict that succumbing to this desire will lower my self-esteem. Under certain conditions, therefore, it would be rational for me to choose the principled action of remaining faithful.

[29] Instrumental motives can overlay emotional ones to alter individual behavior, however. Thus the fear of criminal prosecution probably manages to forestall some intrafamily violence, despite its overwhelmingly emotional roots. Similarly, individuals can take other peoples' likely emotional reactions into account in planning their own strategic action.

[30] This section is drawn from Friedman, Hechter, and Kanazawa (1994).

[31] I am grateful to Diego Gambetta for pointing out this implication.

[32] For an intriguing study of the behavioral consequences of the fear of death, see Solomon, Greenberg, and Pyszczynski (1991).

REFERENCES

Ammerman, Nancy Tatom. 1987. *Bible Believers: Fundamentalists in the Modern World.* New Brunswick, NJ: Rutgers University Press.

———1990. *Baptist Battles: Social Change and Religious Conflict in the Southern Baptist Convention.* New Brunswick, NJ: Rutgers University Press.

Bellah, Robert N., Richard Madsen, William M. Sullivan, Ann Swidler, and Steven M. Tipton. 1985. *Habits of the Heart: Individualism and Commitment in American Life.* Berkeley and Los Angeles: University of California Press.

Berger, Peter L. 1969. *The Sacred Canopy: Elements of a Sociological Theory of Religion.* Garden City, NY: Anchor.

Butler, Jon. 1990. *Awash in a Sea of Faith: The Christianization of the American People, 1550–1865.* Cambridge: Harvard University Press.

Caplow, Theodore, Howard M. Bahr, and Bruce A. Chadwick. 1983. *All Faithful People: Change and Continuity in Middletown's Religion.* Minneapolis: University of Minnesota Press.

Carter, Stephen L. 1993. *The Culture of Disbelief: How American Law and Politics Trivialize Religious Devotion.* New York: Basic Books.

Chaves, Mark, and David E. Cann. 1992. "Regulation, Pluralism, and Religious Market Structure: Explaining Religious Vitality." *Rationality and Society* 4 (July): 272–290.

Christiano, Kevin J. 1987. *Religious Diversity and Social Change: American Cities, 1890–1906.* Cambridge, England: Cambridge University Press.

Davidman, Lynn. 1991. *Tradition in a Rootless World: Women Turn to Orthodox Judaism.* Berkeley and Los Angeles: University of California Press.

Dolan, Jay P. 1985. *The American Catholic Experience: A History From Colonial Times to the Present.* Garden City, NY: Doubleday.

Finke, Roger. 1994. "The Consequences of Religious Competition: Supply-side Explanations for Religious Change." Paper presented at the Sundance Workshop: Assessing Rational Models of Religion.

Finke, Roger, and Rodney Stark. 1988. "Religious Economies and Sacred Canopies: Religious Mobilization in American Cities." *American Sociological Review* 53 (February): 41–49.

———1989. "How the Upstart Sects Won America: 1776–1850." *Journal for the Scientific Study of Religion* 28 (March): 27–44.

———1992. *The Churching of America, 1776–1990: Winners and Losers in Our Religious Economy.* New Brunswick, NJ: Rutgers University Press.

FitzGerald, Frances. 1986. *Cities on a Hill: A Journey Through Contemporary American Cultures.* New York: Simon and Schuster.

Greeley, Andrew M. 1989. *Religious Change in America.* Cambridge: Harvard University Press.

Hadden, Jeffrey K. 1987. "Toward Desacralizing Secularization Theory." *Social Forces* 65 (March): 587–611.

Harrell, David Edwin, Jr. 1985. *Oral Roberts: An American Life.* San Francisco: Harper and Row.

Hatch, Nathan O. 1989. *The Democratization of American Christianity.* New Haven: Yale University Press.

Herberg, Will. 1960. *Protestant, Catholic, Jew: An Essay in American Religious Sociology*. Second edition; Garden City, NY: Anchor.

Hoge, Dean R., and David A. Roozen, eds. 1979. *Understanding Church Growth and Decline, 1950–1978*. New York: Pilgrim Press.

Holifield, E. Brooks. 1994. "Toward a History of American Congregations." In *New Perspectives in the Study of Congregations*, volume 2 of *American Congregations*, James P. Wind and James W. Lewis, eds. Chicago: University of Chicago Press: 23–53.

Hunter, James Davison. 1983. *American Evangelicalism: Conservative Religion and the Quandary of Modernity*. New Brunswick, NJ: Rutgers University Press.

Iannaccone, Laurence R. 1986. "A Formal Model of Church and Sect." *American Journal of Sociology* 94 (supplement): s241–s268.

Iannaccone, Laurence R. 1994a. "Why Strict Churches Are Strong." *American Journal of Sociology* 99 (March): 1180–1211.

————1994b. "Rational Choice: Framework for the Scientific Study of Religion." Paper presented at the Sundance Workshop: Assessing Rational Models of Religion.

Kelley, Dean M. 1977. *Why Conservative Churches Are Growing*. Second edition; San Francisco: Harper and Row.

Marler, Penny Long, and C. Kirk Hadaway. 1992. "New Church Development and Denominational Growth (1950–1988): Symptom or Cause?" in *Research in the Scientific Study of Religion*, vol. 4, Monty L. Lynn and David O. Moberg, eds., Greenwich, CT: JAI Press: 29–72.

McKinney, William, and Wade Clark Roof. 1990. "Liberal Protestantism's Struggle to Recapture the Heartland." In *In Gods We Trust: New Patterns of Religious Pluralism in America*, Thomas Robbins and Dick Anthony, eds. New Brunswick, NJ: Transaction Books: 167–183.

Neitz, Mary Jo. 1987. *Charisma and Community: A Study of Religious Commitment Within the Charismatic Renewal*. New Brunswick, NJ: Transaction Books.

Neitz, Mary Jo. 1990. "Studying Religion in the Eighties." In *Symbolic Interaction and Cultural Studies*, Howard Becker and Michal McCall, eds. Chicago: University of Chicago Press: 90–118.

Niebuhr, H. Richard. 1929. *The Social Sources of Denominationalism*. New York: Henry Holt.

Olson, Daniel V. A. 1989. "Church Friendships: Boon or Barrier to Church Growth?" *Journal for the Scientific Study of Religion* 28 (December): 432–447.

Perry, Troy D. 1972. *The Lord Is My Shepherd and He Knows I'm Gay*. Los Angeles: Nash.

Roof, Wade Clark. 1978. *Community and Commitment: Religious Plausibility in a Liberal Protestant Church*. New York: Elsevier.

Roof, Wade Clark, and William McKinney. 1987. *American Mainline Religion: Its Changing Shape and Future*. New Brunswick, NJ: Rutgers University Press.

Sherkat, Darren E., and Christopher G. Ellison. 1991. "The Politics of Black Religious Change: Disaffiliation from Black Mainline Denominations." *Social Forces* 70 (December): 431–454.

Smith, Timothy L. 1971. "Lay Initiative in the Religious Life of American Immigrants, 1880–1950." In *Anonymous Americans*, Tamara Hareven, ed. Englewood Cliffs, NJ: Prentice-Hall: 214–249.

Stark, Rodney. 1994. "Bringing Theory Back In." Paper presented at the Sundance Workshop: Assessing Rational Models of Religion.

Stark, Rodney, and William Sims Bainbridge. 1985. *The Future of Religion: Secularization, Revival, and Cult Formation.* Berkeley and Los Angeles: University of California Press.

———1987. *A Theory of Religion.* New York: Peter Lang.

Stout, Harry S. 1991. *The Divine Dramatist: George Whitefield and the Rise of Modern Evangelicalism.* Grand Rapids, MI: Eerdmans.

Warner, R. Stephen. 1972. "The Methodology of Max Weber's Comparative Studies." Unpublished PhD Dissertation; University of California, Berkeley, Department of Sociology.

———1979. "Theoretical Barriers to the Understanding of Evangelical Christianity." *Sociological Analysis* 40 (Spring): 1–9.

———1983. "Visits to a Growing Evangelical and Declining Liberal Church in 1978." *Sociological Analysis* 44 (Fall): 243–253.

———1985. "Dualistic and Monistic Religiosity." Pp. 199–220 in *Religious Movements: Genesis, Exodus, and Numbers*, Rodney Stark, ed. New York: Paragon House.

———1987. "Teaching Theory in an Empirically-Oriented Graduate Program." *The American Sociologist* 18 (Spring): 37–41.

———1988. *New Wine in Old Wineskins: Evangelicals and Liberals in a Small-Town Church.* Berkeley and Los Angeles: University of California Press.

———1990. "The Korean Immigrant Church in Comparative Perspective." Paper presented at colloquium on "The Korean Immigrant Church: A Comparative Perspective." Princeton Theological Seminary, February 16–18.

———1991a. "Starting Over: Reflections on American Religion." *Christian Century* 108 (September 4–11): 811–813.

———1991b. "Oenology: the Making of *New Wine.*" In *A Case for the Case Study*, Joe Feagin, Anthony Orum, and Gideon Sjoberg, eds. Chapel Hill: University of North Carolina Press: 174–199.

———1992. "Congregating: Walk Humbly at Rock Church." *The Christian Century* 109 (October 28): 957–958.

———1993a. "Work In Progress Toward a New Paradigm for the Sociological Study of Religion in the United States." *American Journal of Sociology* 98 (March): 1044–1093.

———1993b. Review of Finke and Stark 1992, in *Journal for the Scientific Study of Religion* 32 (September): 295–297.

———1993c. "Introducing the New Ethnic and Immigrant Congregations Project." Working Paper; University of Illinois at Chicago, Office of Social Science Research.

———1994. "The Place of the Congregation in the American Religious Configuration." In *New Perspectives in the Study of Congregations*, volume 2 of *American Congregations*, James P. Wind and James W. Lewis, eds. Chicago: University of Chicago Press: 54–99.

———1995. "The Metropolitan Community Churches and the Gay Agenda: The Power of Pentecostalism and Essentialism." Forthcoming in Mary Jo Neitz and Marion S. Goldman, eds., *Sex, Lies, and Sanctity: Deviance and Religion in Contemporary America.* Greenwich, CT: JAI Press.

Warner, R. Stephen, and James S. Pappas. 1993. "Congregating: Seeing the Word." *The Christian Century*, 110 (June 30–July 7): 663–665.

Wedam, Elfriede, and R. Stephen Warner. 1994. "Sacred Space on Tuesday: A Study of the Institutionalization of Charisma." Forthcoming in *I Come Away Stronger: How Small Groups Are Shaping American Religion*, Robert Wuthnow, ed. Grand Rapids, MI: Eerdmans.

Wuthnow, Robert. 1988. *The Restructuring of American Religion: Society and Faith Since World War II*. Princeton: Princeton University Press.

Yamane, David, and Megan Polzer. 1994. "Ways of Seeing Ecstasy in Modern Society: Experiential-Expressive and Cultural-Linguistic Views." *Sociology of Religion* 55 (Spring): 1–25.

ASSESSMENT

part II

ECONOMIC MAN AND THE SOCIOLOGY OF RELIGION

A Critique of the Rational Choice Approach

Mary Jo Neitz and Peter R. Mueser

RATIONAL CHOICE theory provides a powerful tool for taking another look at some traditional problems in the sociology of religion. The work of Iannaccone, Finke, and Stark elegantly explains some of the persistent problems in the sociology of religion, and rational choice theory, combined with empirical analyses, offers a systematic theoretical alternative to the theories of secularization which have dominated the field since its inception.

However, like R. Stephen Warner, we see the contributions of rational choice theory as ultimately part of a larger body of work, a new paradigm in the sociology of religion (Warner, 1993). Of the two of us, Neitz is a sociologist who, while not identifying with the rational choice framework, finds some of her recent findings consistent with those produced by rational choice theorists, and Mueser is an economist whose own work rests on the assumption of rational choice. In this chapter, we hope to convey our appreciation for rational choice theory—especially where it complements our own work in religion. We do not accept, however, the methodological and theoretical exclusivity that rational choice theorists promote along with their findings. We believe that the rational choice perspective cannot provide a full picture of religion. In this paper, we hope to show how other theoretical perspectives are essential for raising important questions that are too easy for a researcher working within the confines of rational choice theory to ignore. In addition, we argue that inductive and ethnographic approaches produce qualitative understandings of religious phenomena which complement the findings of the rational choice theorists.

CONGRUENCE WITH RATIONAL CHOICE THEORY
Challenges to Secularization Theory

Secularization theory stated that plausible religion is based in religious monopoly, and that it existed in premodern Europe and not in modern developed countries. The classical theories assumed a linear (secular) trend away from religion with the advance of modernization (e.g., Berger 1967; Wilson, 1982). This thesis has been challenged on two fronts. On the one hand, a reading of recent European historians' work on popular religion in medieval and early modern times (work based primarily on inquisition documents) suggests that the institutional church was less successful than the thesis posits at creating a single plausibility structure to which all subscribed (e.g., Ginzberg, 1980; LeRoy Lauderie, 1979).

On the other hand, studies of late twentieth century communities also show the possibility for individual religious commitment and plausibility structures at a subcultural level in a pluralistic religious environment. Precious Blood Prayer Group, the Catholic Charismatic Renewal prayer group upon which *Charisma and Community* (Neitz, 1987) is based, is an example of what that book identifies as "communities of choice." Similar to what the supply-side arguments predict, communities of choice are strong religious groups arising in a pluralistic context. Precious Blood Prayer Group was constituted by members who made a self-conscious choice to be there.

Yet understanding what it is about communities of choice that attracts adherents is not easily achieved by referring to market structures. How these groups build and maintain ties, how they produce meaning in the face of the human limitations of cognitive, moral and physical abilities, and how they inspire individuals to participate in activities which are not in their transparent self-interest are questions better addressed by qualitative approaches.

Conversion as a Rational Process

Another aspect of *Charisma and Community* that is congruent with rational choice theory is its view of conversion as a rational process. Neitz's analysis shows that people undergoing religious conversion are individuals engaged in a rational process; they do not experience a sudden transformation of the kind attributed to Paul on the road to Damascus. Yet there are different understandings in the social sciences about what it means to say that decisions are rational. The understanding of the nature of rationality that informs *Charisma and Community* is based in the tradition of Alfred Schutz and Harold Garfinkle rather than economic theory. Here rationality is in part a sense-making activity, and as such is more concerned with process, whereas the rationality posited by rational choice theorists usually focuses on outcomes.

Garfinkle, for example, describes the following common sense ways of assessing information: categorizing and comparing, working out tolerable degrees of error, assessing the goodness of fit between an item and an explanation, searching for means, analyzing possible consequences, working out strategies for achieving goals, being concerned about timing, attempting to predict outcomes, and attempting to provide grounds for choice—all within the context of imperfect information (Garfinkle, 1967: 363–366). While this understanding shares rational choice theory's idea of "purposive rationality" (the notion that people do the best they can given the circumstances) it shifts the focus. Rather than assuming a well-defined decision problem, the approach in *Charisma and Community* looks at the processes people use to arrive at choices—processes which are tied to their attempts to understand who they are and where they are.

FEMINIST CRITIQUES OF RATIONAL CHOICE THEORY

As seen in the works of Stark, Finke, and Iannaccone, rational choice theory presents a world that is astonishingly ungendered. The pursuit of the leanest formal models pushes toward rendering factors such as race, class, and gender as largely exogenous. In this section of the paper, we examine feminist critiques of rational choice theory for their relevance to the sociology of religion at two levels. The first is at the basic level of the question, "Where *are* the women?" The second, more analytical level suggests yet another conceptualization of rationality itself, one based on a model of the self as relational or connected rather than "separative" and autonomous.

Presumably, even though the theory is stated in gender-neutral terms, gender could logically be introduced in many places as a variable. In fact, Larry Iannaccone does suggest elsewhere that if one of the characteristics of people who are attracted to strict churches is that they have less to lose outside the church, then we might expect women, minorities, and young people to be more attracted to strict churches (1994: 1201). In many cases, researchers could profitably "add women and stir": they could increase our understanding of how religious practices are gendered by more often considering gender as a variable.

For example, feminists are concerned with how structural constraints have limited the kinds of choices that women have been able to make. Certain kinds of constraints can easily be modeled within the context of rational choice theory. Labor market discrimination in other than clergy roles, for example, increases the desirability of clergy roles for women in religious traditions where ordination is possible. Similarly, the lack of opportunities for women in secular society may cause nonpaying roles in churches to appear more desirable.

At another level, feminists have criticized rational choice theory because the implicit model of the person is based on the male experience. A number of feminist theorists have argued that women display a personality structure that differs from men's in that it is more "relational." Women interact with their environment based on feelings of connection to others and, consequently, make moral decisions differently (e.g., Chodorow, 1978; Gilligan, 1982). While not all feminists make these claims, such objections do form the basis of one significant feminist criticism of rational choice theory.

In exploring this criticism of rational choice theory, we do not argue that women are not rational in their decision making. Nor do we want to portray the case as simply a matter of women being constrained. To do so implies that women freed from certain constraints would act like men. The question we pose is, To what extent can one take this criticism seriously and remain within the frame of rational choice theory?

Addressing the question of how inequality between men and women is reproduced, Nancy Chodorow used object relations theory to explain gender development in children as a process based in the experience of being mothered by a woman. Chodorow argues that one of a very young child's developmental tasks is to acquire a sense of identity, which requires coming to see the self as separate from the mother. Males and females accomplish this task in somewhat different ways. Both male and female children initially identify with the mother. Boys develop gender identity and a sense of themselves as separate in part by repudiating the mother and all that is feminine. Because of a lack of available male role models as daily caregivers, male identity depends on being "not feminine." (This is the reason why being called a "sissy" is so much worse than being called a "tomboy.") Male autonomy comes at the cost of separating the self from the mother and that which is feminine.

Girls, on the other hand, also need to differentiate themselves from their mothers, but, the theory tells us, they accomplish this in a much less severe way. Since they do not have to repudiate all that is feminine, they can continue to identify with their mothers as women while coming to see themselves as separate individuals. The consequence is that boys sense themselves more as separate persons acting autonomously in the world, while girls develop a sense of self that is more relational, less separate or autonomous, and more connected to other people. Girls' psychological boundaries are more permeable, encouraging empathy and altruism, and, in the words of Chodorow's title, facilitating "the reproduction of mothering."

Chodorow's theory is corroborated in psychologist Carol Gilligan's work on moral development. Gilligan, a student of Lawrence Kohlberg's, was puzzled by the fact that when Kohlberg's scales of moral development were administered to girls as well as boys, girls tended to come out lower on the scale. Not willing to accept the conclusion that girls were morally stunted compared to boys, Gilligan asked herself what it was about the scale (and the theory upon which it was based) that might yield such results. Gilligan's own experiments suggested that women's moral reasoning was based on an ethic of caring and responsibility toward others coming out of experiences of caring for others, rather than on an ethic of noncoercion coming out of experiences of autonomy.[1]

For feminists, a model of the relational self challenges the separative-self model in a number of ways that bear on rational choice theory. Paula England (1989) has articulated some of the feminist concerns in a revised version of rational choice theory. England points out that most economic analyses are based in the model of the separative self, which she links to the separation between emotion and reason in Western thought. In contrast, she argues that the model of the relational self emphasizes connections to others and rejects the dichotomy between emotion and reason—a dichotomy which is false for men as well as women.

For England, adopting the model of the relational self leads to a revision of the conception of rationality but not the rejection of the rationality assumption itself. England argues:

> [The] feminist position would find economists' conception of rationality problematic to the extent that rationality is seen as radically separate from emotion...The theory...creates a radical separation between two spheres of subjective events. In one sphere are the "tastes" (preferences, emotion, desires, values) that determine one's ends. In the other sphere are the cognitions, the calculations about what means will achieve the ends satisfying the demands of the first sphere. The rationality principle resides in the second sphere...It is this radical separation of tastes from everything else that distorts the conceptualization of rationality. (1989: 21)

The claims of England and other feminists are echoed within traditional economics. Robert H. Frank (1988) argues that human emotion can be understood within the rational choice framework if it is analyzed in strategic terms. Emotions constrain human behavior—to some degree limiting short-term rational choices—but by doing so allow profitable human interaction. Although Frank does not do so, it is evident that male and female differences in emotional makeup discussed above could easily be fitted within his framework.

More broadly, economists studying game theory have for many years recognized that in games involving coordination between players, where mutual expectations play a critical role, culture, history, background, as well as symbolic significance, may influence outcomes, even when they do not directly affect the formal game structure. The assumption of rationality is simply not sufficient to predict behavior.[2] The feminist claim that women are relational in their approach to interactions may be interpreted to imply that they may behave differently even if they are rational and have the same end goals that men have. While game theory tells us that cultural differences can be important, it provides no way to explain or understand them; and for most economists, questions about gender differences simply don't come up.

So why should it matter to sociologists of religion? Because if males have primarily autonomous selves and women relational selves, both conversion and deconversion processes probably occur for them in substantially different ways (see Davidman and Jacobs, 1993). Furthermore, the questions of where we find an ethic of care and what kinds of differences it can make in the organizations and practices of religious people is relevant for the sociology of religion (see Wedam, 1993). Some of Neitz's current work explores the ways that religious experiences themselves are gendered. Examining some of the traditional spiritual practices that emphasize the submission of the will—such as fasting or abstaining from sex—reveals that these practices have very different meanings for women than they do for men, whose spiritual seeking occurs in the context of a separative and autonomous self (Neitz, 1995).

To say that men and women have different human capital or face different structural constraints—the language of the rational choice model—may acknowledge some of these factors, but it also effectively puts them outside of the analytic frame. While that may allow us to focus on some of the consequences of gender differences, such an approach provides little insight into the processes of reproduction, negotiation, and interpretation of gender in religious practices and beliefs. Furthermore, for the most part, the core assumptions of the rational choice model prevent such questions from even coming up. Feminist perspectives do not conceptualize the actor as the individually maximizing, autonomous person known as "economic man." The feminists' alternative conception—the relational, connected person—has the advantage of leading to additional questions about how religions produce and use empathy, emotion, and altruism. These, in turn, can help us to understand how religious groups function, not simply as economic institutions, but as communities in the modern world.

RATIONAL CHOICE THEORY AND QUALITATIVE ANALYSIS

Rational choice theory is often viewed as providing a challenge to traditional analyses of religion, and especially to the work of qualitative researchers. In the foregoing sections, we have argued, first, that existing qualitative analyses by no means reject the idea of rational choice. In fact, the explanations provided by rational choice theory overlap substantially with empirically grounded qualitative work. Second, we have focused on a particular substantive area—analyses considering gender differences and gender relations—where rational choice models fail to address some of the processes that are most critical in understanding observed group behaviors and individual interactions.

In this final section, we focus more directly on the existing rational choice models of religion, attempting to examine them on their own terms. We find that, far from providing a fully formed alternative to qualitative analyses, rational choice theory poses questions that it cannot answer. In doing so, it highlights the importance of continuing to pursue qualitative research that addresses these issues.

Understanding the Religious Production Process

Iannaccone's work follows in the tradition of economic modeling, in that it takes as given both individuals' preferences and the production process. He has shown how this approach can yield a variety of implications, providing a unified explanation for observed patterns of individual religious practice and religious organizational structure. However, the resulting picture of religion remains incomplete to the extent that as it leaves unexplored the heart of the productive process—religious participation itself. In large part, the goal of qualitative research revolves around this heart: explaining how religious inputs combine to produce what Iannaccone labels "religious commodities."

In considering tangible goods, traditional economic analysis examines markets for both inputs (e.g., labor, raw materials) and for outputs, most commonly consumer markets. Supply and demand analysis can be applied to each market, with worker and consumer preferences playing well-defined and separate roles. Although the production process ties these analyses together, economists are generally content to leave explication of the productive process to experts (e.g., engineers, chemists). As Iannaccone correctly observes, the production of religious commodities differs from the production of most tangible goods in a variety of ways.

The most basic difference is that the very character of religious output is subject to interpretation. Whereas common sense may suffice to measure output of cars or shoes (with adjustment for quality or other attributes), simple observation is not sufficient to even define what is produced by a church. Some kind of theory incorporating intent, belief, emotion, and symbolism—all complex conceptual categories—is necessary to render the varied activities of church members understandable as a "religious commodity." Iannaccone's analysis of religion cannot even begin without an implicit set of assumptions that allows activities of the Sunday service to be distinguished from zen meditation, visits to an astrologer, or even social interaction at the local bar.

The production and consumption process for religious commodities is, moreover, governed by the cultural and social structures that actors inhabit. Much of qualitative work focuses on understanding such relations. In Iannaccone's terms, individuals have varying kinds of "religious human capital," which is produced by individual and family investment, as well as an overarching cultural milieu. Iannaccone's model, while it provides a label, is unable to predict the character of this human capital or how alternative forms will interact.

Another important difference between the standard economic analysis of tangible goods and the economic analysis of religion is that, in the case of religion, producers and consumers are, to a large degree, the same individuals, with consumption and production intertwined. In traditional economic analysis, distinct prices for inputs and outputs can be observed, and their separate impacts can be gauged. In contrast, whatever "price" applies to a religious participant must reflect both willingness to supply what is needed by the church (e.g., labor, devotion), as well as the participant's evaluation of the benefits the church provides.[3] In the absence of measurable prices, what goes on inside the church (its production function) naturally becomes critically important in understanding the religious market.

Iannaccone's (1994) innovative analysis of church strictness shows the inherent limitations of an analysis that ignores the processes of religious production. The analysis provides an elegant answer to the intuitively reasonable question of why a strict church may succeed in attracting members when strictness clearly increases the costs of participation. Strictness, Iannaccone argues, may increase the benefits a church can offer by solving a free-rider problem. He argues persuasively that important patterns of religious behavior and institutional structure are explained by this claim. His basic theoretical conclusions depend only on the barest minimum assumptions, that religious production/consumption is often joint (meaning that output depends on coordinated activity), that participants cannot be prevented from receiving religious benefits, and that the individual pricing of those benefits is not feasible.

However, viewed in terms of its own rational choice perspective, the model raises a number of interesting questions that it cannot answer. Iannaccone notes that his model implies an optimal level of church strictness, but that not all churches attain the optimal level (1994: 1201–1204). If so, some factor outside the model must be preventing individual churches from reaching this optimal level. To explain such variation one might look to differences among churches, perhaps deriving differences in bureaucratic structure or religious practice from a church's historical experience.

An alternative approach, one we find attractive, would be to push the rational choice assumption one step further than does Iannaccone. Rather than assume that churches make systematic errors, that, for example, the old-line Protestant churches have, as a group, failed to retain efficient standards to prevent free-riding, we may assume that each church has chosen its optimal level of strictness. Differences among churches therefore derive from variation in the very processes by which religious commodities are produced and consumed, and the nature of the output produced. The study of that productive process—the heart of the qualitative analysis of religion—is again central.

In concrete terms, we are suggesting that Unitarian and Assemblies of God churches produce a different product, and, as a result, attract different kinds of members. Market analysis tells us that churches will occupy niches, and that there will be a matching between the preferences of adherents and the product produced. But we need to study both the products and the consumers to know why optimal levels of strictness will differ.

Once we acknowledge differences among churches in the productive process and the output produced, the question arises of whether the observed positive relationship between a church's growth and its strictness is truly causal. High levels of strictness are optimal only where a church is able to produce a product viewed as highly desirable by a sufficient number of potential customers. The strict, fast-growing churches may be growing largely because they have an attractive product, one that could not be offered by the old-line Protestant denominations. Of course, this is exactly the claim made by Warner (this volume), who argues that factors other than strictness explain differential church growth.[4]

The foregoing argument is not meant to denigrate the contributions made by rational choice theorists to understanding religious behavior. Iannaccone has successfully exploited the power of his models. His success rests, in part, on his willingness to recognize and incorporate conceptual and empirical work outside his own inductive system. But because his presentation often downplays the role of complementary research, we wish to reaffirm the central role that this research plays. It is qualitative research that allows us to address such questions as: What causes religion to be a joint product (i.e., when is free riding a problem)? What kinds of people are likely to be attracted to various kinds of "religious products"? What kinds of religious human capital are similar?

Religious Markets: Explaining the Differences in Competitiveness

The view of religion as operating in a market, with churches and congregants forming supply and demand, has provided a useful lens through which to examine variations in religious activity. According to this view, religious monopoly, like monopoly in other markets, leads to inefficiency and diminished activity, while competition selects suppliers who cater to the needs of customers, creating a growing and vital market. The analysis has been successfully applied, explaining changes over time, and variation across countries.

The striking contrast between the high levels of religious activity in the United States, where competition between religious movements has been common, and Europe, where state or monopoly religion more frequently has dominated, seems to be a clear demonstration of these arguments. We agree that market structure is an important proximate cause of these observed differences in religious participation. We wish to suggest, however, that there are other important national differences in the roles that religion plays, and market structure may be as much a result as a cause of these differences.

The government-supported churches of Europe survive within active democratic states. Granting that the vagaries of politics may induce some arbitrary variation in government policy, and that established religious bureaucracies may succeed in lobbying to retain privilege, popular opinion must nonetheless play an important role in retaining state support. We suspect that state support of religion is viewed very differently in the European countries than in the United States. Such differences are reflected in a multitude of the indicators of religious behavior, and the difference in market competition is only one element of this difference.

Perhaps reference to a more conventional market will clarify the argument. In the developed countries of Europe, health care is either provided by the state or is under its close supervision. As we might expect, health care in these countries displays many of the characteristics of monopoly markets. A smaller array of services is available and individuals with special needs may have limited options. Yet many Europeans view the benefits that accrue from government control—an ability to centralize delivery and provide universal coverage—as ends worth this cost. Should it surprise us that Europeans are also more comfortable with a controlled religious market than are Americans?

Finke (this volume) quotes the Bishop of Stockholm as saying, "The Established Church is like a post office...people don't rush to it when it opens...They are just happy it's there" (Lamont, 1989: 164). In contrast to Finke, who cites this as proof that the clergy faces little incentive to mobilize support, we suggest that this may reflect a legitimate basis for support of the state church for a substantial portion of Swedish voters. According to this interpretation, the difference between American and European churches is partly demand-driven. The Europeans may ask different things of religion than do Americans, and their demands may be more successfully satisfied by monopoly religion. Their preferences are reflected both in their direct participation in religion and in the state policies toward religion negotiated through the political process.

Again, please note that our claim is not that the market analysis of religion is incorrect, but rather that it is incomplete. If we are to have a truly full explanation of what makes American religion different from its European counterpart, we cannot be satisfied to know only how the markets are different. We must understand why they are different, and how cultural differences and ideas about religion interact with the political process and the religious market to produce national differences in the religious environment.

Narrative and Theorizing About Religion

Rational choice models are generally structured around a set of listed axioms, followed by deductive conclusions, which purport to predict empirical relations.

They therefore conform, at least formally, to Popper's standard of providing falsifiable propositions by which a theory can be tested. Stark (this volume) explicitly argues that such a structure is the hallmark of scientific theory construction.

We wish to suggest that while the generation of falsifiable implications plays an important role in the development of scientific theory, adherence to the formal structure common in rational choice models is neither necessary nor even sufficient for theoretical progress. It is now widely recognized that, contrary to the implication of Popper's argument, no single definitive test succeeds in causing the rejection of a theory. Even as Stark was adopting Popper as his standard of science in sociology, Thomas Kuhn (1962) was arguing that, in the natural sciences, the development and adoption of theory rested on a complex process not adequately described by the much-celebrated "scientific method."

The difficulty of evaluating theory in the light of data is illustrated by the story of an exchange between Albert Einstein and the author of a study empirically refuting one of Einstein's theoretical predictions. Einstein is said to have responded acknowledging that the empirical results were inconsistent with his prediction but noting that some source of error of unknown origin could have caused the apparent contradiction. In fact, Einstein was correct, although at the time he had no direct empirical basis for defending his theory.

Donald McCloskey argues the case in economics: "Economists do not follow the laws of enquiry their methodologies lay down. A good thing, too" (1983: 482). Theories are not evaluated on the basis of simple, well-defined empirical tests. The construction of what McCloskey terms "rhetoric"—persuasive argument based on a wide variety of factors—plays an important role in determining acceptance of any theoretical proposition. Ironically, the rational choice assumption, so central to economics, has now been squarely refuted in controlled experimental environments (see Thaler, 1991). Nonetheless, economists are unwilling to discard it.[5]

As in physics and economics, no set methodology exists by which theory and empirical data can be combined to insure progress in the study of religion. Whether or not a theory is explicitly derived from rational choice assumptions, its power, usefulness, and plausibility can only be judged in terms of a broad theoretical and empirical context. The rhetoric in which the theory is embedded, the character of the story it tells, is rightly central in determining its persuasive power.

While it may be convenient to specify a theoretical argument as a set of axioms and conclusions deduced from it, such form cannot substitute for careful analysis and thoughtful commentary. Even the most vacuous parts of Freudian theory, when applied to specific observations, can be cast in terms of assumptions and propositions—which, of course, fit the data perfectly. However "scientific" the form of its presentation, conceptual categories and theoretical structures that appear to have been rigged to yield an observed data point will strike us as *ad hoc*, and the theory will fail to persuade.

While we disagree with Stark's methodological claims, we are in agreement with many of his substantive arguments. We often find his conceptualizations elucidating and his underlying claims persuasive. However to insist that the conversation in the sociology of religion conform to the narrow standards of his stated methodology would be a mistake.

Even highly general deductive theory, in order to have empirical meaning, must be applied with a sensitivity to the details of particular cases, and for that reason must often be rooted not in axiomatic propositions alone but in careful case study. Clifford Geertz, known for his advocacy of "local knowledge," defines the task of ethnography as "thick description." Following an extended discussion of the philosopher Ryle's description of the differences between winking and faked winking, Geertz observes:

> Between what Ryle calls the "thin description" of what the researcher (parodist, winker, twitcher…) is doing ("rapidly contracting his right eyelids") and the "thick description" of what he is doing ("practicing a burlesque of a friend faking a wink to deceive an innocent into thinking a conspiracy is in motion") lies the object of ethnography: a stratified hierarchy of meaningful structures in terms of which twitches, winks, fake-winks, parodies, and rehearsals of parodies are produced, perceived, and interpreted, and without which they would not…in fact exist, no matter what anyone did or didn't do with his eyelids. (1973: 7)

We submit that understanding the differences between winks and twitches is as important to the sociology of religion as is the development of deductive propositions and general theories with predictive power. In fact, we believe that the latter, in large part, depends on the former.

NOTES

[1] Others have suggested that it may not only be women who demonstrate these characteristics but also members of any group socialized outside the dominant culture. See Tronto (1987).

[2] An early, and perhaps still the best, discussion of this issue is provided in Thomas Schelling (1960), especially chapters 3 and 4. Modern game theorists often confront problems for which rational choice assumptions are unable to produce determinate predictions, i.e., in which the formal models have "multiple equilibria." David Kreps (1990) comments, "The solution to the problem of multiple equilibria…lies in the individual's strategic expectations and social and normative environment. (772)

[3] Iannaccone points out that religious activity is, in this sense, a special case of household production (Becker, 1965), in which the family produces things it values for its own consumption. (In the case of both religious activity and household production, the output may be tangible, e.g., a meal, or intangible, e.g., social interaction, peace of mind.) Some economists have argued that because of the problems of separating consumption

and production, the household production model can be misleading (Pollak and Wachter, 1975). Notably, Iannaccone's analysis is successful in avoiding these difficulties.

[4] Warner (this volume) points out that "Baptist growth in the [nineteenth century] was accompanied by a considerable relaxation of standards…"

[5] We are among those who believe it should not be discarded. Its continued use is justified by the elegance and power of the theory, combined with its broad success in explanation and prediction, and the absence of any attractive alternative. The case for continuing to assume rational choice in most economic models is overwhelming, even though it cannot be based on a mechanistic analysis of empirical evidence. See Mueser (1995).

REFERENCES

Becker, Gary. 1965. "A Theory of the Allocation of Time." *Economic Journal* 75 (September): 493–517.

Berger, Peter. 1967. *The Sacred Canopy*. Garden City, NY: Anchor Books.

Chodorow, Nancy. 1978. *The Reproduction of Mothering*. Berkeley: University of California Press.

Davidman, Lynn, and Janet Jacobs. 1993. "Feminist Perspectives on New Religious Movements." In David Bromley and Jeffrey Hadden, eds., *A Handbook of Sects and Cults in America: Assessing Twenty Years of Research*. Greenwich, CT: JAI Press.

England, Paula. 1989. "A Feminist Critique of Rational Choice Theories." *The American Sociologist* 20 (Spring): 14–28.

Frank, Robert H. 1988. *Passions within Reason: The Strategic Role of the Emotions*. New York: W.W. Norton.

Friedman, Debra, and Carol Diem. 1993. "Feminism and the Pro-(Rational) Choice Movement: Rational-Choice Theory, Feminist Critiques, and Gender Inequality." In Paula England, ed., *Theory on Gender: Feminism on Theory*. Hawthorne, NY: Aldine de Gruyter: 91–114.

Garfinkle, Harold. 1967. *Studies in Ethnomethodology*. Englewood Cliffs, NJ: Prentice Hall.

Geertz, Clifford. 1973. *Interpretations of Culture*. New York: Basic Books.

Gilligan, Carol. 1982. *In a Different Voice*. Cambridge: Harvard University Press.

Ginzberg, Carlos. 1980. *The Cheese and The Worms*. Baltimore: Johns Hopkins University Press.

Iannaccone, Laurence R. 1994. "Why Strict Churches Are Strong." *American Journal of Sociology* 99 (5) (March): 1180–1211.

Kreps, David M. 1990. *A Course in Microeconomic Theory*. Princeton: Princeton University Press.

Kuhn, Thomas S. 1962. *The Structure of Scientific Revolutions*. Chicago: University of Chicago Press.

Lamont, Stewart. 1989. *Church and State: Uneasy Alliances*. London: The Brodley Head.

LeRoy Lauderie, Emmanuel. 1979. *Montaillou: The Promised Land of Error*. New York: Vintage.

McCloskey, Donald N. 1983. "The Rhetoric of Economics." *Journal of Economic Literature* 21 (June): 481–517.

Mueser, Peter R. 1995. "Understanding Apparent Violations of Rational Choice Theory." Paper presented at the Meetings of the Western Economic Association.

Neitz, Mary Jo. 1995. "Feminist Theory and Religious Experience." Forthcoming in Ralph Hood, ed., *Handbook of Religious Experience: Theory and Practice*. Knoxville, TN: Religious Education Press.

Neitz, Mary Jo. 1987. *Charisma and Community*. New Brunswick, NJ: Transaction Publishers.

Pollak, Robert A., and Michael L. Wachter. 1975. "The Relevance of the Household Production Function and its Implications for the Allocation of Time." *Journal of Political Economy* 83 (2) (April): 255–277.

Schelling, Thomas. 1960. *The Strategy of Conflict*. Cambridge: Harvard University Press.

Thaler, Richard H. 1991. *Quasi Rational Economics* New York: Russell Sage.

Tronto, Joan. 1987. "Beyond Gender Difference to a Theory of Care." *Signs* 12: 644–663.

Warner, R. Stephen. 1993. "Work in Progress Toward a New Paradigm for the Sociological Study of Religion in the United States." *American Journal of Sociology* 98: 1044–1093.

Wedam, Elfriede. 1993. "Moral Cultures and The Movement Against Abortion." Unpublished Doctoral Dissertation, Department of Sociology, University of Illinois, Chicago.

Wilson, Bryan, 1982. *Religion in Sociological Perspective*. London: Oxford University Press.

RELIGIOUS CHOICE AND RELIGIOUS VITALITY

The Market and Beyond

Nancy T. Ammerman

AMONG THE many propositions of rational choice theories of religion, one of the most controversial has been the idea that pluralism leads not to religious decline but to religious vitality.[1] To put the options in their most stark (pardon the pun) form: Is pluralism good for religion or not? The "old paradigm,"[2] exemplified by secularization theories such as that found in Peter Berger's *The Sacred Canopy* (1969) argues that pluralism weakens the plausibility of religion, making any given religious alternative merely a preference. (In fairness to Berger, it should be noted that this is no longer his position and has not been for some time. It is nevertheless still associated with Berger, as a result of his earlier work.) The "new paradigm," according to Warner and the rational choice theorists, argues that the presence of multiple alternatives makes for healthy competition and allows individuals to find a match for their own religious impulses. The possibility of choice makes attachment both more likely and stronger once made.[3]

I would like to suggest a middle ground between these two opposing views. It seems to me that our task is to ask *under what conditions* the presence of multiple religious alternatives enhances the position of religion, and to ask that question both at the level of organizational health and at the level of individual commitment (two realities that are interrelated, but distinguishable).

This paper sketches some possible answers to that question and, in so doing, takes stock of the contribution rational choice theory can and cannot make in the sociology of religion. I should begin, however, by noting my initial biases. I am wary of any theory that apparently posits rationality as its central premise. I am aware that rational choice theorists can define rationality quite broadly, but there is still a real danger in assuming that human social life is best understood in terms of cognition and reason, leaving aside intuition, affect, transcendent experience, and the like.[4] Those omissions seem particularly serious when it comes to religion.

On the other hand, designating religious choices as rational may be a needed corrective. For far too long people participating in religious practices have been relegated to the heap of pre-modern, nonrational anachronisms. The rational choice perspective at least restores the active agent to the picture and posits that there just might be some real rewards to be had in associating oneself with religious beliefs and practices.

My other major reservation about rational choice theory, however, has to do with the use of economic metaphors for explaining social life. They are very powerful metaphors, capturing in a common sense way the dynamics of much of what we do. But the very fact that they seem so commonsensical makes me suspect that what we have here is a grand metaphor that uses one major cultural symbol system to explain other cultural symbol systems.[5] Its strength as metaphor may give rational choice theory a good deal of explanatory power, but not necessarily the theoretical predictive power it claims.[6] Its explanatory power may derive from the dominance of this metaphor in contemporary society, not from any inherent characteristics of human beings.

Nevertheless, as a metaphor that is generating a growing body of research, rational choice propositions seem well worth exploring. What I offer here are some suggestions about how the simple either/or dilemma—is pluralism good for religion or not—needs to be nuanced. To illustrate some of those nuances, I will draw on data from the communities and congregations and individuals we have studied in the Congregations in Changing Communities project, a research effort funded by the Lilly Endowment under the auspices of the Institute for the Study of Economic Culture at Boston University.

THE EFFECTS OF DIVERSITY: THE CULTURAL CONTEXT

The first published tests of the pluralism hypothesis have assumed that the character of the religious institutional market itself is the primary determining factor in predicting religious participation and that the market's effects are uniform across cultures. The more brands to choose from, the more likely people are to find something they like and therefore enter the religious market. I think it is not so simple, however. We need to take a number of additional factors into account in assessing this relationship.

The first of these factors are variables I would call *cultural* (although rational choice theorists might view them as simply part of the "structure of the market"). For instance, religious institutions are affected not just by the current presence or absence of a monopoly (versus a free market), but also by the history of market competition in a given place. As Laurence Iannaccone (1991: 163) points out, state churches have their effects long past the day when they are officially enforced. People who define religion in terms of ascription do not move easily into defining it as a choice. Nor do people who have depended on state support for religious institutions soon take to the notion that they themselves may need to pay their clergy, provide upkeep on their buildings, and the like. Iannaccone explains this in terms of the investment of "human capital." While that explanation is plausible, it remains partial; it is culture that defines the value of various human activities and culture that defines the costs and benefits of participation.

In a 1994 conference addressing the question of whether Europe is the one place where classic theories of secularization actually work, researchers from a number of European countries presented data on belief and belonging in their countries. Places like Sweden exemplify societies long dominated by one (or a very few) religious alternatives and now ostensibly open to all comers. But the very same "upstart sects" that thrive in the United States have found such cultures very difficult territory in which to grow.[7] In part, as Chaves and Cann (1992) point out, this is the result of continuing state regulation and support of religion. But it is also, I would contend, the result of well-entrenched cultural patterns. After a long history of churchgoing as a civic duty, not a voluntary choice, people in such places have difficulty recovering either the notion that religion might be more personally meaningful or the desire to exercise this form of voluntary participation in society. In these cultures, pluralism has neither killed religion, nor may it be able to revive it. We can agree with the rational choice theorists that religious monopoly and high levels of religious regulation are inimical to the health of religious institutions, but we must go beyond that to note that the mechanisms seem to be more than structural.[8] The effects seem also to be lodged in culture—in patterns of action that after a time need no explicit structural support, remaining in place despite the current absence of such supports.

Analogous locations exist even in the U.S., in certain heavily Catholic urban areas, for instance.[9] When a neighborhood becomes an ethnic Catholic enclave, other religious organizations decline, and a quasi-monopoly is created. Rodney Stark has argued that such an enclave situation is also detrimental to Catholic levels of commitment—the more concentrated the Catholic population, the fewer priests that diocese ordains.[10] Even after the enclave character of the neighborhood changes, the dearth of religious institutions may not immediately be altered. Such neighborhoods do not usually look like especially fertile ground to Protestant "church planters" (the denominational bureaucracies' version of religious entrepreneurs). And other factors may inhibit the growth of the religious market, as well.

One such neighborhood is Allston–Brighton in Boston. In the latter half of the nineteenth century, it became a Catholic enclave, dominated by Irish and Italian immigrants. The area's historic Protestant churches slowly declined, and today they constitute a tiny struggling remnant. Three large Catholic parishes dominated the cultural life of the community through the 1950s, but have since declined as well. The once traditional sight of a Saints-day festival parade winding through the streets is a rarity. In recent years, the neighborhood's traditionally Catholic Irish and Italian families have been replaced by transient students from nearby Boston University, Boston College, and Harvard University, along with waves of South American and Asian immigrants. In 1992, when we surveyed the congregations in this neighborhood, the total combined weekly religious service attendance amounted to barely 5 percent of the population.

The high student population in the neighborhood makes this inhospitable soil for any sort of religious institution building. The immigrant population, on the other hand, requires the sorts of specialized institutions that are relatively difficult to create. As new immigrant communities form and shift and form again, religious institutions (like other immigrant creations) may find survival challenging. In addition, since many of these immigrants are Catholic and seek to remain Catholic, they are subject to the decisions made by the Church's centralized monopoly religious system. If the archdiocese decides that their language group should worship across town, they are very unlikely to develop their own local alternative (although they may become especially good candidates for Protestant conversion). Here the rational choice assumptions about the suppressor effects of monopoly again seem to hold. But note that those effects are highly specific. Religious monopolies can have their effects even when they are not *actually* a monopoly in the population. Both specific religious institutions and specific subcultures may carry the traditions of monopoly structures, even when the larger context actually includes diversity.

At the opposite extreme are communities where diversity is the norm, and religious institutions enjoy high rates of participation. It is upon such communities that rational choice theorists base their argument about U.S. religious culture in general. What I have suggested so far is that this situation may be specific to certain segments of the U.S. population and not to others. I also wish to suggest that both the diversity and the high rates of participation may be the product of a common antecedent factor, a factor inherent in the culture, rather than in the structure of the market itself. In much of the U.S. cultural context, a strong religious culture may produce both diversity and participation.

Certainly American society has been pluralist almost from the beginning. Jon Butler (1990: 174) observes that by 1760, American pluralism reflected nearly as much diversity as Europe taken as a whole and far more than in any single European nation. By the time American nationalism had taken hold, it accommodated a plethora of religious forms not tolerated in any of the societies from which the colonists had come. When the U.S. Constitution was written, that diversity was protected from the imposition of established religion, and the American course was set.

In the years that followed, there was enormous institutional growth in the religious sector. Between 1780 and 1860, congregations sprang up all over the expanding landscape, church buildings raised their spires, denominational and voluntary organizations multiplied, colleges were founded, newspapers and books flourished—all far outpacing population growth in the new nation (Butler, 1990: 272). As Americans were establishing their identity as a nation, they were establishing voluntary religious institutions as a vital part of their common life.[11]

Recent accounts of the nineteenth century have noted that this institutional proliferation was closely tied to the democratic impulses of the new nation. Nathan Hatch (1989) notes that all sorts of independent religious promoters outdid the educated, credentialled, established clergy. The people's insistence on their own right to decide extended into things religious and led to this proliferation. This argument is picked up by Roger Finke and Rodney Stark (1992, especially chapter 3), who make a convincing case for why the "upstart sects" had an advantage over the post-establishment churches. Hatch points to the democratic character of the religious institutions that grew in the nineteenth century. By being intellectually open to ordinary folk and inspired by popular leaders, new religious movements rapidly penetrated the American landscape. These democratic impulses were given concrete form in folk rituals such as gospel music and vernacular preaching. And they were given tangible form in mass-market printed material. People scattered over vast territories, emboldened by ideals of democracy, were able to hear the gospel in a language they could understand, sing the gospel in a style they could master, and take the gospel home to read at leisure. Both local congregations and a whole complex of other religious institutions proliferated in nineteenth-century America, establishing an enduring cultural pattern.

During this same period, the meaning of church membership was also shifting. Earlier, in the seventeenth and eighteenth centuries, much of U.S. Protestantism had been dominated by a Congregationalist (Puritan) model that counted only "communicants" as real members. As a result, attendance was often a good deal higher than actual membership. Over the course of the nineteenth century, such strict requirements for membership were relaxed, and membership percentages began to climb. Holifield (1994) argues that *attendance* rates have probably been fairly stable over the course of American history, hovering between 35 and 40 percent. *Membership* rates, however, have been quite susceptible to the influences of both the culture and the religious organizations themselves. When culture and congregation define membership as normative, rates rise. Where culture discourages membership or congregations make it difficult, rates fall. In nineteenth-century America, enormous institutional growth coincided with the growth of norms that made some sort of religious involvement expected of most Americans. In other words, the whole of American culture may be seen as fostering religious membership and attendance in a way that other national cultures did not.[12] Because of the unique combination of early de-regulation of the religious market, a century of immigration, and wide open frontiers that seemed to invite innovation, both religious diversity and religious participation became the American norm.

Nowhere does that more clearly remain the case than in the two Indiana communities of Anderson and Carmel. Both have a high degree of diversity (nearly one denomination per 1000 residents), a proportionately high number of congregations (42 in Carmel and 121 in Anderson) *and* a high rate of overall attendance—50 percent in Carmel, at least 34 percent in Anderson.[13] Carmel's denominational market has a heavy concentration of independent evangelicals, but also includes a representative sampling of mainline Protestants and, more recently, Catholics. Anderson's selection of denominations is concentrated among Holiness, Methodist, and independent evangelical churches. Anderson, especially, is the heir of the nineteenth-century revivals, having become the headquarters for the Church of God. But some churches in both communities still hold modified camp meetings each summer. For over a century, as each new wave of settlers arrived in the territory, and as each new revivalist travelled through the countryside, new religious traditions have been added to the mix.

The real growth in Carmel's religious diversity did not begin, however, until the 1960s, when small-town Carmel began to become affluent suburban Carmel. Since then, the range of religious choices has expanded exponentially. The finely tuned shopping habits of affluent Carmelites, grafted onto the revivalist heritage of the town, soon broadened the range of religious alternatives. Here the market metaphor works well. Since the culture strongly fostered participation, and the population was increasingly diverse, religious institution-building followed.

This midwestern culture of diversity contrasts sharply with a similar suburban area outside Atlanta. Gwinnett County is also a rapidly-growing affluent area. Its level of denominational diversity, however, resembles Boston more than Indiana, although the monopoly in Gwinnett is Baptist and Methodist, rather than Catholic. And because the culture of southern evangelicalism, in contrast to the culture of urban ethnic Catholicism, encourages regular church going, rates of participation are substantially higher in Gwinnett than in Boston. Our survey of the congregations in eastern Gwinnett county in 1992 turned up an attendance rate of about 25 percent—five times the rate in Boston's Allston-Brighton. Both have a history of quasi-monopoly, with recent increases in the diversity of the population. In other words, the *structure* of these two religious markets is quite similar. But the *content* of the religious culture is different enough to create very different patterns of participation.[14]

My suggestion, then, is that both rates of diversity and rates of participation exist in specific cultural contexts that define desirable religious behavior. In one context, people may participate despite a limited range of choices, while in another, all the choice in the world may not be able to lure them through church doors.

THE EFFECTS OF DIVERSITY: BRINGING THE DEMAND SIDE BACK IN

Not only do cultural contexts shape the meaning of choice, but so does the interplay of supply and demand. Understanding the effects of diversity requires attention to the relationship between the particular populations present in a community and the particular kinds of institutions that may or may not suit their religious needs. Much of the theorizing to date has over emphasized the supply side, forgetting that supply and demand always interact with each other. Institutions shape preferences, and preferences shape institutions.[15] And more important, preferences are not an undifferentiated universal out there waiting to be shaped by whatever institutions may come along.

For instance, the generalization that high commitment institutions necessarily enjoy greater health tends to flatten our understanding of the nature of religious demand. Stark argues that religious institutions uniquely provide certain supernatural "compensators," and that institutions which downplay those supernatural elements are necessarily at a disadvantage.[16] Iannaccone's model (1988), similarly implies that church-like institutions, in contrast to sects, offer few unique (spiritual) rewards, proferring only social rewards already available elsewhere in the culture, and thereby inviting institutional weakness. In addition, Stark and Finke argue in *The Churching of America* that rigorous sectarian groups grew at the expense of less-demanding establishment churches. All of this suggests an undifferentiated religious market defined by certain inherently religious impulses. The more institutions there are to serve that market, the more the impulses will be expressed; and the more nearly those institutions stick to the particular product they uniquely can offer, the more the institutions themselves will thrive.

I am not, however, convinced that this matching of a universal quest for supernatural compensators with sectarian religious institutions is as straightforward as the rational choice model seems to suggest. I *am* convinced that the U.S. populace varies greatly in the degree to which they want religious institutions of the supernaturalist, sectarian variety. Therefore, extensive markets exist for both high- and low-commitment religious institutions. I would suggest, in fact, that the larger culture establishes low commitment as the norm, and groups that seek more from their members than the cultural norm have to work hard to justify that demand. Groups that demand little do, indeed, have all the problems Finke and others have raised,[17] but as long as they can generate just enough resources to supply just enough services, they will survive. They are actually helped by the fact that their expectations of low commitment match the expectations present in a large segment of the market.

This seems to be especially true in middle-class suburban locations. While there are certainly thriving sectarian congregations located in such communities, there are also thriving mainline Protestant and Catholic congregations that expect minimal belief and participation from their members. Their members join churches as an extension of their efforts at raising their children, as an expression of their attempts to be good citizens and moral persons, and as an affirmation of their often vaguely conceived conviction that something transcending human life exists, some power or presence to which they wish to be related.[18]

One community that nicely illustrates such patterns is Carmel, Indiana. Of the 39 Protestant churches, one third are best classified as "mainline" or "church-like," while the remainder could safely be categorized as "sect-like." Our study included one from each camp: Carmel United Methodist and Northview Christian Life Church (an Assembly of God congregation). Northview clearly exceeds Carmel UMC in the amount of time and money it is able to extract from its members. Northview's members are also more likely to talk about feeling separate from the surrounding culture, not really a part of the community. Northview also has a larger core of active members, and those active members contribute more to the church than Carmel UMC's inner core. On all of those measures, Iannaccone is right about the differences between church and sect.

But the fact is that in many ways the two congregations are remarkably similar. They are both very affluent and well-educated.[19] Both are large, with Northview at about 800 in average attendance slightly exceeding Carmel UMC's 600. Both have booming programs for children and youth. And despite the higher levels of participation at Northview, it is still quite possible to slip into and out of the congregation without making a commitment, to sample evangelical religion as a selective consumer just as Carmel UMC's members are sampling more liberal fare. What this suggests to me is that the culture of Carmel establishes a certain range of acceptable religious involvement. Within that range are both high- and low-commitment options (although the two may be more similar than they at first appear). If only sectarian groups existed, a large segment of the market might drop out entirely. If only church-like groups existed, sectarians would probably invent new options that better suited their needs.

Recognizing that there is demand for both high- and low-commitment religiosity is only the beginning of recognizing the complex ways in which demand interacts with supply. Both communities and institutions shape preferences through their expectations about religious participation. Likewise, the accumulation of preferences may induce institution-building. Darren E. Sherkat's work on preferences is clearly establishing that choices are made within the context of social relationships.[20] Simply having more choices available does not necessarily induce religious mobility. One has to take into account the place of those choices in a particular social ecology. What does it mean to join X—as a daughter in this family, as a current member of Y, as a resident of this community, as a woman, as an immigrant, as a gay person, and so on? The relationship between the supply of religious organizations and the overall vitality of those organizations is, I am suggesting, a complex matching of demands with supply. The basic point that greater diversity leads to greater overall participation holds true only as long as the particular diversities in the population come close to matching the particular diversities in the supply of religious institutions. A diverse supply of ethnic Catholic parishes would fail to thrive in the midst of a diverse population of yuppie Protestants. That same population might also fail to respond to the efforts of entrepreneurial sectarians or the plans of a far-away church bureaucracy. The mere presence of a supply of religious institutions will not always induce participation.

What this implies is that the social ecology of a given community—and the life histories represented by that social ecology—will affect the relationship between institutional supply and religious participation. One such factor to be considered is the balance of various cohorts, especially by age and longevity. Just as the character of monopoly and free market structures linger in a culture, it may also linger in an individual. People who grew up in a monopoly may experience diversity differently from those who grew up where diversity was the norm, even though both groups now live in the same community.[21] These factors will affect the demand side and therefore overall religious participation in the community.

Finally, paying attention to the demand side means that levels of religiosity in a population cannot be measured entirely by institutional participation. While rational choice theories do not presume to explain more than the institutional participation they actually measure, emphasis on the supply side has the effect of diverting attention from sources of religious expression not (yet) fully institutionalized.

This omission is especially problematic as the unaffiliated sector in the American religious scene grows. Phillip E. Hammond (among others)[22] has noted that 88 percent of Americans say you can be a good Christian or Jew without attending a church or synagogue. This insistence on "personal autonomy" is even stronger among the younger cohort, and the consequence is weaker parish (and other local) ties. Few dispute that the "unchurched" sector is growing, although this sector is also notoriously unstable. The unchurched seem to keep finding places for themselves in existing religious institutions. As Reginald Bibby has put it, the problem with *nothings* is that they keep becoming *somethings*. They marry a *something* and then have kids that become *somethings*.[23] "Nones" (those who have no religious preference) are less successful at reproducing their stance across generations than are affiliates.[24]

But far more important than the question of who is dropping out and for how long is determining what happens outside organized religion more generally. That seems to be a subject that supply-side economic theory is ill-equipped to handle. We know, for instance, that even the Baby Boomers who have dropped out and not returned seem still to be remarkably "religious." They believe in God (80 percent say yes, and another 16 percent are uncertain, but think so), they are likely to describe themselves as "spiritual," and they say that problems of meaning in life are things they think a good deal about. Wade Clark Roof (1993) describes faith as "the continual activity of composing meaning," and the Baby Boomers he studied do not seem to be totally devoid of such faith—even when they are not involved in any organized religion. Similarly, Daniele Hervieu-Leger has noted the prevalence of new religious movements and the appropriation of religious symbols and identities in numerous societies throughout Europe. At the same time that traditional institutions are being vacated, new-traditional pilgrimages and rituals are springing up.[25] Stark and Iannaccone (1994) report that what they call "potential demand" (levels of belief, despite lack of belonging) are remarkably high throughout Europe. Reginald Bibby (1993: 170ff.) notes similar levels of unofficial belief in the face of official institutional decline in Canada.

To use the economic language of rational choice theory, there appears to be more religious demand than suitable institutions available to meet that demand. Or are these religious practitioners perhaps the equivalent of people who prefer to "grow their own" rather than purchase "store bought" goods? However we characterize them, their presence points to a missing piece in the picture painted by rational choice theorists, a missing element in the attempt to discern whether institutional diversity leads to greater religious participation. By "participating" in religious beliefs and practices that fall outside officially recognized institutions, this growing segment of the American population remains simply an "error term" in the rational choice equation.

CONCLUSION

So what is the relationship between pluralism, with its implied religious choices, and religious vitality? Does having a choice weaken institutions and lower levels of religious commitment, or the reverse? What I have tried to suggest is that the answer goes beyond a simple correlation between diversity and participation. The meaning and effects of choice vary depending on the cultural situation in which they are lodged—the degree of monopoly that has characterized the past, as well as the present, and the degree to which the culture supports diversity and participation as twin goods. Also critical are the interplay of population groups and the particular institutions available to be chosen; specialized populations and people prone to low-commitment participation may alter the equation. Both supply and demand must be taken into account. Finally, we cannot fully understand the religious vitality of a population by examining only the existing religious institutions.

Some attention must also be given to demand-side pressures that have not yet led to new organizational forms. All of this argues that sociologists of religion should listen to the voices of the people in the population who are actually making these choices, discovering from them whether and how the presence of multiple alternatives enhances their likelihood of religious participation.

NOTES

[1] Roger Finke and Rodney Stark ("Religious Economies and Sacred Canopies: Religious Mobilization in American Cities, 1906," *American Sociological Review* 53 (February 1988): 41–49) began the debate, followed by Kenneth C. Land, Glenn Deane, and Judith R. Blau ("Religious Pluralism and Church Membership: A Spatial Diffusion Model," *American Sociological Review* 56 (April 1991): 237–249). The arguments are probably most clearly articulated in Laurence R. Iannaccone ("The Consequences of Religious Market Structure: Adam Smith and the Economics of Religion," *Rationality and Society* 3, no. 2 (April 1991): 156–177), with the clarification offered by Mark Chaves and David E. Cann ("Regulation, Pluralism, and Religious Market Structure: Explaining Religion's Vitality," *Rationality and Society* 4, no. 3 (July 1992): 272–290).

[2] I adopt here the terminology of R. Stephen Warner ("Work in Progress toward a New Paradigm for the Sociological Study of Religion in the United States," *American Journal of Sociology* 98 (March 1993): 1044–1093).

[3] Mary Jo Neitz argues in *Charisma and Community* (New Brunswick: Transaction, 1987) that people who are aware that conversion is a choice are more attached to those choices than are those who perceive religious affiliation as inevitable.

[4] Mary Jo Neitz (this volume) elaborates this particular shortcoming of rational choice theory.

[5] In a discussion at the Center for the Study of American Religion at Princeton, April, 1994, John Schmaltzbauer noted that rational choice theories seem especially well-suited to explaining the religious phenomena of nineteenth-century evangelicalism. Since that was also the era in which American entrepreneurial capitalism flourished, establishing its hegemony in economic life, one might expect entrepreneurial metaphors to work well in explaining other cultural phenomena of that era.

[6] Mark Chaves, in "On the Rational Choice Approach to Religion" (forthcoming in *Journal for the Scientific Study of Religion*) argues that rational choice claims to being a unified, deductive theory are over-stated. While rational choice arguments often provide plausible explanations, they rest as much on substantive assumptions about the way religion works as on theoretical premises derived from rational choice propositions.

[7] "Secularized Europe: The Great Exception?" conference sponsored by the Erasmus Institute, the University of Rotterdam, and the Institute for the Study of Economic Culture, in Rotterdam, March, 1994. In a recent study of Sweden, Hamberg and Pettersson report that where there is increased religious competition, church attendance rates are in fact higher ("The Religious Market: Denominational Competition and Religious Participation in Contemporary Sweden," *Journal for the Scientific Study of Religion* 33 (3) (1994): 205–216). Those rates, however, still barely reach 10 percent.

[8] Chaves and Cann (1992) note this cultural effect in the differences among Catholic countries with similar pluralism and regulatory structures. The religious market does not explain everything, and there is no particular reason to insist that it must.

[9] Note that Land, Deane, and Blau (in "Religious Pluralism and Church Membership") found that "percent Catholic" was a confounding variable in their attempt to measure the effects of religious diversity on adherence rates. Catholics have very high adherence rates *and*

are disproportionately urban, creating multi-collinearity in the equations. I would note that they are also likely to be highly concentrated in given sections of a city, and that high adherence rates are not necessarily related to high participation rates, at least in the U.S.

[10] Rodney Stark and James C. McCann, "The Weakness of Monopoly Faiths: Market Forces and Catholic Commitment," quoted in Rodney Stark, "Do Catholic Societies Really Exist?," *Rationality and Society* 4, no. 3 (July 1992): 261–271.

[11] This, of course, was de Tocqueville's oft-cited observation in *Democracy in America*, 1969 edition, trans. George Lawrence (Garden City, NY: Doubleday, 1835).

[12] This enduring effect of national culture is also found by Robert Campbell and James Curtis in "Religious Involvement Across Societies: Analyses for Alternative Measures in National Surveys," *Journal for the Scientific Study of Religion* 33 (3) (1994): 215–229.

[13] Note that these rates exceed the national averages estimated by C. Kirk Hadaway, Penny Long Marler, and Mark Chaves, ("What the Polls Don't Show: A Closer Look at U.S. Church Attendance," *American Sociological Review* 58, no. 6 (December 1993): 741–752). Since we used estimates of attendance from knowledgeable congregational sources, it is safe to assume that our totals for church attendance may represent slight exaggerations, but should be relatively close to actual counts.

[14] Christopher G. Ellison and Darren E. Sherkat, in "The 'Semi-Involuntary' Institution Revisited: Regional Variations in Church Participation Among African Americans," (A paper presented to the Association for the Sociology of Religion in Miami, Florida, August, 1993) argue that black southern culture was also a quasi-monopolistic religious system. In this case, the religious monopoly was further complicated by the segregation that made black churches central community institutions. African Americans who leave the rural south, entering a world of greater religious diversity, are *less* involved in institutional religion than those "back home." Southern evangelicals in general, but black churches in particular, seem to have encouraged high levels of participation despite low levels of religious diversity.

[15] Darren Sherkat (this volume) goes a long way toward correcting this failure to consider the choosing agent.

[16] Although his theory is elaborated in a number of sources, his essay in this volume gives a good overview of relevant points.

[17] Finke (this volume) points to various institutional difficulties in nonsectarian religion, but goes a long way toward refining the simple equation of high membership standards with growth.

[18] This argument is elaborated in Nancy T. Ammerman, "Golden Rule Christianity: Lived Religion in the American Mainstream," a paper presented to the conference on Lived Religion at Harvard Divinity School, September, 1994, and forthcoming in a volume to be edited by David Hall.

[19] Richard Lee's attempt (in "Religious Practice as Social Exchange: An Explanation of the Empirical Findings," *Sociological Analysis* 53, no. 1 (Spring 1992): 1–35) to claim that sectarian groups turn "what is" (their low social status) into "what ought to be" is simply wrong. His use of Southside Gospel Church (see Nancy T. Ammerman, *Bible Believers: Fundamentalists in the Modern World*. New Brunswick: Rutgers University Press, 1987) as an illustration of that point is a serious misreading of the data presented on that church. Both they and the members of Northview Christian Life are misdescribed by efforts to paint them as low in social status.

[20] Darren E. Sherkat and John Wilson, "Preferences, Constraints, and Choice in Religious Markets: An Examination of Religious Switching and Apostacy," Unpublished Paper (n.d.).

[21] This is the difference often captured by the distinction between "local" and "cosmopolitan." See, for example, Wade Clark Roof, *Commitment and Community* (New York: Elsevier, 1978).

[22] Wade Clark Roof and William McKinney report this finding in *American Mainline Religion* (New Brunswick: Rutgers University Press, 1987). Hammond elaborates on the consequences for parish involvement in *Religion and Personal Autonomy* (Columbia, SC: University of South Carolina Press, 1992).

[23] Reginald Bibby addressing the conference on "Baby Boomers and Religion" at the Louisville Institute for the Study of Protestantism and American Culture, March, 1994.

[24] Warner (1993), citing Roof and McKinney (1987).

[25] "Is the notion of secularization still relevant in order to appreciate the evolutions in the religious field in Europe?" presented to the conference "Secularized Europe: The Great Exception?" in Rotterdam, March, 1994.

REFERENCES

Ammerman, Nancy T. 1987. *Bible Believers: Fundamentalists in the Modern World*. New Brunswick, NJ: Rutgers University Press.

————1994. "Golden Rule Christianity: Lived Religion in the American Mainstream." Paper presented to the conference on Lived Religion. Harvard Divinity School, September.

Berger, Peter L. 1969. *The Sacred Canopy*. Garden City, NY: Anchor Doubleday.

Bibby, Reginald W. 1993. *Unknown Gods: The Ongoing Story of Religion in Canada*. Toronto: Stoddart.

Butler, Jon. 1990. *Awash in a Sea of Faith*. Cambridge: Harvard University Press.

Campbell, Robert A., and James E. Curtis. 1994. "Religious Involvement Across Societies: Analyses for Alternative Measures in National Surveys." *Journal for the Scientific Study of Religion* 33 (3, September): 217–229.

Chaves, Mark. Forthcoming. "On the Rational Choice Approach to Religion." *Journal for the Scientific Study of Religion*.

Chaves, Mark, and David E. Cann. 1992. "Regulation, Pluralism, and Religious Market Structure: Explaining Religion's Vitality." *Rationality and Society* 4 (3, July): 272–290.

Ellison, Christopher G., and Darren E. Sherkat. 1993. "The 'Semi-Involuntary' Institution Revisited: Regional Variations in Church Participation Among African Americans." A paper presented to the Association for the Sociology of Religion. Miami, FL: August.

Finke, Roger, and Rodney Stark. 1988. "Religious Economies and Sacred Canopies: Religious Mobilization in American Cities, 1906." *American Sociological Review* 53 (February): 41–49.

————1992. *The Churching of America, 1776–1990*. New Brunswick, NJ: Rutgers University Press.

Hadaway, C. Kirk, Penny Long Marler, and Mark Chaves. 1993. "What the Polls Don't Show: A Closer Look at U.S. Church Attendance." *American Sociological Review* 58 (6, December): 741–752.

Hamberg, Eva M., and Thorleif Pettersson. 1994. "The Religious Market: Denominational Competition and Religious Participation in Contemporary Sweden." *Journal for the Scientific Study of Religion* 33 (3, September): 205–216.

Hammond, Phillip E. 1992. *Religion and Personal Autonomy*. Columbia: University of South Carolina Press.

Hatch, Nathan O. 1989. *The Democratization of American Christianity*. New Haven: Yale University Press.

Holifield, E. Brooks. 1994. "Toward a History of American Congregations." In *American Congregations: Congregations in Context*, James P. Wind and James W. Lewis, eds. Chicago: University of Chicago Press: 23–53.

Iannaccone, Laurence R. 1988. "A Formal Model of Church and Sect." *American Journal of Sociology* 94 (supplement): s241–s268.

————1990. "Religious Practice: A Human Capital Approach." *Journal for the Scientific Study of Religion* 29 (3): 297–314.

————1991. "The Consequences of Religious Market Structure: Adam Smith and the Economics of Religion." *Rationality and Society* 3 (2, April): 156–177.

Land, Kenneth C., Glenn Deane, and Judith R. Blau. 1991. "Religious Pluralism and Church Membership: A Spatial Diffusion Model." *American Sociological Review* 56 (April): 237–249.

Lee, Richard R. 1992. "Religious Practice as Social Exchange: An Explanation of the Empirical Findings." *Sociological Analysis* 53 (1, Spring): 1–35.

Neitz, Mary Jo. 1987. *Charisma and Community*. New Brunswick, NJ: Transaction.

Roof, Wade Clark. 1978. *Community and Commitment*. New York: Elsevier.

————1993. *A Generation of Seekers*. San Francisco: Harper Collins.

Roof, Wade Clark, and William McKinney. 1987. *American Mainline Religion*. New Brunswick, NJ: Rutgers University Press.

Sherkat, Darren E. and John Wilson. n.d. "Preferences, Constraints, and Choice in Religious Markets: An Examination of Religious Switching and Apostasy." Unpublished Paper.

Stark, Rodney. 1992. "Do Catholic Societies Really Exist?" *Rationality and Society* 4 (3, July): 261–271.

Stark, Rodney, and Laurence R. Iannaccone. 1994. "A Supply-Side Reinterpretation of the 'Secularization' of Europe." *Journal for the Scientific Study of Religion* 33 (3, September): 230–252.

Tocqueville, Alexis de. 1835. *Democracy in America*. 1969 edition. Translated by George Lawrence. Garden City, NY: Doubleday.

Warner, R. Stephen. 1993. "Work in Progress toward a New Paradigm for the Sociological Study of Religion in the United States." *American Journal of Sociology* 98 (March): 1044–1093.

PHENOMENOLOGICAL IMAGES OF RELIGION AND RATIONAL CHOICE THEORY

Lawrence A. Young

I CAME to the sociology of religion in the mid-1980s with little familiarity or interest in the subdiscipline. What drew me to the subject was two projects, both of which called for a familiarity with the sociology of religion. I had, first, the opportunity to study the organizational demography of the Catholic clergy and, second, an interest in how normative mechanisms functioned in higher education, particularly in colleges and universities with explicit religious identities.

As a relative newcomer to the field, then, I can provide perspective on what the sociology of religion looked like to a graduate student just beginning to read the literature in the mid-1980s. One of the most arresting notions I encountered was of religion's continuing vitality. Thus, while most scholars agreed that religion had undergone a process of institutional differentiation and privatization, that shift did not necessarily mean that religion was in decline, either as a personal force shaping action or as an organizational phenomenon. In fact, when social theorists did point to dire consequences, those consequences were primarily rooted in macro-level concerns and questions such as how society would sustain social cohesion given pluralism and what was the future for a public sector that seemed increasingly detached from a hegemonic cultural base rooted in the religious. However, even theorists expressing such concerns were open to the possibility that the extent of institutional differentiation and privatization had been overstated.

The bottom line was that while most sociologists tended to ignore religion as an important social force, those sociologists who did study religion did so because they felt it continued to be important. More often than not, if they mentioned the notion of secularization as religion in decline, it was to suggest that this old, worn-out concept demanded replacement (Hadden, 1987; Hadden and Shupe, 1986; Warner, 1993).

What this meant for the sociology of religion as a field in the mid-1980s was that a new generation of students (myself among them) were likely to employ the religion-in-decline version of secularization theory as a foil rather than a guiding framework. Among the major social events we had observed were the resurgence of the religious right in the United States, an Islamic revolution that extended beyond the borders of Iran and challenged communism as the major ideological event of our century, an ongoing liberation theology that influenced politics throughout the developing world, and the central role of churches in the process that led to the downfall in several Eastern European countries of state-sponsored communist regimes.

At the same time, we were being introduced to new research which told us that religion matters. Caplow, Bahr, and Chadwick (1983) told us that religion mattered in Middletown. Robert Bellah and his colleagues (1985) told us that individual-level religion mattered, even if organized religion had less of a hold in the last few decades than earlier in this century. Stark and Bainbridge (1985) told us that the future of religion would be a lively one. And while Roof and McKinney (1987) pointed out that the ascribed origins of individual religious identity had weakened by the 1960s, they also told us that the ideological dimensions of religious identity seemed to have increased in importance. Steve Warner (1988) unfolded a picture of resurgent vitality in a Presbyterian congregation in Mendecino, California. Nancy Ammerman (1990) told us about the fundamentalist takeover of the largest Protestant denomination in the United States—largely in reaction to the forces of modernity. Mary Jo Neitz (1987) described the normalcy of charismatic religious expression among secular professionals. Demmerath and Williams (1992) documented the continuing vitality of religion in shaping community politics. Andrew Greeley (1990) and Helen Rose Ebaugh (1991) both argued that the post-Vatican II Catholic Church was characterized by heightened vitality among its laity. And the stories go on and on.

And so, as we were socialized into the discipline, we simply didn't hear much about religion in decline. And mostly, we were told again and again by fellow graduate students and faculty members that bringing religion back into the sociological mix made great sense. Thus we became revisionists. When we did cite those who suggested that religion had drifted into the backwaters of social life, we typically did so to illustrate the need to reassess the place of religion, given past failures to do so adequately. Obviously, as a grounding for our discussion of religion, many of us looked beyond secularization theory for a new foundation.

This book considers the alternative approach that has enjoyed the greatest attention in recent years—namely, the rational choice approach. But it is not the only alternative, and this chapter considers another approach which has influenced many sociologists over the years—namely, a phenomenological or experiential image of religion.

Note I refer to image rather than theory. In defining the phenomenological approach as an image rather than theory of religion, I follow the lead of organizational analyst Gareth Morgan (1986). In explaining the concept of image, Morgan points towards something more fluid than a formal model of organizations. He argues that an image of organizations "rests in a way of thinking rather than in the mechanistic application of a small set of clearly defined analytical frameworks." Morgan points out that while any particular image of organizations represents a "distinctive" way of seeing or understanding, it is only a "partial way." A comprehensive understanding of organizations "depends on an ability to see how...[these images] coexist in a complementary or even a paradoxical way" (Morgan, 1986: 16, 12).

According to Morgan, the dominant approaches to organizational analysis are usually grounded in images of organizations rather than formal models. The same has generally been true of the sociology of religion. But because empirical research is necessarily guided by formal models of organizations or religious action, the use of theories which focus on general ways of seeing rather than on the "clearly defined analytical frameworks" of formal models means that the transition from theory to empirical research is not clearly mapped out for the researcher.

Clearly, one of the major contributions of the rational choice approach to religion is that it comes much closer to being a "clearly defined analytical framework" or formal model, making the link to research more straightforward and potentially more fruitful (see Warner, 1993). Nevertheless, alternative images which fall short of theory have the potential to expand our ways of seeing and enhance our level of understanding—tasks which are of great benefit even if the underlying images only address issues of "description or codification" (see Stark, this volume). In the remainder of this chapter, I will discuss the work of several scholars who are identified with the phenomenological image of religion and then consider the relationship of the phenomenological image to rational choice models of religion. The phenomenological tradition includes influential individuals such as William

James, Rudolf Otto, Martin Buber, Jocham Wach, and more recently, Thomas O'Dea, Mircea Eliade, Clifford Geertz, Peter Berger, and Andrew Greeley, among others.

What all of these scholars agree on is that any meaningful discussion of the nature of religion must begin with a recognition that nonrational religious experience exists at the core of all religions. Greeley (1989a) powerfully clarifies by simplifying the essential nature of religion to four words: experience, image, story, and community. He argues that the origin of religion, its raw power, is experience. Religion's core is religious experience, a part of the nonrational (or pre-cognitive) portion of human experience. Experience leads to imagery in the imperfect attempts to communicate and preserve the experience through stories. Religions, then, are story-telling communities rooted in these core experiences. The imagery in these stories is symbolic of a reality beyond itself—of raw, pre-cognitive experience.

In his classic study of human encounters with the numinous, Martin Buber (1970) observes that the imperative to capture this experiential phenomenon within symbols and stories is the sublime melancholy of the dialectical nature of religion. That is, when we attempt to preserve the unique source of vitality in religion by naming it or placing it within ritual, we lose the actual experience—we leave the numinous encounter since the phenomenon always transcends the communicative capacity of symbols and stories. By attempting to preserve the experience, however, we remember the encounter and provide structured pathways back to it.

Thomas O'Dea (1961) expresses a similar view, arguing that the very thing that makes possible the survival of religion—namely, its institutionalization—also potentially undermines the essence of religion. In the process of fleshing out this dilemma, he reveals the phenomenological nature of his own sociological understanding of religion. He states, "religion is first of all a response…to the ultimate and the sacred which are grasped as relevant to human life and its fundamental significance" (O'Dea, 1961: 273). Furthermore, religious response to the ultimate or sacred is religion's "constitutive element and out of [religious response] proceeds the process of the elaboration and standardization of religious institutions" (O'Dea, 1961: 275). O'Dea suggests that since

> this experience involves the deep engagement of the person involved with a "beyond" which is sacred, it is unusual in a special sense. It would remain a fleeting and impermanent element in human life without its embodiment in institutional structures to render it continuously present and available. (O'Dea, 1961: 275)

But it is this very process which produces the central dilemma:

> In bringing together two radically heterogeneous elements, ultimacy and con-
> crete social institutions, the sacred and the profane, this necessary institution-
> alization involves a fundamental tension... (O'Dea, 1961: 275)

Out of the basic tension involved in translating religion's constitutive nonrational encounter with the sacred into an institutional form, O'Dea then unfolds his classic discussion of specific dilemmas encountered by any organized religion.

Andrew Greeley also discusses the preconscious foundations of religion. Greeley (1989b), building upon the early work of Clifford Geertz (1968), suggests that religion

> is a set of symbols which provide answers to issues of the ultimate meaning of
> life, symbols which explain imaginatively what the world is about and provide
> templates for shaping human response to the world... [That is,] religion is an
> imaginative "cultural system"—a collection of directing "pictures" (Greeley,
> 1989b: 484–485).

But what are the origins of the symbols or directing "pictures"? Greeley tells us that

> While these "pictures" may produce theological and ethical codes, they are
> pre-propositional and metaphorical. The codes are derivative, the superstruc-
> ture, if one wishes, built on an imaginative and preconscious infrastruture(485).

Again, Greeley proposes an image of religion clearly grounded in pre-cognitive experience.

Of course, some sociologists would argue for bracketing out any phenomenon that cannot be observed with empirical tools. They would be uncomfortable with the sort of sociological image of religion that Buber, O'Dea, and Greeley propose. On the other hand, some sociologists are equally uncomfortable with an overly restrictive sociological view of religion. Both Peter Berger and Richard Schoenherr have argued against reductionistic trends. For example, even as he argues that "at the heart of the religious phenomenon is prereflective, pretheoret-ical experience," Peter Berger (1980: 34) also argues for the normalcy of including such phenomenon in the study of human action.

The Heretical Imperative (1980), presents Berger's clearest exposition of this position. He draws upon Alfred Shutz's concept of multiple realities which posits that individuals do not experience reality as a single unified whole. Rather, reality is composed of zones or strata with greatly differing qualities. Shutz labels the reality of ordinary, everyday activities "paramount" or "mundane" reality because this zone has the strongest plausibility structure and most of the time we experience it as the more real of the realities we encounter. This mundane reality is the point of departure and orientation for other realities, and it is the one returned to. "Other realities" are experienced as alien zones, enclaves, or holes within mundane reality. Finally, mundane reality is experienced as being both massively real and very precarious—it can be lost as easily as falling asleep.

The other realities (or what William James would call "subuniverses") are defined in contrast to and experienced as ruptures of mundane reality. These other realities are very difficult to describe because language has its roots in mundane experience. They include, but are not limited to, experiences of theoretical abstraction, aesthetic experience (music/art/nature), the experience of the cosmic, and physiological experiences (i.e., dreams, joy, and pain). These experiences are very difficult to describe to someone who has not also experienced them. Yet we still try. However difficult to describe, we recognize these experiences as real, not fantasy.

Berger goes on to argue that religion, when defined as the breakthrough to the sacred, is one such experience. Furthermore, it makes sense for sociologists to try to describe this experience and understand it as part of the whole spectrum of human experience, well worth studying despite the inherent difficulties. Berger illustrates the effort involved with Rudolf Otto's (1976) description of the experience of the sacred—or *mysterium tremendum*. Otto describes the experience of the holy rather than the holy itself because he suggests that the holy can not be reduced to rational categories. Furthermore, Otto suggests that his discussion of *mysterium tremendum* will not resonate for those who have not also experienced the holy. Nevertheless, to paraphrase Mircea Eliade (1959), Otto argues that to leave a discussion of the holy out of a theory of religion would be to study a religious system as if it were dead, a defunct myth system.

In describing the family of "other realities," Berger suggests that all these experiences are characterized by an ecstatic quality—a sense of standing outside the ordinary world. From within the experience of one of these ecstatic ruptures, the ordinary world is relativized—mundane reality appears tenuously put together, full of holes, easily collapsed into unreality. These experiences set boundaries on mundane reality and expose its flaws or absurdities.

Berger argues, then, for a sociological image of religion in which religion's essence is understood to be first and foremost grounded in experience which stands outside of mundane reality. But, he acknowledges, religion is more than just "prereflective, pretheoretical experience." It is also experienced as tradition. "Religious experience," Berger (1980: 43) explains,

> in consequence [of its nonrational nature], comes to be embodied in traditions, which mediate it to those who have not had it themselves and which institutionalize it for them as well as for those who have…The special character of religious experience, however, creates a number of problems…[R]eligious experience breaches the reality of ordinary life, while all traditions and

institutions are structures *within* the reality of ordinary life. Inevitably, this translation…tends to distort.

Traditions may be imperfect vehicles, but as Berger (1980: 45) later suggests, that distortion serves a purpose:

> The insertion of the supramundane into mundane reality inevitably distorts it, but only by virtue of this distortion can even a faint echo of the original experience be retained amid the humdrum noises of everyday life.

Richard Schoenherr, my primary mentor in the sociology of religion, has also been engaged in the conversation concerning the phenomenological approach. Schoenherr (1987: 54) has argued that the approach "assumes that religious experience as a complete event cannot be empirically verified and yet can be known by a human action as absolutely real." If Schoenherr is correct, herein lies the dilemma for sociologists. While we can empirically measure belief in and consequences of symbols and stories, the core of the religious phenomenon, that is, religious experience itself, is not directly measurable, despite being real.

How then do we incorporate its elusive reality into a sociology of religion? How are we to capture the numen which is not only "experienced as an objective presence, [but] is also experienced as 'totally other,' that is, as incapable of being limited by, or of occupying normal time and space…" (Schoenherr, 1987: 54)?

Schoenherr (1987: 54) frames this question within "Kant's epistemological doctrine…[which], has had a decisive influence on the development of methodological tools for the humanities and social sciences." He first explains Kant's basic stance in relation to religions experience:

> Kant is correct in concluding from his analysis of pure reason that the existence…of any numen cannot be proven by scientific reason. But in his *Critique of Practical Reason* he went on to demonstrate that explanations based on pure reason do not exhaust all of reality. (Schoenherr, 1987: 54)

Schoenherr then sketches the thinkers who have modified Kant's epistemology for the social sciences:

> Kantian epistemology has been corrected and refined by Schleiermacher's analysis of intuition; Dilthey's hermeneutics for interpreting inner experience; Otto's classic treatment of the religious *a priori*; Husserl's prescriptions for a phenomenological *epoche* when judging the factual truth of objects of belief…and finally by Eliade's brilliant melding of the German history of religion…and phenomenology of religion in his monumental studies of myth,

rites and symbols in primitive and archaic religions. (54; *bibliographic references in original deleted*)

In the end, Schoenherr (1987: 52) argues that understanding power and authority in organized religion necessitates understanding the rootedness of religious power in religious experience which cannot be assessed through a "reductionistic epistemology for empirical analysis." This leads him to endorse "a basically phenomenological and therefore antireductionist theory of religion."

As the length of this brief overview establishes, phenomenologically oriented social thinkers represent a central and major perspective within the sociology of religion—and one which is not dependent on either secularization theory or rational choice theory. Of course, many of these scholars, having considered the implications of modernity and pluralism on religion, would appropriately be included in a discussion of secularization. But the heart of their perspective—namely, that the essence of religion or its constitutive element is contained in precognitive, nonrational experience—does not depend upon a discourse with secularization theory. The remainder of the chapter seeks to open a dialogue between the phenomenologically grounded tradition in the sociology of religion and rational choice models of religion. To date, this conversation remains underdeveloped, a situation which accounts for some of the current uneasiness between various groups of scholars.

First, proponents of a rational choice approach can reasonably claim that if religion is constituted by preconscious, nonrational experiences, the forces that lead to, as well as the consequences of, those experiences correspond with the predicted intentions, behaviors, and collective outcomes contained within rational choice models of religion. Furthermore, rational choice models seem not to be particularly dependent upon a recognition of this correspondence in order to generate a fairly comprehensive set of testable predictions.

I am reminded of Eileen Barker's (1984) description of conversion to the Unification Movement. She notes that her model of conversion is not dependent upon positing the existence of God. If God does exist and enters into the process of Moonie conversions, apparently he or she chooses to do so through observable social mechanisms. Proponents of a rational choice approach to religion may make much the same claim with respect to the phenomenological image of religion. That is, the rational choice model does not depend upon positing the existence of religious experience as the constitutive element of religion, since to whatever extent religious experience does drive religion, the process still unfolds in a fashion consistent with observable social mechanisms that fit the rational choice approach. Thus, rational choicers may be able to describe and predict religious behaviors even if they do not utilize the style of thick description that phenomenologically oriented social scientists find more appealing.

Second, some social scientists may suggest that attempts to incorporate religious experience into a rigorous, empirically grounded theory of religion will be counterproductive. That is, the problems encountered in trying to measure the experience of the holy are too great and lead to the misrepresentation and distortion of reality through the misapplication of reductionistic methods to a phenomenon that is inherently preconscious and nonrational. In addition, such measurement efforts may block the development of a social scientific model of religion by misdirecting the attention of researchers away from the scientifically doable into a methodological morass.

Assuming that the nonrational cannot at least be indirectly included in social theory, however, would seem to be inconsistent with the recent efforts of economists such as Larry Iannaccone (this volume) to incorporate complex commodities such as "love" and "recreation" into their models of household production.

Furthermore, a careful dialogue between proponents of rational choice explanations of religious behavior and proponents of a phenomenological image of religion will benefit both approaches. For example, recognizing that religious experience is a "thing-in-itself" clarifies its status as a reward or benefit that can induce willingness to bear significant costs.

The dialogue also leads one to ask, "To what extent can religious experience be classified as a risky commodity?" (See Iannaccone's chapter in this volume for a full discussion of religious capital.) If we take the phenomenological explanations seriously, the full value of religious experience cannot be appreciated by an individual prior to its actual consumption. Drawing on Martin Heidegger's model of knowledge and thinking, the consumption of religious experience would bring with it religious capital in the form of non-rational knowledge of religious experience as a thing-in-itself, namely, a knowledge that can only be acquired experientially. Once an individual acquires such religious capital, the continued pursuit of religious experience becomes rational. But because of the inability to fully assess the worth of this commodity prior to its initial consumption and the fact that one must invest time, energy, and emotion in its uncertain pursuit, religious experience is a risky commodity. Social mechanisms such as testimonials may be necessary to induce the pursuit of the commodity prior to the initial experience of consumption which transforms it into religious capital.

The dialogue between the rational choice and phenomenological approaches makes possible in other ways a fuller appreciation of the value placed upon religious experience. For example, while phenomenologists describe religious experience as a precognitive thing-in-itself which is intrinsically rewarding or self-validating, the rational choice approach alerts us to the possibility that constraints associated with the consumption of the good (persecution, political penalties, excommunications, etc.) might alter the demand over time. In some instances, constraints may even undermine the perceived legitimacy of symbols and rituals which lead to the experiences or that provide an interpretive framework for the experiences. Under such conditions, an individual may place lower or even no value upon the continued consumption of religious experience. For example, feminist images of God have served as a structured pathway to religious experience for some Mormons but recent attacks on such images by Mormon Church leaders, including the excommunication of some proponents of those views, may lead some individuals to place lower or even negative value upon the continued consumption of religious experience flowing out of such images.

Religious experience may also be interpreted through symbols and stories to be an indicator of the reality of other risky commodities. Thus, a believer may adhere to a symbol system in which the encounter is understood to demonstrate unobservable realities such as the existence of God or of life beyond the grave. In this case, religious experience becomes part of the legitimation process for an uncertain good or risky commodity. Similarly, the encounter might be interpreted as a prerequisite for the acquisition of certain risky commodities such as being saved. Individuals who adopt such interpretations would be expected to place enhanced value upon religious experiences and have a greater propensity to seek them out. Again, while religious experience can be wholly valued as an end-in-itself, as illustrated by Maslow's (1964) agnostically grounded discussion of peak experiences within religious settings, the application of rational choice concepts to a phenomenological interpretation of religion brings with it insight and clarity.

The concern with the free-rider problem illustrates another way in which a dialogue between the rational choice approach and the phenomenological image can enhance an understanding of the social conditions surrounding religious experience. The phenomenological image of religion has argued that individuals value religious experience and depend upon religious communities or organizations for symbols, stories, and rituals to facilitate religious experience. According to rational choice theory, a religious group may restrict access to symbols, stories, and rituals which act as structured pathways to religious experience in order to induce the costs of full participation within the community. All of this serves to help us understand why costly membership can draw rather than drive away adherents.

Another area in which rational choice models can clarify the thinking of those social theorists who draw primarily upon phenomenological images of religion is by articulating the conditions under which religious experience is most likely to occur. Specifically, because demand is viewed as being relatively constant by rational choicers, rational choice theory suggests that the propensity for the occurrence of religious experience is relatively constant under conditions of stable supply. However, in unregulated religious markets with high levels of competition among suppliers, niche-specific symbols and stories which resonate for specific subpopulations are more likely to be developed. Thus, Stephen Warner (1993) argues that American religion has not become rootless or arbitrary in the face of pluralism. Rather, he suggests that the breakdown of ascription-based religion may be welcomed when, like members of the Metropolitan Community Church [which serves the gay and lesbian community], its beneficiaries are convinced that they have been freed to acknowledge their true nature…In this way, the breakdown of ascriptive ties to religion can enhance, rather than reduce, the elemental nature that believers attribute to their experiences. From this point of view, social ascription that denies one's true being is seen as arbitrary, while a new-found religion is self-affirming. (1078)

The point is that while phenomenologically grounded descriptions of religious experience may be accurate, contributing to our understanding of the nature of religion in a way that rings true, it is the supply-side version of rational choice theory which describes the conditions under which both mass and virtuosi forms of religious experience are most likely to flourish. Rational choice theory helps us predict which segments of the population are most likely to be exposed to the sacred as a result of an active, lively religious market, while the phenomenological images provide a discourse or language that helps us understand or sense why the encounter with the sacred is perceived to be rewarding.

Finally, the utility of the phenomenological approach and its capacity to be integrated with rational choice models of religion probably rests upon the degree to which the phenomenological approach can generate testable predictions. Far from being scarce, such predictions abound. Several illustrations follow which flow out of the discussion contained in this chapter. Note that some of these testable predictions have already been empirically established:

Proposition 1: *Because religious experience is encountered as a benefit, religious attachment will be higher among those individuals reporting religious experience.*

Proposition 2: *Because religious experience is a risky commodity prior to its initial consumption, the value placed on religious experience will increase after self-reports of initial consumption.*

Proposition 3: *Members of religious organizations that rely on religious experience to legitimate risky commodities or far-off compensators will have higher rates of self-reported religious experience.*

Proposition 4: *Because religious experience is a deeply personal phenomenon that is self-legitimating and has multiple possible interpretations, religious organizations which encourage the pursuit of religious experience will a)seek to exercise greater control over religious symbols and stories and/or b)experience higher rates of sect formation.*

Of course, all of these propositions may be modified given specific constraints. For example, with proposition 4, one might add that under conditions of modernity, sect formation and efforts to control the symbolic apparatus may increase for religious organizations which depend upon religious experience.

In summary, many social scientists engaged in the analysis of religion have been highly influenced by phenomenological images of religious experience. With the development of rational choice models as an emerging new paradigm within the sociology of religion, adherents of the phenomenological approach may feel that their intellectual underpinnings are being threatened. At the very least, those wedded to a phenomenological image of religion are haunted by the question of whether or not the capacity of rational choice theory to predict religious behaviors should be viewed as the equivalent of tapping into the sociological essence of religion. While some social thinkers rooted in the phenomenological tradition may tend to pursue an agenda of rejection with respect to rational choice models of religion, in this chapter I have argued for an agenda of dialogue and integration that could benefit both rational choicers and phenomenologists.

REFERENCES

Ammerman, Nancy Tatom. 1990. *Baptist Battles: Social Change and Religious Conflict in the Modern World*. New Brunswick, NJ: Rutgers University Press.

Barker, Eileen. 1984. *The Making of a Moonie: Choice or Brainwashing?* Oxford: Basil Blackwell.

Bellah, Robert N., Richard Madsen, William M. Sullivan, Ann Swidler, and Steven M. Tipton. 1985. *Habits of the Heart: Individualism and Commitment in American Life*. Berkeley: University of California Press.

Berger, Peter L. 1980. *The Heretical Imperative*. Garden City, NY: Doubleday Anchor Books.

Buber, Martin. [1923] 1970. *I and Thou*. New York: Scribners.

Caplow, Theodore, Howard M. Bahr, and Bruce A. Chadwick. 1983. *All Faithful People: Change and Continuity in Middletown's Religion*. Minneapolis: University of Minnesota Press.

Demmerath, N. J., III, and Rhys H. Williams. 1992. *A Bridging of Faiths: Religion and Politics in a New England City*. Princeton: Princeton University Press.

Ebaugh, Helen Rose, ed. 1991. *Vatican II and U.S. Catholicism: Twenty-five Years Later*. Greenwich, CT: JAI.

Eliade, Mircea. 1959. *The Sacred and the Profane*. New York: Harcourt, Brace and World, Inc.

Geertz, Clifford. 1968. "Religion as a Cultural System." In *Religious Situation 1968*. Edited by Donald Cutler. Boston: Beacon.

Greeley, Andrew M. 1989a. ASA Conference.

———1989b. "Protestant and Catholic: Is the Analogical Imagination Extinct?" *American Sociological Review*. 54 (August): 485–502.

———1990. *The Catholic Myth: The Behavior and Beliefs of America's Catholics*. New York: Scribner's.

Hadden, Jeffrey K. 1987. "Toward Desacralizing Secularization Theory." *Social Forces* 65 (March): 587–611.

Hadden, Jeffrey K., and Anson Shupe. 1986. "Introduction." In *Prophetic Religions and Politics*. Jeffrey K. Hadden and Anson Shupe, eds. New York: Paragon House.

Maslow, Abraham. 1964. *Religions, Values and Peak-Experiences*. New York: Viking.

Morgan, Gareth. 1986. *Images of Organization*. Beverly Hills, CA: Sage Publications.

Neitz, Mary Jo. 1987. *Charisma and Community: A Study of Religious Commitment within the Charismatic Renewal*. New Brunswick, NJ: Transaction.

O'Dea, Thomas. 1961. "Five Dilemmas in the Institutionalization of Religion." *Journal for the Scientific Study of Religion* 1: 30–39.

Otto, Rudolf. 1976. *The Idea of the Holy*. London: Oxford University Press.

Roof, Wade Clark, and William McKinney. 1987. *American Mainline Religion: Its Changing Shape and Future*. New Brunswick, NJ: Rutgers University Press.

Schoenherr, Richard A. 1987. "Power and Authority in Organized Religion: Disaggregating the Phenomenological Core." *Sociological Analysis*. 47 (March): 52–71.

Stark, Rodney, and William Sims Bainbridge. 1985. *The Future of Religion: Secularization, Revival, and Cult Formation*. Berkeley: University of California Press.

Warner, R. Stephen. 1988. *New Wine in Old Wineskins: Evangelicals and Liberals in a Small-Town Church*. Berkeley: University of California Press.

————1993. "Work in Progress toward a New Paradigm for the Sociological Study of Religion in the United States." *American Journal of Sociology* 98 (March): 1044–1093.

RELIGION AND RATIONAL CHOICE THEORY[1]

Michael Hechter

CONSIDERING ITS exalted and special position in classical sociological theory, the study of religion holds a surprisingly marginal status in present-day American sociology. In country after country, the early sociologists seized on religion to support their contention that social life could not be adequately explained on the basis of the individualist methodologies of economics and psychology. As articulated most persuasively by Talcott Parsons (1937), the classical consensus was that religious behaviour could not be understood as an outcome of individually rational action.

This claim is difficult to assess, however, because there is little consensus about the meaning of rationality in social science, let alone among commentators on rational choice theory. One fundamental controversy, highly relevant to the study of religion, pertains to the status of beliefs in definitions of rational action. Some (like Elster, 1989: 37–39) limit their definition of rationality to actions that are based on scientifically justifiable beliefs. This seems too narrow. Others (like Boudon, 1994: 254–257) merely require that rational agents have good reasons for making their choices. This seems too broad. A more reasonable definition lies between these two extremes. The hallmark of rational action consists in its instrumentality. Thus, people are rational to the degree that they pursue the most efficient means available to attain their most preferred ends. These ends may be material or nonmaterial. People are irrational when they pursue a course of action regardless of its consequences. It cannot be rational, therefore, to "value for its own sake some ethical, aesthetic, religious, or other form of behaviour, independently of its prospects of success" (Weber, [1922] 1968: 24–25).[2]

Most (but not all) classical sociologists not only regarded religion as irrational; they also considered it to be an emergent rather than an individual phenomenon. Sacredness, that quintessentially distinctive religious attitude, could not be attributed to an individual's preference for a specific good, but necessarily referred to a socially constructed source of sanctity (Parsons, 1937: 711). Parsons' claim carried with it the notion, unpalatable to many contemporary sociologists, that religion is a subject that is unsuitable for any kind of positive analysis.

The papers by Stark, Iannaccone, and Finke (this volume) reveal that rational choice theory can be used successfully to explain a variety of religious phenomena. In fact, the rational choice approach has become a leading contender in the sociology of religion. Yet the denouement is even more surprising. The prominence of rational choice theorizing in sociology has grown steadily, if slowly, in the last decade. One might expect that the most rapid growth would have been in the sphere of economic and political sociology, but it turns out that some of its greatest strides instead have been in the sociology of religion. This rapid progress is due to the ready availability of survey and census data about religious attitudes and behaviour, to the profoundly antirational strain in the study of religion that provides rational choice scholars with first-mover advantages, and to the skill and perspicaciousness of these new theorists of religion. Their evolving research program is welcome not only for its contributions to sociological versions of rational choice theory, but also for its contributions to sociology as a whole. In a discipline at risk of balkanizing into a congeries of separate substantive areas having too little common knowledge to sustain an intellectual community, this research program directly ties the study of religion to that of many other kinds of social phenomena. Hence, it helps to stem the centripetal tide that threatens sociology's intellectual coherence.

In such a context, any effort based on general theory that has the promise of launching a research program in sociology represents progress, even if one doubts the carrying capacity of the theory. I have few doubts about the carrying capacity of this one. The research summarized at Sundance is impressive in its scope, its ambition, and even some of its empirical results.

THE RATIONAL CHOICE APPROACH TO RELIGION

The Sundance applications of rational choice theory assume that, even though they sometimes may produce distinctive kinds of goods, religious groups are faced with problems fundamentally similar to those of firms, clubs, and other voluntary associations. Like all these groups, religious ones must manage to obtain and allocate the jointly produced goods (in this case, religion) that sustain their membership. Therefore, they must overcome obstacles to goods production, such as free-riding and poor coordination (Hechter, 1987).

Adequate explanations in social science require specification of the mechanisms that produce the causal relations between variables that are the focus of empirical research (Kiser and Hechter, 1991). These mechanisms, however, tend to be unobservable. This means that they cannot be inferred through induction. The role of general theory in sociological explanation is to suggest plausible mechanisms. For example, the assumption that all groups face similar problems in the realm of goods production enables the rational choice theorist to consider an armamentarium of mechanisms—based on the theories of clubs, public goods, and group solidarity—to account for a wide range of observable phenomena. The adequacy of the mechanism postulated in the given case can only be assessed empirically, however. Even though mechanisms are seldom directly measurable, we are persuaded of their efficacy when they lead to observable implications that are unique and consistent with the available evidence.

For example, Iannaccone discusses how strict churches deter free-riders. His central premise is that religion is a jointly produced commodity. The adherent's satisfaction depends both on his or her own inputs and those of others:

> The pleasure and edification that I derive from a Sunday service does not depend solely on what I bring to the service (through my presence, attentiveness, public singing, etc.); it also depends on how many others attend, how warmly they greet me, how well they sing or recite (in English, Latin, Hebrew, Arabic, etc.), how enthusiastically they read and pray, and how deep their commitments are. However, it also extends to religious belief and religious experiences—particularly the most dramatic experiences such as speaking in tongues, miraculous healings, prophetic utterances, and ecstatic trances—all of which are more sustainable and satisfying when experienced collectively. (Iannaccone, 1994: 1184)

Joint production of a good is likely to induce free-riding, however. One way to solve this free-rider problem is for churches to penalize or prohibit alternative activities that compete for members' resources (Iannaccone, 1994: 1187). The prohibition of alternatives increases levels of commitment within the group by two different mechanisms. The first operates by screening out the less committed. The second raises the cost of consuming externally-provided commodities, thereby shifting the demand for commodities from external providers to internal ones. This outcome depends on the existence of a close substitute for the demanded commodity (Iannaccone, 1994: 1187). For instance, if sex is a demanded good then the group can increase member commitment by adopting a policy that encourages internal sexual liasons at the expense of external ones. Without close substitutability, there will be no shift in demand and hence no increase in member commitment.

Similarly, Finke (this volume) argues that state regulation ultimately serves to decrease levels of religious participation. His conclusion is driven by straightforward market logic. Unlike producers in competitive markets, monopolists don't have a strong incentive to worry about market share. Monopolistic producers will be less responsive to consumer demand: they won't specialize so as to maximize demand.

> It will be obvious that a set of specialized firms will, together, be able to appeal to a far greater proportion of consumers than can be the case when only one faith is available without risk of sanctions. Moreover, because so much of the religious product necessarily is intangible and concerns the far distant future, vigorous marketing activity is needed to achieve high levels of consumption. (Stark, 1994: 3)

On this account, religious monopolists should be expected to turn out a less attractive product than producers in more competitive markets. The sale of papal indulgences prior to the Protestant Reformation is a famous case in point. Since monopoly limits the quality of the joint good, as well as consumer demand (via its effects on price), religious participation is suboptimal. Predictably, the introduction of competition into religious milieux would rapidly swell rates of religious participation.

Although ideas like these are suggestive, they only begin to tap rational choice theory's potential for analyzing religious phenomena. Take, for instance, the fact that the strategy of treating religious groups as fundamentally similar to firms is limiting and limited. In key respects, religious groups are different from nonreligious ones as well as from one another. Rational choice theory may help account for the distinctiveness of religious groups, as well as their similarity to other kinds of groups.

The very existence of a competitive market for religion raises challenges for conventional rational choice models. How can markets ever arise for inscrutable goods—those whose quality it is impossible for consumers, and even producers, to discern?

> Inscrutable commodities are generally regarded as *sui generis*, special realms of human activity unsuitable for rational choice analysis. This is a reasonable atti-

tude. It is arduous for agents to rank the alternatives on the basis of quality, thus they have no rational way to decide whether to enter an exchange. Moreover, the fact that suppliers themselves are unsure about the quality of their services adds an insurmountable impediment because there is no way they can send honest signals to customers helping them to make up their minds. There is no clear ground on which the notion of "honesty" itself can be constructed. (Gambetta, 1994: 354)

How do consumers choose between churches that claim to produce the same good? The producers of inscrutable goods can overcome these formidable obstacles by employing several different strategies. They can attempt to rely on a reputation for delivering a high quality product, but this is not so easy for religions because so many of their products are intangible.

The character of the producer often stands as proxy to the quality of the product. The accuracy of many promises made by a priest cannot be checked readily, since they often refer to events taking place in the hereafter. This assessment problem can be eased if the priest is also engaged in activities where his performance and trustworthiness can be monitored; he may earn a reputation for reliability, and this by association renders his less tangible promises also more reliable (Schlict, 1991: 25).

Another challenge to the use of a conventional rational choice model for the study of religion has to do with the assumption that religious goods are highly substitutable. To some extent the assumption is plausible: the goods offered by religious groups, indeed, do appear to be close substitutes for those offered by political and social groups. Like other groups, religious ones provide their members with welfare, entertainment, prestige, and relief from loneliness, among other goods. Evidence in a number of conference papers lends some empirical support to the assumption.

But how substitutable are the various goods produced by different religions? Will a Fundamentalist Protestant join the Lubavitchers if he or she can gain greater instrumental benefits by doing so? My conjecture is that this happens less frequently than conversions of Democrats to the Republican Party. Conventional rational choice theory has little to say about questions of this sort. The most it can postulate is that *if* the various joint goods are (regarded by consumers as) close substitutes, then the implications highlighted by Iannaccone, Finke, and Stark will follow. But if the various goods are not so regarded, then very different outcomes should obtain.

One's allegiance to a religion is on average *stickier* than loyalty to a particular brand of coffee. Disputes over religion are far more likely to breed violence than disputes over health care initiatives; people are more wont to give up their lives for their religion than for their firm. All told, religious commitments are sometimes far more intense and salient than secular social commitments. This certainly was the contention of Durkheim, for whom the concept of the sacred was the crucial *differentium*. Weber, for his part, found it necessary to distinguish traditional and affective values from the instrumental (*zweckrational*) ones that motivate the rational choice models under consideration here (Kalberg, 1994).

Although rationality requires an instrumental orientation to action, the end or goal of this action is left quite unspecified in rational choice theory. Some people like to play golf, others like to play piano; some people are materially acquisitive, others get pleasure from giving away their wealth; some people like to bask in the limelight, others are content to play a supporting role. Rational choice theory does insist that actors be utility maximizers, but the concept of utility is substantively empty. In effect, then, an instrumental orientation to action is one which merely implies means/ends rationality. Although this sounds like a weak and unexceptionable assumption, it rules out exclusively emotional and value-rational (*wertrational*) orientations to action (Weber, [1922] 1968).[3] Even so, assuming instrumental rationality often is justified in macrosociological analysis (Hechter, 1994; 1995).

Many rational choice models also assume that people's values (invariably termed utilities in more formal models) are both stable over time and homogeneous across individuals. This is an overly restrictive assumption, however; certainly such an assumption is not necessary to drive the macro outcomes which interest rational choice theorists. All that must be assumed in such models is that some subset of these values (instrumental ones, in fact) are held in common, and that any remaining idiosyncratic (noninstrumental) values are distributed through the given population independently with respect to constraints (Hechter, 1994). Because money, power, and prestige tend to satisfy these assumptions, the theory assumes rational action in the pursuit of them.

What can such a theory tell us about the peculiar salience of religious affiliation? It is hard to think that we can predict people's religious behaviour without understanding their values and beliefs. On this account, Stark and Bainbridge (1985) find it useful to introduce novel concepts like *compensators* in their theory of religion. They claim that people with large endowments of wealth are much less willing to exchange supernatural compensators for material rewards than those who are less well endowed. Can this purely instrumental logic account for the actual degree of income and occupational heterogeneity found in existing churches and sects? This is an empirical question, but I suspect that additional mechanisms are likely to be at play, and that these probably have something to do with people's *immanent* values—ends that are valued for themselves alone, rather than for what they can yield in exchange.

William James provides an eloquent description of the immanent value of religion:

> For when all is said and done, we are in the end absolutely dependent on the
> universe; and into its sacrifices and surrenders of some sort, deliberately looked

at and accepted, we are drawn and pressed as into our only permanent positions of repose. Now in those states of mind which fall short of religion, the surrender is submitted to as an imposition of necessity, and the sacrifice is undergone at the very best without complaint. In the religious life, on the contrary, surrender and sacrifice are positively espoused: even unnecessary givings-up are added in order that the happiness may increase. (James, 1902: 51)

For James, religion clearly represents an immanent rather than an instrumental good—how else to account for the fact that "surrender and sacrifice are positively espoused"? Note the difference between James' conception and Iannaccone's. Iannaccone argues that strict churches can provide a better product than lax ones, but he never suggests that the members' sacrifices produce happiness *directly*.

If James' insight is correct, we can begin to understand more reasons for religion's salience. In fact, perhaps the newest frontier in rational choice theory concerns the incorporation of such immanent values into individual utility schedules. So far there has been precious little agreement on how to proceed, yet progress is being made on several different fronts. Due to the difficulties of reliably measuring peoples' values (Hechter, 1992; Hechter et al., 1993), some rational choice theorists find it useful to invent novel value assumptions to explain why people rationally choose to remain unemployed (Akerlof and Yellin, 1993), or why they continue having children when the net instrumental benefits of both choices are negative (Friedman, Hechter, and Kanazawa, 1994). Others are attempting to find reliable independent measures of individual values and their determinants that might some day be incorporated into utility functions in formal models. Both lines of research are important and well worth doing.

AN UNCERTAINTY-REDUCTION THEORY OF RELIGION

In the remainder of this chapter, I will sketch how immanent values can be incorporated by assumption (as opposed to direct measurement) in a rational choice theory of religion. The particular assumption I will use is uncertainty reduction. Decision making under uncertainty is decision making without knowing the odds of the various alternative consequences in the set of choices.[4] This is to be distinguished from decision making under risk, in which a decision maker can attach probabilities to alternative consequences. Failure to achieve desired ends can occur in both states. However, under risk the decision maker knows (or believes he or she knows) the odds of failure, whereas under uncertainty the decision maker cannot judge these odds. In choosing between alternative courses of action, then, the rational actor first must ascertain all potential consequences of a single course of action; second, he must assess the desirability of these consequences; and third, he must assign a subjective probability to each of these consequences. The judgment is under risk whenever any of these probabilities lies between 0 and 1. Given such conditions, the rational actor will choose that course of action with which the highest expected value is associated. Under uncertainty, however, such rational calculation is precluded because the third step in the process—assigning probabilities to the potential consequences—is impossible. Therefore, under uncertainty, people cannot use a utilitarian calculus to guide their behaviour.

To proceed rationally, one must be able to assess risk. For this reason, rational actors prefer risky to uncertain situations. States of the world can be uncertain as well, and beyond the actor's ability to change. Indeed, one may argue, as did Knight ([1921] 1971: 313), "We live in a world full of contradiction and paradox, a fact of which perhaps the most fundamental illustration is this: that the existence of a problem of knowledge depends on the future being different than the past, while the possibility of the solution of the problem depends on the future being like the past."

Yet even this extreme state of objective uncertainty does not stand in the way of the actor's quest to reduce uncertainty in his or her life. Insofar as actors have it in their power to change an uncertain state to a certain (albeit risky) state, they will do so. This is the uncertainty-reduction assumption. Because people value uncertainty reduction as an end in itself rather than merely as a means to various other ends, it is an immanent rather than an instrumental value.

Actors can reduce uncertainty in two ways. First, they can try to gather information that transforms uncertainty to risk for a local choice problem. Religion cannot reduce uncertainty in this way. Second, they can pursue global strategies designed to reduce uncertainty regarding whole strings of future courses of action. Although no actor can make the future more certain by his or her actions alone, the desire to reduce uncertainty impels actors to bind themselves to courses of action that are largely independent of future states of the world. This is the kind of uncertainty-reduction that religion can provide.

More than any other good, religion can offer relief from existential uncertainties about the meaning of life, and about death and its aftermath. These are the primary uncertainties of life.

Although uncertainty is not measured easily, its implications for religious behaviour are amenable to measurement. Most of us value both our work and our family lives. This creates conflict when we are compelled to choose between these sources of reward. Selecting between equally attractive alternatives is the essence of hard choices, which are famously difficult to make on rational grounds. The story of Buridan's ass is an archetypical example of the limits of rational choice theory. When this animal was faced between the choice of two equally attractive bundles of hay, it couldn't decide what to do and starved to death. Religion can help resolve hard choices, however, because it provides an external criterion for ordering values. In this sense Maimonides' noted text, "A Guide to the Perplexed," was aptly titled. Further, the venerability of many religions might encourage rational actors to privilege religious values precisely because they have survived the test of time, and therefore are presumptively adaptive.

To the extent that a religion enunciates a clear vision about the meaning of life by providing a hierarchy of values, it reduces actors' uncertainty in making critical life choices. To the degree that this indeed is a reason why people are attracted to religious groups, then the demand for religion should be highest among people who routinely face harder choices. To some degree, the prevalence of hard choices is a function of one's location in the social structure. Buridan's ass was incapacitated by bundles of hay, but the values driving human action are far more subtle and various. One important source of hard choices is role conflict. If we make the reasonable assumption that role conflict is fostered in culturally diverse but tolerant societies, such as the United States, and inhibited in culturally homogeneous and/or intolerant societies, such as Japan, then we should expect to find much more religious commitment in the former than in the latter types of societies. Such an analysis also yields the counterintuitive implication that modern societies should be more religious than pre-modern ones.[5] (Note that this line of thinking provides an alternative rational choice explanation to that offered by Finke and Stark for their findings on the effects of religious regulation.)

Both casual observation and social theory instruct us that the fear of death is among the strongest human sentiments, if not absolutely the strongest. Hobbes used death aversion as his fundamental behavioral assumption. Weber argued that Calvinists' uncertainty about their salvation led to the extreme forms of behaviour that helped create the institutions of capitalism. Rather more prosaically, the fear of death is ultimately responsible for the growth of health care expenditures in the welfare state, for taxpayers' disproportionate willingness to support defense and health care as opposed to other kinds of public expenditure, and for massive shifts in consumer behaviour, such as the decreased consumption of beef and other forms of red meat in American society.

Religion can reduce uncertainty about death in several ways. For Weber, it offers an image of the afterlife and a road map showing people how to get there. For James, religion provides a different kind of benefit:

> We are all…helpless failures in the last resort. The sanest and best of us are of one clay with lunatics and prison inmates, and death finally runs the robustest of us down. And whenever we feel this, such a sense of the vanity and provisionality of our voluntary career comes over us that all our morality appears but as a plaster hiding a sore it can never cure, and all our well-doing as the hollowest substitute for that well-*being* that our lives ought to be grounded in, but, alas! are not. And here religion comes to our rescue and takes our fate into her hands. There is a state of mind, known to religious men, but to no others, in which the will to assert ourselves and hold our own has been displaced by a willingness to close our mouths and be as nothing in the floods and waterspouts of God. In this state of mind, what we most dreaded has become the habitation of our safety, and the hour of our moral death has turned into our

> spiritual birthday. The time for tension in our soul is over, and that of happy
> relaxation, of calm deep breathing, of an eternal present, with no discordant
> future to be anxious about, has arrived. Fear is not held in abeyance as it is by
> mere morality, it is positively expunged and washed away. (James, 1902: 47)

Although we are all uncertain about our fate after death, death is not equally
vivid to all of us, nor is it equally vivid at all times. The uncertainty—and atten-
dant anxiety—generated by the contemplation of death is differentially distributed
in a population. It stands to reason, then, that people who are most aware of death
will be more likely to be religious than others, *ceteris paribus*. This includes old people, those who have recently witnessed death due to accident or illness, and people with terminal illnesses. More specifically, this analysis suggests that the relationship between religiosity and the experience of death should take the form of
an inverse U-shaped curve. Two kinds of people—those having had little experience of death (high school students), and those whose massive experience of death
has habituated them to it (oncologists and geriatricians)—should be less religious
than people whose exposure to death is more sporadic.[6]

How can propositions like these about the structural sources of differential religiosity be tested empirically? Only with the greatest difficulty. The key problem
lies in the measurement of religiosity. This is an long-standing concern among students of religion:

> The truth must at last be confronted that we are dealing with a field of expe-
> rience where there is not a single conception that can be sharply drawn. The
> pretension, under such conditions, to be rigorously "scientific" or "exact" in
> our terms would only stamp us as lacking in understanding of our task. Things
> are more or less divine, states of mind are more or less religious, reactions are
> more or less total, but the boundaries are always misty, and it is everywhere a
> question of amount and degree. (James, 1902: 39)

As this paper makes clear, the fact that people can join a church *both for instrumental and immanent motives* plays havoc with our interest in theory testing. Data about
church attendance have no necessary relevance for religiosity because a person can
be motivated to attend church largely or entirely for its secular (that is, instrumental) benefits. The same is true for measures of compliance with religious doctrine
or obligations: While such compliance *may* be motivated by religiosity, it may also
be motivated by purely instrumental considerations. ("What would the neighbours
think if they saw us driving on the Sabbath?") Rational choice theory allows for
both kinds of influences—indeed, it predicts both kinds.

CONCLUSION

Does rational choice theory have much to offer sociologists of religion? Certainly. If the sociology of religion follows the lead of demography—a field that uses many of the same kinds of evidence and data reduction techniques—then we should expect to find rational choice explanations inspiring ever more empirical research. One need think only of the immense catalytic role played in the analysis of fertility shifts, for example, by the (somewhat different) rational choice theories of Becker (1960) and Easterlin (1966). As is the case in demography, not all results of this research on religion will confirm these theories, of course. Neither we nor Karl Popper's ghost should be too surprised or disappointed about this. Occasional empirical disconfirmation will only serve to whet the appetites of empirical researchers. All told, the approach will motivate studies on religion that otherwise never would have been carried out, for it will suggest questions that had never been considered by scholars of religion. Ultimately, everyone in the field—both friends and foes of rational choice—will benefit from the continued development of this research program.

As I have tried to argue, however, the study of religion can offer much to the development of rational choice theory, in return. Rational choice theorists have gotten themselves into a rut by treating every group as if it were a firm and by focusing their models exclusively on the attainment of private, instrumental goods like wealth. Rational choice theory does not offer a single explanation of religion. Religious behaviour potentially offers a rich lode of evidence about the difficulties in producing and marketing inscrutable goods, and about the salience of immanent values—like uncertainty reduction—that can help rational choice theorists to enrich their models, thereby making them empirically more robust.

Such applications provide an opportunity to establish interactions between those who are immersed in the substantive knowledge of a given field and those whose vision is relentlessly general and substantively abstract. This promise, so seldom realized, may perhaps come to pass as a consequence of conferences like the one at Sundance.

NOTES

[1] I am grateful to Diego Gambetta and Federico Varese for comments.

[2] Principled action need not be considered to be irrational under this definition. If I place a high value on being a faithful husband, then this may enable me to resist the temptations of an affair at the office. Although I may be attracted to the promise of an affair, I can predict that succumbing to this desire will lower my self-esteem. Under certain conditions, therefore, it would be rational for me to choose the principled action of remaining faithful.

[3] Instrumental motives can overlay emotional ones to alter individual behavior, however. Thus the fear of criminal prosecution probably manages to forestall some intrafamily violence, despite its overwhelmingly emotional roots. Similarly, individuals can take other peoples' likely emotional reactions into account in planning their own strategic action.

[4] This section is drawn from Friedman, Hechter, and Kanazawa (1994).

[5] I am grateful to Diego Gambetta for pointing out this implication.

[6] For an intriguing study of the behavioral consequences of the fear of death, see Solomon, Greenberg, and Pyszczynski (1991).

REFERENCES

Akerlof, George A., and Janet L. Yellin. 1993. "The Fair Wage/Effort Hypothesis and Unemployment." In M. Hechter, L. Nadel, and R.E. Michod, eds. *The Origin of Values*. Hawthorne, NY: Aldine: 107–134.

Becker, Gary S. 1960. "An Economic Analysis of Fertility." In Universities–National Bureau Committee for Economic Research, ed., *Demographic and Economic Change in Developed Countries*. Princeton: Princeton University Press (for the National Bureau of Economic Research): 209–231.

Boudon, Raymond. 1994. *The Art of Self-Persuasion*, translated from the French by Malcolm Slater. Cambridge: Polity.

Easterlin, Richard. 1966. "On the Relation of Economic Factors to Recent and Projected Fertility Changes." *Demography* 3: 131–153.

Elster, Jon. 1989. *Nuts and Bolts for the Social Sciences*. Cambridge: Cambridge University Press.

Friedman, Debra, Michael Hechter, and Satoshi Kanazawa. 1994. "A Theory of the Value of Children." *Demography* 31: 375–401.

Gambetta, Diego. 1994. "Inscrutable Markets." *Rationality and Society* 6: 353–368.

Hechter, Michael. 1987. *Principles of Group Solidarity*. Berkeley: University of California Press.

———1992. "Should Values be Written out of the Social Scientist's Lexicon?" *Sociological Theory* 10: 214–230.

———1994. "The Role of Values in Rational Choice Theory." *Rationality and Society* 6: 318–333.

———1995. "Explaining Nationalist Violence." *Nations and Nationalism* 1: 53–68.

Hechter, Michael, Lynn Nadel, and Richard E. Michod, eds. 1993. *The Origin of Values*. Hawthorne, NY: Aldine.

Iannaccone, Laurence R. 1994. "Why Strict Churches Are Strong." *American Journal of Sociology* 99: 1180–1211.

James, William. 1902. *The Varieties of Religious Experience*. New York: Modern Library.

Kalberg, Stephen. 1994. *Max Weber's Comparative-Historical Sociology*. Cambridge: Polity.

Kiser, Edgar and Michael Hechter. 1991. "The Role of General Theory in Comparative-Historical Sociology." *American Journal of Sociology* 97: 1–30.

Knight, Frank H. [1921] 1971. *Risk, Uncertainty and Profit*. Chicago: University of Chicago Press.

Parsons, Talcott. 1937. *The Structure of Social Action*. New York: McGraw-Hill.

Schlict, E. 1991. "Economic Analysis and Organised Religion." Paper prepared for the fourth workshop on Demography, Economics and Organised Religion, Linacre College, Oxford, 14–15 June.

Solomon, S.J. Greenberg, and T. Pyszczynski. 1991. "A Terror Management theory of Social Behavior: The Psychological Functions of Self-Esteem and Cultural Worldviews. *Advances in Experimental Social Psychology* 24: 93–159.

Stark, Rodney. 1994. "Rational Choice Theories of Religion." *The Agora* (Newsletter of the Rational Choice Section of the American Sociological Association) 2: 1–5.

Stark, Rodney, and William Bainbridge. 1985. *The Future of Religion*. Berkeley: University of California Press.

Weber, Max. [1922] 1968. *Economy and Society*, translated by G. Roth and C. Wittich. New York: Bedminster.

STARK AND BAINBRIDGE, DURKHEIM AND WEBER

Theoretical Comparisons

Randall Collins

THE WORK of Stark and Bainbridge (1985, 1987) is a landmark in the sociology of religion. It is the most systematic general theory yet to appear, with its axiomatic–propositional form and its derivation of a wide range of consequences. It stands out in the literature of sociology and related disciplines in testing and supporting so many aspects of its general theory by a long series of empirical researches, both directly and by reference to a secondary literature.[1] Among the classic sociologies of religion, Emile Durkheim and Max Weber overlap Stark and Bainbridge's work in theoretical and empirical scope, while falling short of it in several respects.

Durkheim's treatment of religion is analytically central to his entire sociology, but it was not a general theory of the variants and dynamics of religion *per se*. It was a pathway into the heart of Durkheim's theory of social solidarity and symbolism, and its main inheritors have been the sociological tradition of studying ritual in non-religious spheres, pursued by such thinkers as Lloyd Warner, Goffman, and Mary Douglas. Max Weber, on the other hand, studied the empirical variations of religion on a historical scale far beyond Stark and Bainbridge, whose empirical base is essentially the United States of the past two centuries. Weber's focus was on religion in the context of other social institutions, above all on the ways it led or failed to lead from the alleged economic fixity of agrarian-coercive societies to the dynamics of industrial capitalism. Weber's massive comparative studies of the world religions are only obliquely concerned with the project of a general theory of religion which Stark and Bainbridge pursue straightforwardly.

Of course Weber could be an awesomely systematic writer too; *The Sociology of Religion*, excerpted from *Economy and Society*, purports to lay out the basic motivations, social conditions and dynamics of religion across a universal scale. Nevertheless, Weber tends to give more taxonomy than causality. *The Sociology of Religion* is pulled askew, too, by its persistent side-glances at the effects of one religious variant or another upon rationalized capitalism. And—with all due respect to Weber's imposing ghost—Weber's empirical evidence for his generalizations are often no more than scattered examples, not untainted at times by prejudices and stereotypes. Weber's sheer historical range leaves him largely unchallenged on his chosen turf;[2] but in principle he is far from unchallengable on many empirical and theoretical points. In addition, Weber's purported methodology of historicist ideal types (which he did not always follow himself) deflects criticism and deters revision; Weber's inheritors have tended to withdraw from the field of a truly general theory of religion, ceding the systematic terrain to others.[3]

The differences among our three theories express the differences between three of the major traditions of sociological analysis. Stark and Bainbridge count as a major empirical–theoretical triumph of the rational/utilitarian tradition. (Durkheim is the fountain-head of the opposing tradition which emphasizes a sub-surface of non-rationality, emotion, and the seeking of social solidarity. Accordingly, Durkheimian sociology of religion is much more reductionist and anti-supernatural than Stark/Bainbridge, who in effect make agnosticism into a theoretical basis for explaining belief in religious compensators.) Weber, finally, is an historicist, blending (some say inconsistently) idealist–interpretive and materialist–conflict theories of society.

Presumably our interest is not in the purity of intellectual traditions but in the truth of a sociology of religion. We should be open to the ways in which specific points of these disparate theories may turn out to reinforce one another to be saying the same thing in different terms. When this happens (as we shall see in regard to the role played by social solidarity in both Stark/Bainbridge and in Durkheim) it raises the issue of what the most general theoretical propositions should be. In other cases, a specific lack in one theory may be supplied from another; such strategic transplants again raise questions on a higher level of theoretical generality.

Among these approaches, Stark/Bainbridge versus Durkheim are the most anti-thetical. Stark/Bainbridge explicitly criticize and reject Durkheim. In part this is directed against the functionalist side of the Durkheimian lineage: the style of analysis promoted by Parsons and others, which proceeds from the needs of the whole to the behavior of the parts; the emphasis upon a shared culture and under-lying value system shaping the motivations of individuals over and above their per-sonal self-interest; the emphasis upon religion as a source of social integration. In explicit contrast Stark and Bainbridge build theoretical explanations from moti-vated, self-interested individuals outwards into larger social institutions, and they recognize that religions can just as well be disintegrating as integrating, both with-in their own ranks and in relation to the larger society. I am fully in agreement with Stark and Bainbridge's rejection of functionalism; and their antithesis to this side of the Durkheimian lineage is clear.

Nevertheless there is another branch of Durkheimian analysis, which was for-mulated most explicitly in *The Elementary Forms of the Religious Life*, and carried forward by sociologists like Goffman, that operates independently of macro-func-tionalism. This is the theory of ritual solidarity within the local group; it displays a causal mechanism whereby emotional interactions are focused into feelings of group loyalty and expressed in symbols. Here there is no priority to values and cul-ture; on the contrary, these are produced and carried by the varying intensities of group interaction. There is no functional causality by reference to consequences, but a causal mechanism which produces, or fails to produce, solidarity—depend-ing upon antecedent conditions. Since it is local groups which are integrated, these same groups may well be in conflict with the larger society, and thus can contribute to societal disintegration as well as integration; and locally, the degree of integrtion within the group is not a constant but a variable consequence of ritual processes.

Stark and Bainbridge are aloof from this kind of micro-Durkheimian explana-tion of religion too; for it would shift the center of motivation to the dynamics of social solidarity and away from the rewards of supernatural compensators. Nevertheless, part of the Stark/Bainbridge model depends crucially upon the dynamics of membership solidarity, and their recruitment model shows priority of social attachments over beliefs, which are the sphere of supernatural compensators. I will attempt to show that the Stark/Bainbridge theory can be strengthened by revision in the direction of more explicit treatment of ritual–emotional mecha-nisms of social solidarity. This discussion will be similar to a more general tack, now being broached, of bringing emotional dynamics into rational actor theory.[4]

Weber is analytically closer to Stark/Bainbridge. In general, Weber's view of reli-gious motivation is similar to the theory of generalized compensators for worldly suffering, and his analysis of religious variations by social class generally supports a central part of the Stark/Bainbridge model. Where Weber's work diverges from Stark/Bainbridge is in the religious variants catalogued by his much wider histor-ical comparisons, which help bring to light some of the areas of incompleteness in

Stark/Bainbridge. In pre-industrial societies, religion was not only otherworldly compensation and worldly magic; it was also closely entwined with the dominant forms of worldly social status—a point which cuts against the grain of class dynamics of secularization in the Stark/Bainbridge model. In addition, Weber focuses attention upon forms of religion which were historically quite central, but now have sunk to the standing of cults—mysticism and monasticism. These theoretical divergences follow the shift in focus from Weber's concern with pre-industrial societies, and Stark and Bainbridge's focus on the capitalist–industrial world in which religion is institutionally much less central than previously. Paradoxically, today's religion is much more concerned with otherworldly compensators than it was in Weber's medieval–agrarian societies, where religion was a bulwark of the main organizational structure, and the church was a direct route to power, wealth, and prestige.

Another strand which Weber captures (without fully developing), and which Stark/Bainbridge downplay, is religion as the source of ethical action, of morality, including moralistic movements. Viewed in the modern context of secularization, in which the liberal churches are weakened by watering down supernatural doctrine into a purely ethical message, ethics appears to be a deviation from the religious essence, and Stark and Bainbridge make it a minor part of their theory of religion. On the other hand, ethical doctrines and motivations are among the most important effects which religion has had upon society, and it is valuable to understand theoretically how this comes about. Weber's typology of various paths to salvation (ritualistic, mystical, ascetic) at least gives a start for understanding the branches of these various dynamics. What Weber offered on these points was little more than a sketch; for a truly general theory of religion it needs to be carried further.

STARK AND BAINBRIDGE'S GENERALIZED COMPENSATOR THEORY

Religion, for Stark and Bainbridge, provides supernatural general compensators. Magic provides specific compensators. People prefer real rewards, but sometimes they cannot get them. Even more importantly, people's explanations of how to obtain rewards are difficult to evaluate, especially if the rewards are rare or imagined to exist in some distant time or realm; and the more general the explanation, the more that individuals must depend upon other persons, rather than on direct experience, for assessing its validity. A generalized compensator is an imagined reward, a substitute for unavailable earthly rewards, framed in a way that makes impossible to unambiguously evaluate the possibility of obtaining it. Such are the general compensators of eternal life, heavenly bliss, and moral superiority over persons who control worldly rewards. There are also specific compensators, substituting for particular rewards, magical means for attaining health, love, success, revenge and the like. Religion and magic are two overlapping forms of social exchange, which individuals purchase compensators, according to their level of demand and at the best rate available.

The empirical germ of the theory probably comes from Malinowski's observation that people use rational technologies when they know how to work them, and fall back upon magic when they cannot—in addition to findings that the pattern of religious involvement differs among social classes. In general, wealthier and more powerful persons have less need for compensators; although they still have some need, since everyone is subject to death, illness, old age, and personal difficulties. Hence the typical conflict within churches: the upper classes seeking greater accommodation so they can enjoy the things of the world; the lower classes seeking greater tension through more exclusive focus upon compensators. The dynamics of individual recruitment, and the ups and downs of religious organizations follow from this stratification of demands and resources. Although the lower classes in general have more need for compensators, it is the upper classes who are best able to put together a successful organization or to rise to dominance within it; and in any case a successful religion amasses wealth and organizational power for its full-time leaders, so they too tend over time towards greater accommodation with worldly success.

The Stark/Bainbridge theory is an outstanding example of deriving non–obvious macro-patterns from micro-level principles. The authors distinguish between sects (high-tension movements based on traditional religious culture) and cults (those creating new religious culture). Since the main processes are the same for both, I will refer mainly to sects. Recruits typically join when their other social attachments are low or in flux; for higher class persons, these moments are episodic, connected to mobility or life-cycle turning points, and thus tend to make for short-lived attachment to a high-intensity cult. On the other hand, lower class persons will have more enduring needs for compensators, but less to offer a group.[5] Recruitment takes place most successfully when there are chains of ties in which one recruit brings in others; yet it is social isolation or lack of social skills that motivates many joiners in the first place. From this kind of contradiction Stark and Bainbridge derive many of the typical dynamics of cults and sects over time. Lower class or isolated individuals are easiest to attract, but they do little for the further growth of the group. Where sects compete for membership, they often spend a great deal of attention upon their newest members, thereby raising the level of social rewards for those individuals; but the elevated rewards are temporary, and many persons with low social resources become chronic seekers, moving from one group to another. Because of these self-undermining processes, the membership of cults and sects tends to be constantly in turnover; at any point in time, a majority of any sect may be composed of seekers rather than the fully committed.

Sects and cults go through cycles of internal evolution; at the same time there may be large-scale stability or even growth in their total distribution. For each group's history there is a balance point, on one side of which sects accelerate towards churchlyness, on the other side towards extreme social tension and encapsulation. New cults and sects become for a while increasingly isolated and self-contained—what Stark and Beinbridge call a "social implosion"; among other reasons for this tendency, there is a "social evaporation" as the dissatisfied depart, leaving a higher level of satisfaction and social bondedness among those who remain—providing that the group is on the far side of the point where it becomes swamped by chronic seekers. Among those especially likely to leave are its higher class members, whose comparative low tension with the outside world puts them in low status within the group. If this continues, the group will tend towards increasing tension and isolation; that in turn makes recruitment more difficult. Eventually isolation becomes irreversible, and the group will survive at all only if it finds a self-sufficient economic niche. On the other side of the balance point, the preponderance of higher class members or the worldly rewards of the leadership pulls them back churchwards, and this process ends with the seccession of the minority who demand more otherworldly compensators.

Whenever there are relatively open market opportunities, the macro-distribution of religious movements is driven by a series of self-undermining processes: some groups ending in complete isolation; many movements failing because of high costs of recruiting low-payoff members; among successful movements, a tendency for split-offs by the minority who wants either more or less otherworldliness than the majority. Moreover, it is by apprenticeship in previous movements that new organizational leaders acquire their skills and network opportunities; hence the greater the number of successful cults and sects, the more potential there is for still further groups to be created. The process feeds on itself, keeping up a high degree of competition among such groups. The great majority of sects and cults fail, or remain small; out of their competition, only a few grow for the several generations it takes to become a major religious movement and eventually a church. Where the religious market is unmonopolized by a state-enforced church, there will be a continuum of churches and sects from the low-tension socially accommodating to the high-tension worldly-rejecting end, together with cults which formulate entirely new systems of religious compensators.

Stark and Bainbridge envision not only small-scale cycles within specific groups, but also a large-scale cycle, taking hundreds of years, in which the most successful religious movements become low-tension churches, thereby losing commitment from their members; weakening ties in these churches feeds an unchurched population; and out of that in turn are recruited adherents to sects or new religious movements which provide high intensity religious compensators. Many sects and cults compete; a few are successful, these in turn pay the price of diluting the value of their compensators; out of their decline come still further religious organizations purveying high-priced compensators. Whether there is an overall steady-state equilibrium resulting from these intertwining processes, or instead an alternation of waves of boom and bust in the whole religious economy, is a question worthy of further investigation, most feasibly by computer simulation.

DURKHEIMIAN RITUAL SOLIDARITY

In the Durkheimian analysis, the core of religion is social membership or solidarity (in contemporary sociology, the ritual production of emotions). Along with membership goes moral sentiments, dividing insiders from outsiders, good from evil, sacred from profane. Stark and Bainbridge argue that there is no need to postulate a social instinct, although they waffle on this point, conceding that affectual ties are a major reward which bind members to a religious group. Their line of theory would prefer to do without much emphasis upon social rewards, partly because it would undermine their view that the essence of religion is compensators rather than real (if surreptitious) rewards, and partly because they derive the need for social membership from a more fundamental process, the need for social evaluation of compensators (which otherwise cannot be evaluated in the absence of tangible payoffs).

This line of argument is not convincing. If that is all there is to it, the demand for social attachments will vary directly with the demand for compensators (i.e. with the level of deprivation in real rewards); persons who are materially satiated would have no social attachments at all. This flies in the face of the evidence that people are especially likely to join religious groups when they are deprived of social attachments, more so than of material rewards. Stark and Bainbridge also seem to feel that a social instinct is a poor mode of explaining variations in behavior, but that it not necessarily so, if one formulates it such that humans have a physiological propensity to respond to social interaction with contagious emotional arousal, to a degree that varies with the social density of activities. (The principle is not so alien to exchange theory, since it is similar to one of Homans' basic principles.) Neo-Durkheimian theory of interaction ritual would interpret religious groups as specialists in various kinds of ritual solidarity, and thus purveyors of real social rewards; it is merely the symbol system or ideology which cloaks these rewards as supernatural compensators.

It is hard to decide between Stark/Bainbridge compensator theory and Durkheimian ritual reward theory because there is so much empirical overlap. Churches reduce emotional ritual; sects increase it; cults find new ways of producing or interpreting it. Secularization would affect the market for ritual solidarity in much the same way as it affects the market for compensators. However, Stark and Bainbridge implicitly concede the importance of social solidarity at many points, especially in their recruitment model.

(1) *Network ties.* Network ties hold members to the religious group, and those with weak or absent network ties tend to leave (e.g., in the crisis period of a doomsday cult) (Stark and Bainbridge, 1985: 314–315).

(2) *Friendship ties.* The extent of friendship ties within the group correlates not only with belief but with the tendency to have intense religious experiences; this is found not only within sects and cults but also in mainline churches (Stark and Bainbridge, 1985: 320).

(3) *Personal ties.* Personal ties are the most efficacious modes of recruitment in all sorts of religious groups, far more than literature and advertising appealing to ideas. The highly successful Mormon recruitment process shows that the degree of closeness of social ties is highly correlated with the success of recruitment attempts, with the highest level of all (50%) where recruitment is not of individuals but of small groups through family-to-family visits, and doctrine is introduced at the end of the process (Stark and Bainbridge, 1985: 317–318).

(4) *Social ties.* This evidence suggests social ties are prior to ideological beliefs (a point conceded by Stark and Bainbridge at times: e.g., 1985: 151, 309). This is congruent with the Durkheimian point that ideas are symbols of group membership, and grow out of it (Stark and Bainbridge 1985: 311) assert that there must also exist some predisposing deprivation as well as network ties; but this is not as well documented and appears to be the weaker determinant of recruitment. My alternative interpretation is that persons seeking a new religious membership are not necessarily avoiding something negative, but seeking the positive emotional and social benefits of the group. In general theoretical terms, individual motivation is emotional energy-seeking, rather than deprivation-avoiding.

(5) *Social implosion.* Finally, the more restricted part of Stark and Bainbridge's theory dealing with a "social implosion," the encapsulation of a sect or cult and its withdrawal from the larger society, reads like a translation of interaction ritual theory. The beginning is a small number of persons in intimate interaction, assembled for some project (in this case, for a collective attempt to get some scarce or nonexistent reward); failure of the original goals leads to the development of compensators (magical and religious symbols), in the course of exchanging social rewards of emotional solidarity. Intensification of these processes leads to an "implosion" or withdrawal from externally controlling social relations, and thence the consolidation of a novel culture. This is essentially a cumulatively accelerating Durkheimian process, made specific to the religious context by the particular kinds of purposes which brought the group together in the first place, plus the market dynamics of alternative sources of exchange which lead towards the implosion.[6]

One advantage of the Stark/Bainbridge compensator theory over Durkheimian ritual theory is that it tells us what is specific to religious organizations as opposed to secular ones. Durkheimian theory implies every social group with a strong ritual focus produces its own emotional arousal, its own symbols, morality and feelings of membership. The issue did not arise for Durkheim because his empirical archetype was the totemic clan, where religious organization is pretty much coextensive with society. But in secular conditions, pseudo-religious rituals abound, in the form of sporting events, pop-star concerts, or political rallies. Why should there continue to be specifically religious groups, which see themselves as apart from all this, and vastly superior to it?

Stark and Bainbridge would answer that only religious organizations bill themselves as providers of supernatural compensators. This is true, but their own theory implies the proliferation of secular entertainments and movements cuts into the religious market; they explicitly note that religions like liberal Christianity which focus upon social morality are undermined by competition with secular political movements. Since I am hesitant to make the difference derive solely from the nature of the ideology, I would suggest a key social difference is that popular sports, entertainment, and most political participation are episodic gatherings with shifting and rather impersonal membership—whereas religious symbols reflect a publically avowed personal commitment to membership. The personal nature of the gods reflects the social emphasis upon the individual tie; Jesus, Mary, or the Buddha are emblems of the individual seeker, rather than emblems of the compensator.

This still leaves the problem of why religious memberships should claim such high moral status. Whether we interpret them as purveyors of Durkheimian solidarity, or of Stark/Bainbridge compensators, religious commitment is regarded by the faithful, and by many of the non-faithful as well, as ranking higher than anything in the world. If one uses the ideology of compensators, one will say supernatural rewards are higher than any earthly rewards; if one speaks the language of morality (whether in the form of a moralistic religion or a secular or political morality), one will say the greatest thing is to do good even at the cost of material gain or the sacrifice of one's life. There is something underlying here which is best described as social status; the most socially legitimate thing one can do is to avow one's altruism and one's willingness to sacrifice oneself to the symbols of the group.

The strength of the Durkheimian theory is that it points to a larger social process, exemplified in religion but found wherever there is a social hierarchy. Rank is usually based on material possessions and coercive power; but it can only become honored if the holders of rank turn their resources into acquiring the ritual technology which generates group emotions and feelings of morality. In our society there are so many secular ways of doing this that the traditional use of religious ritual is downplayed. The favorite legitimating ritual of today's upper class is the public display of charities. Here we see again religion provides real goods, not only compensators; it provides the emotional/ritual technology for moral legitimation and social impressiveness. This helps explain a point which is something of a puzzle for Stark and Bainbridge: why the upper classes should participate in religion at all, since they control so many real rewards. Stark and Bainbridge argue that individual members of the upper classes still need compensators for personal problems and universal issues such as sickness and death. What this fails to explain is why the upper classes have historically dominated the churches, and why they participate so widely even today.[7] In medieval Christendom, it was the aristocracy which provided most of the saints; in China and Japan, it was the aristocrats who were the famous Zen masters. And still today, in much of the U.S. as well as in many Catholic countries, respectable community membership calls for belonging to a church.

A major reason why sects and cults are socially disreputable is not merely that they are in supernaturally-oriented tension to secular society, but that they are in moral tension with the ordinary claims of social participation. Medieval Chinese Confucians, who saw very explicitly the connection between rituals, social order, and social morality, charged the Buddhist movements with being selfish and immoral, since they withdrew into their inner purity and neglected their obligations to family and society. Sects and cults are regarded in much the same way today, not merely because there is a battle in the market for compensators, but because churches (and some secularly equivalent organizations, such as moralistic political movements) see a genuine moral failing in groups which are separatist, or which focus on the ritual technologies of supernatural bliss to the detriment of real social obligations.

Stark and Bainbridge give moral superiority a minor place in their system; they see it only as a compensator by which the reward-poor turn the tables of social status upon the reward-rich. If morality and its associated social status are not imaginary compensators, however, but real social emotions and sources of real rewards, then the competition between rich and poor, and the dialectical flow between churches and sects, must be seen in another light. The dominants generally get to be more moral than the subordinates—which seems grossly unfair, but it follows from precisely the extent to which the poor really do seek compensators rather than real rewards. Of course the upper classes are frequently hypocrites, wrapping themselves in the rituals of morality, donating to charity out of egotism and without putting their hearts in it. But this has been known to happen in the lower-middle classes as well, and perhaps lower down the economic ladder; and on the other hand the grand self-sacrificing gestures of the saints have usually been reserved for members of the elite, who have had the resources to exploit moral opportunities.

If I am right that the Stark/Bainbridge theory needs to be supplemented by Durkheimian theory of ritual and morality, this does not mean their apparatus is unsound. Much of what I have said about the historical dynamics of mysticism, and about the stratification of ritual and morality, can be put in their framework of rewards and resources, recruitment and movement evolution. Religion becomes more of a market for high intensity emotional rewards and for moral status; in many instances, these work just like the market for compensators, although there are some points of divergence which call for further study.

WEBER'S ROADS TO SALVATION

The central point of Weber's account of religious motivation is very similar to Stark and Bainbridge's. "Since every need for salvation is an expression of some distress, social or economic oppression is an effective source of salvation beliefs, though by no means the exclusive source" (Weber, [1922] 1991: 107). This is again a theory of supernatural compensators, and Weber supports it by observations of the same kind, namely that the higher social classes are less likely to emphasize salvation than the unprivileged. Weber's historical comparisons are congruent with Stark and Bainbridge's point that high social class reduces tension and results in worldly accommodation. But whereas Stark/Bainbridge see this as the side of the cyclical dynamic which leads to religious liberalization and secularization, and thus the weakening of the upper class churches, Weber does not see any weakness in such churches, at least in his historical range of instances. Instead, Weber invokes another "psychological need," for "reassurance as to the legitimacy or deservedness of one's happiness" in one's superior social position (Weber 1922/1991: 107). This is another way to answer the question which Stark/Bainbridge leave hanging, and which I have already raised in relation to Durkheimian theory: why the higher classes should participate so much in churches, far beyond their personal need for compensators. It is conceptually messy to invoke several psychological needs, and a simpler version of Weber's argument is to make the point in terms of social interaction: the higher classes need to legitimate themselves in the eyes of the unprivileged, and hence they use the ritual impressiveness of religion, and its Durkheimian mechanism for generating sacred symbols, as a way of cloaking themselves with the aura of religiosity even if it has little inner significance as supernatural compensators.[8]

So far this is congruent with the line of argument developed by Stark and Bainbridge. Weber complicates matters in relation to social class and religious/worldly tension by the additional observation that salvation religion has "another source besides the social condition of the disprivileged" (116–117): the desire to understand the world as a meaningful cosmos, which arises among intellectuals and therefore primarily among the privileged classes.[9] Weber has in mind Gnosticism in the West (as well as the spiritualism popular among his intellectual contemporaries at the turn of the twentieth century); and in Asia, Buddhism, Jainism, and the Hindu mysticisms, which he correctedly attributes to upper-class intellectuals. Weber attempts to connect this material with his primary argument, that compensators arise in times of distress, by arguing that Buddhism came from a declining military class; this has turned out to be historically incorrect (Buddhism recruited primarily among the Brahmans [Chakravarti, 1987]), and in any case there are too many other instances of supernatural religions which emerge from social groups which are not the distressed part of society.[10]

Weber was not a systematic theory-builder in the sense that Stark and Bainbridge set out to be; if Weber's theory of religion has a somewhat *ad hoc* quality, it is because he was primarily concerned to array the comparative historical material in some order and chart the sources of economic rationalization. Sidestepping the issue of causality, Weber produces a typology which for his purposes serves to indicate which pathways are the progressive ones for world-historical development, and which are dead ends. His typology is full of interest for a general theory, however, since it sketches the range of phenomena which we ought to be able to explain.

(1) *Magical religion.* This is not really a salvation path, but rather the opposite of it. Historically it is important because it incorporates much of early tribal religion, as well as the religion of peasants and the urban lower classes. Stark and Bainbridge do full justice to this category in their analysis of modern cults as well as magical practices in high-tension sects and churches.

(2) *Ritualistic devotional religion,* is that in which ceremonies and sacraments predominate. Weber considers this a major category of historical religions, encompassing the main forms of Confucianism, Hindu caste observances, and Catholic and Eastern Orthodox Christianity. For Weber, this type was the prime religious obstacle to the harnessing of religious tension towards social change and economic rationalization; on the micro level, the key may be in his comment that the ritualistic priest leads a passive congregation of followers. This is a category which Stark/Bainbridge need to develop more explicitly. This highly Durkheimian religious ritualism especially enforces the status honor and sense of group membership boundaries of religious participants, and reinforces their worldly orientation; accordingly, it is this type of religion which has been so prominent among the upper classes. Stark and Bainbridge miss this point, in part because of their antipathy to Durkheimian theory, in part because their data drawn from the twentieth century United States shows that the upper-class congregations are not so much ritualistic (although the Episcopalians fit that description) as theologically liberalized. Here again Stark/Bainbridge shift the attention from religious activity to religious belief, over-emphasizing the cognitive element of what operates primarily as a form of social practice.

(3) *Asceticism* and (4) *Mysticism.* For Weber, both are crucial to societal transformation, since they generate tension, setting off religiously committed persons from the accepted ways of the world. They are also alternatives to each other, and turning points in world history, insofar as mysticism drains off the tension, whereas asceticism, in resisting worldly pleasures and temptations, has the potential for harnessing religious energies to bring the world into harmony with supernatural purposes. Rather than explaining why these various orientations arise in genuinely causal and theoretical terms, Weber is more descriptive in a narrowly historicist sense. In general he wishes to characterize Asian religions as mystical, and Western religions as ascetic—although as ideal types the categories can turn up as minor themes everywhere, and there are Christian and Muslim mystics, as well as Asian ascetics. Honing the category scheme to isolate the aspect of Christianity which Weber thinks is the key to Western development, he cross-classifies asceticism and mysticism with the additional categories of inner-worldly and other-worldly orientation. This gives us a further four-fold sub-categorization:

(3a) *Other-worldly asceticism*: the self-torturing of Indian fakirs or Catholic monks as a means of fleeing the world. For Weber, this is one of the dead ends of religious energies.

(3b) *Inner-worldly asceticism*: linking salvation to the performance of ethical duties in the world. This is Weber's world-transforming force. Unfortunately for his purposes, it is still overgeneralized, since it includes not only economic self-discipline leading to rationalized capitalist development, but also military crusades; among the latter we find Christian as well as Muslim holy wars, Cromwell's armies, and, since Weber's day, modern instances including militant political mobilization among both Christian fundamentalists and the activist Christian left. Weber never satisfactorily addressed the question of when this type of religious motivation turns in a military/political direction, and when it turns in the direction of economic activity.

(4a) *Other-worldly mysticism*. This is the classic mysticism of hermits and monks, associated with the practice of meditation and a doctrine of world-illusion. Weber is interested in this category mainly as another historical dead end.

(4b) *Inner-worldly mysticism*. Weber could scarcely overlook the Pietists, so prominent in German religious history, as well as the Quakers, who muddy the conceptual landscape of his Protestant sects in the period of the capitalist takeoff. In Asia, Taoism (at least in its upper-class form) exemplifies inner-worldly mysticism. For Weber's purposes, this branch of mysticism is another dead end, resulting in quietism and therefore acceptance of the social status quo; one lives in the world but not of the world, going through the motions of living with a spirit of gentle inner withdrawal. Weber does recognize one historically influential aspect of inner-worldly mysticism: he cites it as the source of the ethic of universal brotherly love. ([1922] 1991: 226; cf. 211–214) Weber does not follow up this point, but it implies a surprising significance for mysticism, at least insofar as the ethic of love is taken as the essential message of Christianity. In general, Weber's interest in Christianity is not in this ethical aspect, but in its disciplining of energies into economic activity. Weber makes a point of noting that Christian mysticism does not long stay pure, but tends to turn into the active pursuit of virtue ([1922] 1991: 177). Mystical movements, such as those pioneered by St. Bernard, St. Francis, the Jesuits, or the Baptists, soon turn into activist movements with major social consequences. In theoretical terms, Weber here is engaging in question-begging: his general principle is that mysticism cannot lead to world-transformation; when he finds that it does, he brings in the *deus ex machina* of a Western ethos or tendency to turn mystical movements into activist ones. Unfortunately for the coherence of Weber's model, one may find the same kind of worldly activist consequences in Asia, in the histories of Taoist and Buddhist politics and economics.

Weber was concerned primarily with the economic-development consequences of his typology of salvation paths, rather than with a theoretical explanation of the social processes and conditions which gives rise to each. A general theory of religion, such as Stark and Bainbridge set forth, needs to handle these variants. Stark/Bainbridge, however, are mainly interested in what they see on the contemporary American landscape: magic in its various forms from faith-healing through health cults, plus the continuum from high-tension to low-tension churches, which are essentially within Weber's sub-type of inner-worldly asceticism. As I have indicated above, part of the moderate-to-low tension segment of the American continuum is better described as Weber's ritualism type; part of the low-tension end, with its liberal social activism, fits Weberian world-changing ascetic activism too. Stark/Bainbridge elide these distinctions, lumping everything at the low-tension end into the category of weak supernatural compensators, of prime interest to them in their concern for the cycle of secularization via weakening of commitment in the low-tension denominations. Stark/Bainbridge leave out most of the rest of the Weberian category scheme: both types of other-worldly religion—ascetic and mystical—plus inner-worldly mysticism (except for the bits of the latter found in the contemporary cult fringe). Can the compensator model be adjusted to explain these types of religion?

THE DECLINE OF MYSTICISM

For present purposes, we can treat both other-worldly forms together; both asceticism and mysticism thrive only where full-time practitioners can withdraw from family and ordinary work, forming not congregations but monastic communities. In this discussion, it is not worth going into the differences between self-torturing ascetics and contemplative mystics. Let me consider them together here as monastic forms of religion, with primary reference to the mystical version. Stark and Bainbridge's treatment of the traditional monastic religions is not very satisfactory. Compared to the modern world, the core members of the mainstream "churches" in the period of Buddhism, medieval Hinduism, and pre-Reformation Christianity (and much of later Catholicism as well) were in a very high level of tension with worldly society, equivalent to today's sects at the far end of the continuum. Monks organized their lives around a very encompassing round of devotions, and denied themselves material comforts and even family ties. Yet for centuries these were the dominant religious organizations of their societies, by no means marginal sects.

In the Stark/Bainbridge view, monks would have to be very strongly in need of compensators. But monasteries typically recruited from the upper classes, and maintained membership life-long, not merely during life-cycle turning points. This casts doubt on the suggestion that religion, in these cases, was providing compensators for lack of worldly rewards. Nor was it a matter of monastic movements flourishing during times of general social crisis; on the contrary, the great periods of the expansion of monasticism (pre-Maurya and Maurya India, Sui and T'ang China, Christian Europe in the 12th and 13th centuries) were times of economic growth. Monasteries grew, not because of increasing need for compensators, but because they provided opportunities to expand rewards. Among other reasons, in a society based on patrimonial (i.e. familistic/household) structures, the monasteries were the only extra-familial organization, and had tremendous advantages in recruiting large memberships and amassing wealth and power.

Another reward was supplied intrinsically in the core monastic activity—intense meditation or prayer. This may be regarded not as a mode of escape, but as a form of pleasure-seeking, a technology for producing what the Buddhists call bliss. This technology can only be used when there is considerable investment of material resources, so that the monks can concentrate on developing inner experience. And since monks live as a leisured elite, they are potential targets of jealousy by other social classes; they need protection by religious legitimation, in which the monks themselves are treated as sacred objects, whose veneration by lay persons is counted as an act of religious merit . Monastic religions thus depended upon a special set of resources and rewards, including their comparatively high organizational power in their society, their technology for inner experience, and their ritual impressiveness and monopolization of high social status.

Stark and Bainbridge built their theory upon the study of Protestant sects in a period of secularization; hence they tend to see mysticism as just another fringe cult practice. Although this is true today, the sociological reasons for this historical shift are revealing. After bureaucratic organization broke the tie between the family and the modes of production and political mobilization, monasteries no longer have any organizational advantage, and become resource drains rather than resource creators. The massive investment of time and concentration necessary to perfect the inner-bliss technology is no longer available, and social veneration of monks has disappeared (everywhere except in parts of India), leaving mysticism a private, amoral activity purveyed on a quasi-commercial market. Other-worldly mysticism becomes of necessity inner-worldly mysticism—an attitude practiced by individuals within the hurly-burly of modern life as best one can. Even the inner-worldly version fades; without the high social status given to Taoist literati in traditional China, or the distinctive social recognition accorded to Pietists or Quakers in the 1600s and 1700s, today's inner-worldly mystics find themselves lacking the sense of community, and the distinctive social role, that sustained such mystics in earlier periods.

With their focus upon secularization theory, Stark and Bainbridge believe that mysticism is inherently self-liquidating. In their view, a doctrine of absorption into an all-pervasive spiritual force undermines the bargaining power of the religion; for it is only when there are at least two gods, one good and one evil, that the good god can demand a high exchange ratio. Mysticism is like liberal Christianity, incapable of providing specific compensators for the ordinary problems of life and making the promise of a general compensator too easy to attain. Easy attainment is a drawback, since the value of compensators cannot be assessed in reality and must be set by its social estimation; this in turn must fall when a cosmopolitan, secular society allows a wide range of religious competitors to drive the price of compensators to a very low level.

This dynamic helps explain the further decline of mysticism under modern conditions, where it competes on the general market for supernatural compensators; but present day mysticism has ended up on this market as the result of a structural shift which undermined pre-modern conditions in which monasticism was a major producer of real rewards. That is not to say that mysticism totally loses its attractiveness; it appeals to modern cosmopolitan persons because it reduces the particularistic elements in religion to a miminum. Given a continuing demand for supernatural experience, inner-worldly mysticism will no doubt continue to exist, and professionals will continue to provide enough information and episodic experiential guidance to keep it from going extinct. But without the economic and organizational conditions which once gave monasticism distinct advantages in the production of social and material rewards, modern-day mysticism survives in the popular marketplace of religious cultural choices not as a sustainable organization or even a social movement, but hovering in the limbo of audience cults.

Stark and Bainbridge's overall picture of the modern religious marketplace is one in which all the cheap compensators at the liberal end of the spectrum are gradually driving themselves out of the market through a kind of inflation of religious currency. This leaves the conservative end as the market gainers, at least in the short run; in the long run, as the most successful among them acquire socially dominant members, conservative sects and churches eventually liberalize too, following the paths of the Congregationalists and Methodists over the past centuries, and thus liquidate themselves to make way for yet newer forms of high-tension religion. Liberal religion is constantly dying, while conservative religion is being reborn. Nevertheless, several structural trends in the modern world appear to be undermining conservative religious contents: turning them away from particularism and fixed membership lines towards geographical mobility and intermarriage, increasing generalized standards of tolerance and widespread disapproval of too localistic and overly exclusive group identities. Conservative sects, for all their emotional commitment and tension, are simultaneously adjusting doctrinally towards the more cosmopolitan–universalistic conditions of modern society. For this reason, intrinsically more cosmopolitan practices, including those of mysticism, might be expected to infiltrate back into the array of standard religious techniques.

RELIGIOUS ETHICAL ACTIVISM

A related issue left hanging by Stark and Bainbridge is also connected with left/right political correlates of the high-tension/low-tension religious continuum. In general, their picture is of political liberalism undermining religiously liberal denominations (or co-determining the ongoing decline), while the political right plays piggy-back on the cyclical gains of the religiously conservative. In this view, religious social activism is just another pathway to organizational suicide by the liberal end of the denominational spectrum.

Here Stark and Bainbridge may be reflecting on the political patterns of the United States in the 1970s and 1980s. Their analysis is also rooted in fundamental assumptions of the theory of supernatural compensators, which make ethical motivations for world transformation a relatively minor by-product of religious motivation. Both Weber and Durkheim suggest challenges to this viewpoint. For Durkheim, religion is the source of social ethics as well as of supernatural symbols; hence we should not expect ethical behavior necessarily to undermine religion.[11] Of course Durkheim's testimony is suspect, because his theory does not emphasize compensators at all, instead attributing religious commitment to mediately felt emotional rewards of social solidarity.

Weber is more damaging to the Stark/Bainbridge model. Christianity, as predominantly a form of inner-worldly asceticism has long had a propensity towards political activism; hence church-launched political movements are not necessarily a falling away from intense religious commitment. Weber refers to the type of leadership characteristic of this type of religious movement as "ethical prophecy" (as opposed to the "exemplary prophecy" of the mystical leader), and describes such a charismatic individual as similar to a political orator, stirring up crowds to take action ([1922] 1991: 53). To be sure, Weber leaves plenty of loose ends hanging too. He does not explain why ethical prophecy (i.e. "inner-worldly asceticism") should take the form of exhortation to political action rather than the economic action of minding one's business in a disciplined way while awaiting one's supernatural rewards; and if ethical prophecy does take the form of political action, we are given no clues as to whether it should go towards the altruistic/universalistic causes of the left, or towards the particularistic/authoritarian militancy of the right.[12] In any case, it hardly seems certain that the cycle of secularization-plus-rejuvenation should exclusively mobilize the political–religious right. If this has been the case in recent decades in the U.S., nevertheless the more fundamental principles of the theory of religion do not rigorously determine why this should be so.

CONCLUDING LOOSE ENDS

My theoretical comparison of Stark and Bainbridge, Durkheim and Weber may seem more like an unravelling than an improvement. In truth, there are holes in all three theories. Durkheim is perhaps most incomplete of all, because his theory covers only a mechanism; he gives the fundamental mechanism of the micro-organization of the religious group, but he leaves it to us to find how that mechanism works across the wide range of types of religions and their processess of change. I have suggested how the much wider scope of Stark and Bainbridge's formal theory could be bolstered by explicitly incorporating the Durkheimian mechanism of group solidarity. This still leaves a basic issue: Stark and Bainbridge's focus is upon religious beliefs, the cognitions involved in assessing the exchange value of rewards and compensators, whereas the Durkheimian tradition relegates ideas to a super-structure while the real action goes on at the level of religious action and emotional energy. For Durkheimian theory, religious ideas are always symbols of something else: not something empirically undecidable, as in Stark/Bainbridge, but real, if disguised, social rewards. Whether these two theoretical conceptions can be brought together remains to be seen.

Weber and Stark/Bainbridge are closer on fundamentals. This may not be entirely a good thing, since these are just the points at which the Durkheimian theory holds that both of them need to be corrected. However that may be, Weber's elaborated historical taxonomy implies a series of challenges for Stark/Bainbridge. Stark/Bainbridge deal with only a part of Weber's typology of religions; this leaves a good deal of work to be done in historically broadening the Stark/Bainbridge theory; at the same time, since Weber himself left so many causal questions dangling, the effort to bring the more systematic approach together with Weber's historical sketches should have the effect of turning Weber's pioneering work into a real explanatory theory of religious variants. Since Weber's ideal types of religion also apply analytically to the several strands of contemporary American religion, this has the effect of making the current application of the Stark/Bainbridge theory much messier that it might seem at first glance. In particular, it casts doubt on the flow of the secularization-and-renewal cycle from the weakening liberals to the burgeoning conservatives.

As these questions are worked out, we will probably find that the models so far put forward are too simple. There are multiple religious forms, and numerous historical mixtures and trajectories. Nevertheless there is a theoretical path through this complexity. The systematic marshalling of a set of analytical principles, which Stark and Bainbridge have contributed, is an interim achievement along the path. However they end up being modified, it is an important step that should give the field confidence in what can be accomplished in the future.

NOTES

[1] As Stephen Warner (1993) documents, the orientation which Stark and Bainbridge develop has been emerging across a broad front of researchers in the sociology of religion. Much of this research has been concerned with the particular nature of religion in the United States and with criticism of the older secularization paradigm. My focus here is on general theory; in that regard, the work of Stark and Bainbridge, especially their 1987 book, is the most generalized and systematic.

[2] Obviously I am not referring to the long series of criticisms and revisions of Weber's Protestant ethic thesis, which has overshadowed the rest of Weber's religious sociology in popular estimation, but in fact comprises a relatively small part of it this work.

[3] Most scholars who have pursued Weber's comparative world sociology have cast themselves in the role of Weberian loyalists—not that they have abstained from interpretation and addition, sometimes quite one-sided, and diverging in quite different directions. The result has been little tendency to challenge Weber's general theoretical pronouncements in *The Sociology of Religion*, and instead to overlook them (in the case of scholars not willing to enter the deeper labyrinths of Weberian studies), or else to interpret them in the light of a global conception of what Weber's project is supposed to have been. For Parsons and Bellah, it was all fitted into an evolutionary scheme; for Bendix, the political struggle of status groups; for Schluchter, the master-trend of world rationalization, and so forth.

[4] See the April 1993 issue of *Rationality and Society* (5, No. 2) devoted to "Emotions and Rational Choice."

[5] One major difference between sects (traditionalist schisms) and cults (new religious movements) is that the latter recruit more from the higher social classes. Sects and cults also develop in different geographical regions: sects in areas where traditional religions are strong, cults where traditional belief is low and the proportion of unchurched persons is high. In each of their respective regions, sects and cults feed upon their predecessors by schisms and spin-offs.

[6] Stark and Bainbridge (1985: 183–186), where this is also referred to as the "subculture evolution model". Compare Collins (1993) on the ingredients of an interaction ritual cycling over time: assembly of a face-to-face group; boundaries to outsiders; mutual focus of attention, and shared emotional mood; recycling and mutual intensification of these conditions; resulting in enchanced emotional energy, plus symbols which become sacred objects, emblems of group membership. Given the decay of emotional energy over time (in fact on the scale of days), periodic reassembly of the group is needed if high levels of emotional energy are to be sustained; this provides a motivation for individuals to meet with a frequency proportionate to the level of emotional energy they are seeking from that group.

[7] Stark and Bainbridge (1987: 43–48) are certainly aware of this evidence, and their propositions include the points that religious participation provides some real rewards; specifically, they refer to the income and power which priests derive from their organization, and the status of holding rank within it. But this explains the motivations of religious professionals rather than of their higher class congregations; for the latter, Stark/Bainbridge cite the intrinsic rewards of participation in social occasions—conceding the Durkheimian point; plus "status and legitimate standing in the community"—which would explain why the higher classes have higher than average levels of church participation; but they do not provide the theoretical mechanism to explain why it is this kind of participation that translates into community status. Here again the full Durkheim model appears to be needed.

[8] Stark and Bainbridge note that religious organizations provide rewards as well as compensators, and thus in principle open a way to explain why the higher classes are able to appropriate these rewards as well as those of ordinary non-religious life. In general, their theory would be strengthened by recognizing how central religious organization was in the pre-industrial economy; control of religious organization was not merely a luxury of the upper classes, but a major part of their material base (above all in medieval

Christianity). It departs a little further from the emphasis of the Stark/Bainbridge model to see religion as providing the *primary* means of dramatizing one's status, the chief "means of ritual production" or "emotional production"; in other words, the key again becomes Durkheimian ritual, which provides real rewards rather than compensators.

[9] Weber does make allowance for intellectualism in other social classes; it is when intellectualism occured in combination with the compensation needs found in the non-privileged classes, especially the lower-middle strata of dispossessed Jews in the Roman empire, that the distinctive salvation cosmology of Christianity was created.

[10] Stark and Bainbridge (1985: chapter 18) also note that cults (i.e., new religions, as opposed to renewal movements or schisms within established religions ["sects" in their terminology]), tend to recruit from the higher classes. This somewhat anomalous fact is not really integrated with their theory of compensators, since Stark and Bainbridge's attention is directed to a side issue here; they wish to show that cults are not primarily individual pathology, but part of the cyclical renewal process whereby secularization flows into creating new religions. In general, their model of *successful* new religious movements stresses not the deprivations but the social resources which those movements tap: the education and cosmopolitanism of their leaders, as well as the interpersonal networks which make possible rapid growth.

[11] Warner (1993) points out that some of the most liberalized contemporary churches gain converts precisely because their social/political activist stances attract constituents for these causes. From a Durkheimian viewpoint, political activism too can generate high levels of emotional energy which build organizational commitment.

[12] There is a hint of the complexities here, in Weber's suggestion that inner-worldly mysticism is the source of universalistic brotherly love. Now we get away from Christianity as inner-worldly asceticism, and over into the variants of inner-worldly mysticism. These have been exemplified by the Quakers, but also by some of the ascetic churches on their path towards liberalization: thus the Congregationalists, and even more so their Unitarian schism, became highly active in the anti-slavery movement and other moralistic social crusades of the mid-1800s—at just the time that inner-worldly mysticism became a popular movement in the form of Transcendentalism. This doesn't help much, because we have no general principles as to why a religion would move either to inner-worldly asceticism or mysticism. It does suggest that one would expect the continued mobilization of altruistic social movements, so characteristic of certain parts of the population in the late twentieth century, to have some connection with this religious attitude.

REFERENCES

Collins, Randall. 1993. "Emotional Energy as the Common Denominator of Rational Choice." *Rationality and Society* 5: 203–230.

Chakravarti, Uma. 1987. *The Social Dimensions of Early Buddhism*. Oxford: Oxford University Press.

Durkheim, Emile. (1912) 1954. *The Elementary Forms of the Religious Life*. New York: Free Press.

Stark, Rodney, and William Sims Bainbridge. 1985. *The Future of Religion*. Berkeley: University of California Press.

———1987. *A Theory of Religion*. New York: Lang.

Warner, R. Stephen. 1993. "Work in progress toward a new paradigm for the sociological study of religion in the United States." *American Journal of Sociology* 98: 1044–1093.

Weber, Max. (1922) 1993. *The Sociology of Religion*. Boston: Beacon Press.

NAME INDEX

SUBJECT INDEX